A Discouraging (ɔɪ
Brazilia ɔ

Sebastián Ronderos

Abstract

As political crises and social unrest proliferate worldwide, the appeal of populism grows steadily in various fora, including academic fora. In this respect, an abundance of scholarly publications has sought, through the study of populism, to unravel important aspects of contemporary political and social dynamics. Discourse theory scholars, in particular, have played an important role in pushing the boundaries of populism studies forward. They have challenged objectivist perspectives in the (social) sciences by foregrounding the role of meaning-making and by treating populism as a discursive logic that better characterises the political (dis)articulation of social reality. In situating its analytical focus at the frontier of populism studies, this paper-based dissertation contributes to this literature from both an empirical and a theoretical point of view.

Through the four papers which make up this thesis, I contribute to discourse theory by presenting three main lines of analysis in the study of populism in Brazil, a case that is frequently referenced but which remains under-explored. Firstly, by exploring Brazil's fourth republican period (1946-1964), this thesis shows how populism is best understood as both a concept and a signifier, revealing the way the dynamic interplay of populism discourses shape our sense of social reality. Secondly, by studying a leading magazine with an upmarket readership in Brazil (*Veja*), I explore the affective force running through anti-populist discursive articulations, affirming the value of the category of fantasy from an empirical and analytical point of view. Thirdly, by focusing on the collective candidacy of the *Bancada Ativista* in the Sao Paulo State elections, I explore the potential of the concept of populism, conceived as a logic, to shed light on aspects of political life beyond populist phenomena. Finally, in recognising a gap in the literature in relation to the constitutive role of desire in social meaning-making processes, the fourth paper constructs, through the psychoanalytic category of hysteria, an approach to knowledge production informed by desire, which constitutes the main theoretical contribution to the discourse theory tradition.

By paying close attention to Brazilian politics, this thesis explores some of the distinctive virtues of a discourse theoretical approach to populism by drawing out the normative, ideological, and politico-strategic implications of complex political dynamics and social meaning-making processes within and beyond the study of populist phenomena.

Contents

1. Introduction and Scope of the Thesis

There is no denying that much ink has been spilt in coming to terms with the meaning of 'populism'. However, unfortunately, few conceptual frameworks analytically enrich an already plethoric field which has grown under the label of 'populism studies' with well-defined research agendas, bringing about new and valuable insights into contemporary politics beyond the mere characterisation of players as being populist (or not).

What is more, many of these studies have been rather quick in treating their object of inquiry pejoratively. Be it through a deceiving style (e.g. Weyland, 2001), a Manichean outlook (e.g. Mudde, 2004), fuelled by anti-liberal tendencies (e.g. Müller, 2016) or by forms of unscrupulous and exploitative electoral opportunism (Betz, 1994), a broad array of actors and movements with distinctive political stripes are carelessly classified, ordered and grouped, and negatively evaluated in scholarly publications under the label of 'populism'. In this view, the sovereign *populus*, i.e. 'the people', appears as an ill-equipped, over-emotional and homogeneous political subject (e.g. Mudde and Rovira Kaltwasser, 2017) which, lacking a solid ideology and consistency, ends up subjected to vertical and anti-pluralist forms of (populist) political leadership (e.g. Weffort 1965ab; 1967; Mudde, 2004). Although scholars draw on a wide range of distinctive research traditions, the standard views of 'populism' and 'the people' in populism studies are pejorative.

Still, a growing number of scholars have warned against the 'reification of populism', in which populism is treated as a phenomenon *per se* and often identified as to be the main driving force of social and political dynamics (see De Cleen and Glynos, 2021, p. 179; 182). While some practitioners strongly question the conceptual utility of characterising players and movements as 'populist' (e.g. Cannon, 2018), others have claimed that the concept of populism is so loosely and varyingly used that neither the object of study nor its conceptual significance are properly presented (e.g. Rydgen, 2017). Indeed, calls for its radical renewal or definite abandonment have become all the more frequent amidst an avalanche of research production on populism studies threatening 'to swamp all our analyses of and discourses about contemporary politics, radical or not' (Dean and Maiguashca, 2020, p. 19).

It is in this context that proponents of the discourse theory approach, part of the so-called *Essex School of Discourse Analysis* (hereafter *Essex School*), have intervened in the central debates encompassing studies on populism. In seeking to counteract the tendency to treat populism as a 'thing', discourse scholars invite us to pay attention to the performative dimensions and functions not only of populism but also of discourses *about* populism, tracing their effects in the political and social domains (De Cleen, Glynos and Mondon, 2018; De Cleen and Glynos 2021). Indeed, exploring the performative function of labelling actors as populists has been pointed as a promising analytic scope by discourse theorists to advance in the study of contemporary discourses about populism and their influence over social and political dynamics. In assuming a meaning-making perspective (Laclau, 2014), they also promote a reflexive and critical stance which considers the emotional investments underlying discursive formations which slavishly see populism as an always-central feature of political reality (Glynos and Mondon, 2016; Eklundh, 2020; Ronderos and Zicman de Barros, 2020; Brown and Mondon, 2021).

While highly suggestive, most of these interventions remain relatively brief, and such lines of analysis are still underdeveloped and underexplored in light of concrete case studies. Building on the discourse theory framework, this thesis focuses on the case of Brazilian politics to contribute to a literature that takes its bearing from discourses *about* populism at 'frontier of populism studies'. In other words, I am interested in the performative function of discourses about populism in Brazil. By associating in this thesis the study of discourses about populism with the concept of 'performativity', I am hinting at the need to study populist discourses in a more analytic and empirical fashion (see Laclau 2005a, 97, p. 103; 118). I claim that discourses which refer to populism as a central discursive element are performed in concrete ways, and their structural logics will vary according to the concrete social space in which they are inscribed. This is no small detail, as, for discourse theory, identity comes about discursively and, lacking an objective field of pre-determined meaning, any form of social meaning and identity formation is always politically installed, for the words we use and the ways these are performed help shape the social world and the identities inscribed in it.

When it comes to Brazilian politics, a *populist* descriptor is gaining traction, assuming a central role in discourses in the public sphere and inscribing newspaper headlines with clamorous political predicaments and devastating social prognosis. Regarding academic production, scholars have little hesitation in claiming that the recent rise in Brazilian populism unambiguously stems from the discrediting of major political parties and makes use of extra-constitutional strategies to deceivingly capture the public agenda (see, for example, Borges, 2021; Fuks et al., 2021; Avritzer et al., 2021). However, when reading such studies, one is left wondering about the significance behind this pervasive and staggering word – 'populism' – in the Brazilian context, as no definitional clarity (or defining effort, even) is rendered visible. One thing is certain: when the signifier 'populism' enters the scene, references to representational crisis, social erosion and deceptive political processes tend to take over the foci. With regards to the specialised literature regarding populism studies as a field of research, Brazil is often highlighted as an *ad hoc* host of both left- and right-wing populism, without properly undertaking a more rooted and profound case-analysis of its social and political dynamics (e.g. Mudde, 2019; Mudde and Kaltwasser, 2011, p. 12; Kaltwasser, 2019, p. 43-45).

Today, many seem to think that populism has a privileged role in the Brazilian setting and that the Brazilian case is telling in terms of the conceptual significance of populism as such. Regrettably, however, few analytic efforts have formally committed themselves to developing either the significance of populism in Brazil or the value of Brazilian politics to its research to an agreeable level of detail, nuance and rigour. Given the prominent reference to populism in Brazil by both Brazilian and populism studies literature, the widespread perception of political change in the country and the pervasive character of the words 'populism' and 'populist' in Brazil's public debate (see, for example, Ronderos and Zicman de Barros, 2020), an analysis of discursive repertoires *about* populism and their role in political antagonism in a more profound and localised fashion is extremely necessary.

In exploring the Brazilian case, I am not simply aiming to capture valences and trends related to discursive patterns about populism. Instead, and as portrayed in this thesis' title, I seek to (de)construct (from an affective, meaning-making perspective), some underlying logics enacted in populism-related discursive disputes characterising crucial political dynamics in Brazil. This effort expands methodological and analytical aspects of discourse-theory's approach to political antagonism and discourses *about* populism. Furthermore, this habilitates putative explanations of the Brazilian case that might contribute to other such cases with 'overlapping similarities' and which present salient 'family resemblances' (Wittgenstein, 1953).

In engaging in a deconstructive practice, this paper strives to identify and account for the (dis)articulation of urges to find closure and homogeneity in questions of populism in Brazilian politics. In doing so, I make visible impure and contradictory elements underlying gestures of totalisation, thus delving into a systemic elucidation of the contradictions, tensions and aporias within a social system of meaning. As Derrida points out, if 'totalisation no longer has any meaning, it is not because the infiniteness of a field cannot be covered by a finite glance or a finite discourse, but because the nature of the field—that is, language and a finite language—excludes totalisation' (Derrida, 1978, p. 289). Zooming into gestures of totalisation which allege an insight into society through questions of populism might allow one to reveal concealed moments of structural 'undecidability' (see Gasche, 1986, p. 142-47), explicating ruled-out possibilities and allowing for critical evaluation of the response-ability of subjects in making political decisions (Norval, 2004, p. 154). To be sure, the parentheses given to 'de' in *deconstruction* in this thesis' title relates to a de-constructive practice not merely as a negative gesture of inverting two poles in a binary relationship through the 'clamorous declaration of the antithesis' (Gasche, 1986, p. 171), but instead entails reconfiguring the system of meaning into a novel infrastructure, which bestows a positive gesture of *construction*, bringing about something new of a kind.

Discourse theorists have developed a distinctive reading of deconstruction and its role in political analysis, promoting the full analytical fruition of the Derridean infrastructure of undecidability by articulating adjacent idioms, particularly from psychoanalytic, Lacanian-inspired works[1]. On this account, the question of identity is addressed from a negative ontological standpoint that places affect at the core of identificatory processes and political action.

With the so-called affective turn, questions related to emotions, desire and affect have become very fashionable amongst philosophers, political theorists and thinkers of the social sciences and the humanities. However, despite the growing and visible interest scholars have given to affect when reflecting about social processes, the approaches therein vary to such an extent that they present antithetical ontological stances. Indeed, rationalist perspectives tend to address questions related to affect, emotions and desire as merely strategical or descriptive categories restrained to specific movements and actors which display less rational political processes and highly emotional social articulations. In political theory, while some find an influence in Deleuzian-inflected works, other accounts seek inspiration in neuroscience,

---

[1] This is not to say that the formal articulation of deconstruction by discourse theory scholars has been exempted from debate and discussion. For a glance at debates about the full fruition of the infrastructure of undecidability in the discourse theory framework, please be referred to Norval (2004).

behavioural psychology, constructivism, and much else besides. In so far as the field of populism studies is concerned, dominant strands of literature tend to be openly dismissive of and hostile to emotional expressions in politics.

Following the likes of Lacan, discourse theory approaches affect as an inherent and constitutive dimension of all possible forms of identity and social meaning-making. Two main consequences follow from this: First, as affect is constitutive of identity, the emotion/reason divide becomes obsolete. Second, any effort to bestow a hierarchical distinction between emotional and rational actors appears as an attempt to promote (political) exclusion.

In consequence, for discourse theorists, discourse is not seen as mere patterns of meanings, texts or symbolic representations, but rather as a practice of articulation that links together and modifies (meaningful and affective) elements into relational systems. This articulatory practice, in turn, yields incomplete social systems. In positioning its style of reasoning within a retroductive and post-positivist context, discourse theory scholars promote a problem-driven research approach that counters the tendency to see research purely in terms of empirical generalisations by deductive or inductive means (Glynos and Howarth, 2007).

Following discourse theory inspired works and building on post-structuralism and psychoanalysis, this thesis assumes a retroductive style of reasoning to explain how alleged populist elements have helped shape the contours of political antagonism in Brazil and how approaching such elements through a discourse theory-based, deconstructive fashion, habilitates meaningful insights concerning some salient processes underlying Brazilian politics.

While situated in this rationale, I argue in this thesis contra standard discourse theory views on the centrality of social demands in political articulation. As such, I contend that desire prefigures the formal structuring of social demands. However, I understand desire in this thesis as being always inscribed in a field marked by articulation through historically-constructed

6

libidinal structures. This is to say that, while, in my view, desire prefigures the formal structuring of social demands in political articulation, this desire is always situated in an already articulated context of meaning and habilitated by historically-enlivened libidinal structures, which, ultimately, situate political decision[2].

As Norval (2004) develops in her *Hegemony after Deconstruction*, the concept of undecidability alone can not account in full for a theory of hegemony, as the subjects' experience, decision and responsibility are fundamental in grasping the horizons of such political acts (the democracy-to-come, in Derrida). To be sure, this thesis will not take issue with hegemony-related debates as such, however, my engagement with scholarly and political debates about populism helps formulate essential insights into the theory of political identities and thus expand the scope of discourse theory of hegemony. In practical terms, I contend that my desire-centred approach to political identities expands the discursive analytical frame of hegemony by inscribing political decision in a historically-informed libidinal frame of recognition and representation, all of which are key in exploring and accounting for processes underlying the instalment and contestations of social regimes and practices. Consequently, I argue that placing desire at the heart of the discourse theory edifice brings about non-trivial implications for political analysis in general and current analyses of Brazilian politics in particular.

Given the discursive approach adopted in this thesis, the literature review that follows will seek to construct and problematise key reflections deriving from the articulation of discourse theory with reference to populism. In so doing, I avoid – at least in this more introductory section – a broader engagement with all theoretical traditions and schools of thought encompassing populism studies. This is to prevent this thesis from falling into the trap of presenting a 'superficial acquaintance with a field' that resembles 'a jack of all trades and

---

[2] For a more detaild account please be referred to Paper 4.

master of none' (Laclau, 1991). Once this thesis has acquired a considerable degree of mastery over its central theoretical perspective, I will invite a more critical engagement with other academic discursive repertoires on populism, whether they form part of international debates (Paper 4) or part of a more focussed investigation of the case, entailing engagement with Brazilian scholarly discussions (Paper 1).

The intellectual legacy of Ernesto Laclau and Chantal Mouffe is the primary source of inspiration for this thesis. Before outlining some of their contributions to political theory (Laclau and Mouffe, 1985) and related ideas on populism (Laclau, 1977; 2005), I will first engage with some of the leading intellectual voices through which Laclau and Mouffe found a way to express their thought. In presenting the genealogy of Laclau and Mouffe's subversion of essentialist tendencies in Marxist thought, I first construct critical reflections on ideology as developed by the Italian Marxist Antonio Gramsci through his general theory of hegemony. I then move on to discuss the psychoanalytic intervention, making intelligible some key concepts and theoretical formulation in Jacques Lacan's work to better appreciate the potential benefits of moving from the clinic to the social and political fields, as Laclau and Mouffe did in their work. This section concentrates on Lacan's idea of lack and his *Imaginary*, *Symbolic* and *Real* registers. Having constructed the Gramscian and Lacanian turns, I then turn to Laclau and Mouffe's oeuvre, constructing central features comprising their theoretical framework.

Building on Laclau and Mouffe's work allows me to follow the emerging Essex School literature reflecting on discourses *about* populism (Glynos and Mondon, 2016; De Cleen, Glynos and Mondon, 2018; Ronderos and Zicman de Barros, 2020; De Cleen and Glynos, 2021), strands of literature studying journalistic populism discourses (Stavrakakis, 2018; Nikisanis, Simos, Stavrakakis, Marku and Timitroulia, 2018; Eklundh, 2020; Goyvaerts and De Cleen, 2020; Brown and Mondon, 2021) and debates about the role that emotions, affect and desire play in the constitution of political identities (Žižek, 1989; Laclau, 2005; Glynos,

2001; Glynos, 2008; Glynos and Howarth, 2007; Stavrakakis, 2000; Stavrakakis, 2007; Glynos and Stavrakakis, 2008; Eklundh, 2019; Eklundh, 2020). Specifying this thesis' unique contextual features, this initial review of the literature helps me problematise the tensions and puzzles enlivening the development of a four-step research approach to the study of populism from a discourse theory standpoint.

Following this extended introductory section, I present the practical dimensions in carrying out this research project. In so doing, I present a reflection of my intended aims and research questions. I then delineate the intended contributions of this thesis organised as a function of four (stand-alone) research papers and develop my overall research approach and methodological strategy. This is followed by the four papers that constitute the main body of this thesis.

Reflecting upon the role that the signifier populism plays in the formal structuring of social meaning, paper 1 proposes a distinct conceptual framework to study populism as both a concept and a signifier by drawing on Brazil's Fourth Republican period. Subsequently, paper 2 takes issue with the affective force animating and inviting the articulation of debates centred around populist discursive elements by relying on the psychoanalytic category of fantasy. Through this paper, I focus on the central role media players have in constructing discursive dynamics on the ubiquitous nature of populism, as a signifier, by studying the elite Brazilian magazine *Veja*. Moreover, paper 3 brings back some basic formal principles encompassing the deconstructed conceptualisation of populism as a political logic, as offered by discourse theory, enlivening an analytical initiative in understanding political disputes and collective articulations derived from a period of heated social disruption. Furthermore, paper 4 delves into a theoretical exploration of the role of desire in knowledge production through the psychoanalytic concept of hysteria. Finally, the thesis presents its main concluding remarks.

1.1.Context and State of the Art

In order to formally construct and present the approach developed by Laclau and Mouffe with which to analyse socio-political phenomena, specifically with reference to the question of populism, I will first invite the reader to take a short theoretical detour. In so doing, I aim to present the most prominent intellectual voices inspiring Laclau and Mouffe in articulating their post-Marxist and post-structuralist school of thought. In constructing this contextual background, I clarify crucial concepts and theoretical turns inspiring the reconstitution and radicalisation of the Marxist tradition, further furnishing their novel ontological perspective from where we may critically explain, from a meaning-making perspective, the articulation of social and political reality.

In following this course of action, I first present some key theoretical developments with reference to the role of ideology in the Marxist vein, as given by the Italian thinker Antonio Gramsci through his general reflections on the question of hegemony. Therein, I present the Gramscian conception of hegemony as a principal genealogical root of Laclau and Mouffe's discursive turn. Following this brief navigation through some of Gramsci's contributions to the Marxist theory of ideology, I move to psychoanalytically informed perspectives on subjectivity and identity formation. In so doing, I rely upon the work of French psychoanalyst Jacques Lacan, giving particular attention to the three main concepts he proposes as a means of accounting for the psychic structure. I am namely referring here to the *Real*, the *Imaginary*, and the *Symbolic* registers. Through the Lacanian turn, I present the concept of lack as the main theoretical foundation of Laclau and Mouffe's negative ontological stance.

In closing this rather short but crucial theoretical detour, I then move to the theoretical reflections on hegemony and populism undertaken by Laclau and Mouffe since the early 1970s, culminating in the milestone publications of *Hegemony and Socialist Strategy* (1985) and *On Populist Reason* (2005a). Following this overview of Laclau and Mouffe's oeuvre, I then locate the logic of populism in the discourse theory perspective, presenting such a theoretical turn as this thesis' primary terrain of engagement. Finally, I examine the state of Essex School debates regarding populism, allowing me to articulate and present the rationale and research questions enlivening this research project.

1.1.1. *The Gramscian turn: hegemony as genealogy*

The word 'hegemony' found its place in the seminal debates of the 2nd International (through the work of thinkers such as Luxemburg, Kautsky and Bernstein). It became a greater strategical concept throughout Russian Social Democracy (in the ideas of Plekhanov or Axelrod) and further expanded in later 2nd and early 3rd International and Comintern debates (through Lenin and Trotsky).

Based on a number of laws of historical developments, the Marxist theory was hallmarked by an essentialist conception of historical stages that afforded pre-conceived subjects, with well-established and fixed identities, the firm virtue of discharging social change. Echoing Marx's (1859) somewhat static structure/superstructure metaphor, these theoretical developments were governed by *conditions of necessity*, in which concrete historical dynamics, determined by organised stages of economic development, provided the setting for social transformation through Revolution, with a capital 'r' (see, for example, Plekhanov, 1883/1974; Kautsky, 1909).

While Marxist thinkers were actively attempting to reveal the necessary economistic conditions of structural social shifts, hegemony-related debates provided a theoretical supplement giving nuance to political dynamics in the strategic organisation of socialist struggles. As such, the motifs of hegemony gave Marxism a *logic of contingency* operating in social organisation, inviting the exploration of political interventions related to, for example, the role of the party and class alliance discussions and debates over the function of intellectuals in organising and directing periods of social revolution (see Lenin 1967, p. 84; Luxemburg, 1985, p. 38; Trotsky 1986, p. 72).

However radical the underlying contribution of reflecting on political aspects enacting in the structuring of social relations seemed, the logic of contingency derived from hegemony debates remained restricted to a mere supplement in the 2nd International deliberations. However, while most Marxist approaches to hegemony were rather brief and isolated, Gramsci brought this category to the heart of the Marxist tradition (Anderson, 1976, p. 17), inscribing it onto a much more radical and dangerous scope from where could be addressed the Marxist economistic problematic.

Gramsci produced extended historiographic and political analyses, constituting a corpus of over 30 notebooks which founded a prime contribution to the political theory of the 20th century. Nevertheless, by going through the many references throughout his work, no one succinct definition of hegemony is plainly apparent, as Gramsci's *Prison Notebooks* (1971) were never intended for publication in their present form. While the dreadful pressure of Mussolini's regime did not break the drive that kept the Italian Marxist from analysing the challenging times that marked his era, as Gramsci's writings were mainly produced in prison, they underwent relentless censorship and were subjected to fascist daily scrutiny (Femia, 1983, p. 329; Simons, 2015, p. 22). It is clear, however, that while Lenin took *gegemoniya* (Russian for hegemony) as an obvious strategic alliance of social classes for the establishment of the vanguard party leadership (see Lenin 1967, p. 84), Gramsci extended it as an analytical category to understand the conformation and crisis of power structures (Mouffe, 1979, p. 179; Simon, 2015, p. 25).

By drawing on Machiavelli's Centaur – half-human, half-animal – Gramsci (1971, p. 57; 170) elaborated a distinction between consent (cultural direction) and force (domination by state-legislative or police intervention), as in two distinct modes in which a social group may assume supremacy over others (see also Anderson, 1976, p. 31). Hegemony is conceived in Gramsci's work mainly as 'a relation, not of domination by means of force, but of consent by means of political and ideological leadership' (Simon, 2015, p. 24). Therefore, for a social group to become hegemonic, it has to attain intellectual and moral leadership by transforming the popular consciousness (Mouffe, 1979, p. 190). Such leadership is presumed to be fostered by a set of alliances established with other social groups, requiring an adaptation of 'class interests' in the conformation of a new ideological synthesis. Therefore, for Gramsci, 'politics ceases to be a zero-sum game conducted by classes with fixed identities and interests, and becomes more a process of constructing relationships and agreements' (Howarth, 2000, p. 90).

The theory of ideology persisted marginally through most of the Marxist tradition, as the predominant essentialist scope of the 2nd International took politics and ideology as mere reflections of the forces and relations of production, making of them meagre epiphenomena, only accountable by the dynamics of the economic sphere. In this vein, two main theoretical grids have guided Classical Marxist thought on ideology. The first, reflects on the *contribution to the Critique of Political Economy* (1859) preface in its famous distinction between structure and superstructure. At this point, Marx sees the economic base as an intelligible whole, as a material basis whose dynamics we can discover and which, through a necessary correspondence, determines the legal and political superstructural content. Ideology is, therefore, seen as a by-product of the material conditions enclosed within the forces and relations of production proper.

Just as our opinion of an individual is not based on what he thinks of himself, so can we not judge of such a period of transformation by its own consciousness; on the contrary, this consciousness must be explained rather from the contradictions of material life, from the existing conflict between the social productive forces and the relations of production (Marx, 1859, p. 390).

The second pillar rests on the understanding of ideology as false consciousness. Since all subjectivity is seen to carry a final objective essence determined by the economic base, the non-recognition of this reality is seen as a distortion of ideological character. This is yet another idea present in Marx and Engels' youthful texts, such as *The German Ideology* (Marx and Engels, 1845/1965).

Even when considering Gramsci's 'insistence that hegemonic subjects are necessarily constituted on the plane of the fundamental classes' (Laclau and Mouffe, 2001, p. 137–8; see also Mouffe, 1979, p. 183), his idea of 'organic ideology' carries with it rigid implications concerning the orthodox views of classical Marxist thought and its mechanistic elaboration of ideology based on the structure/superstructure complex. Indeed, 'the whole purpose of what Gramsci called an organic (i.e. historically effective) ideology' brings about the processes in which actors, identities, and projects conform to a new collective will, thus making hegemony 'a 'unity' out of difference' (Hall, 1991, p. 136).

Furthermore, the Gramscian elaboration of hegemony was linked to Gramsci's concern with the condition of the subordination of southern Italy as a critical matter of the national question (see Urbinati, 1998). For Gramsci, hegemony could not merely be conceived of in terms of an alliance of classes, as it requires popular struggles and grievances to achieve national leadership (Gramsci, 1926). We could therefore say that the construction of hegemony, for Gramsci, entails articulating both 'national-popular' and 'social class' dimensions into the conformation of an ethical, moral and intellectual leadership (Simon, 2015, p. 27).

The core of Laclau and Mouffe's seminal reflections until the mid-1980s would find in Gramsci, through his identification of the centrality of the people's democratic grievances in disputing and obtaining national leadership, inspiration for developing a non-reductionist theory of political identities (Laclau, 1977; Mouffe, 1979; Laclau and Mouffe, 1985). Correspondingly, 'Laclau's populism would echo on Gramsci's interest in such dimension' (Stavrakakis, 2017a, p. 538), theoretically embedding Gramsci's envisioning of hegemony as unity out of difference in the construction of 'a popular identity out of a plurality of democratic demands' (Laclau, 2005a, p. 95). Therefore, it is through the post-Gramscian theory of hegemony that the discourse theory approach to *populism* comes about.

1.1.2. *The Lacanian turn: lack as ontology*

While Gramsci's critique on economism took '"popular beliefs" and similar ideas' to be part of material forces (Gramsci, 1971, p. 164-5), Laclau would draw on the impossibility of objectivity to reflect upon ideology as a 'dimension which belongs to the structure of all possible experience" (Laclau, 1997, p. 311). Indeed, Gramsci's theory of hegemony opened up an analytical and strategical engagement with political dynamics by putting forward under-theorised (and neglected) lines of analysis by the Marxist tradition. To a great extent such reflections derived from striving to locate ideology in the Marxist theoretical frame (Mouffe, 1979). In breaking with class essentialism, however, Laclau and Mouffe formulate a whole new ontological perspective, finding in *negativity* the very condition of possibility for social meaning. Such an ontological turn derives from psychoanalytic perspectives, fundamentally relying upon Jacques Lacan's ideas.

The work of French psychoanalyst Jacques Lacan has long transcended the margins of clinical psychoanalytic practice and have been adopted as an analytical grid for the study of social dynamics and political phenomena (e.g. Barrett, 1991; Feher-Gurewich, 1996; Bracher, 2018). Most practitioners and theorists reflecting from a post-structuralist standpoint ascribe to Lacanian theory's great potential in filling in pressing theoretical inconsistencies and lacks in the sciences (Stavrakakis, 2002; Glynos and Stavrakakis, 2018). Inscribed in a rather anti-utopic stance, the Lacanian notion of subjectivity embraces lack as to render intelligible the chimerical and dangerous idea of fullness (Glynos, and Stavrakakis, 2008, p. 260). While objectivist perspectives in the (social) sciences, such as the essentialist Marxist stance, assume the subject as a positively foreclosed entity (as the subject of knowledge), psychoanalysis deals with the drama of precariousness that constitutes subjectivity, reflecting upon identity *via negativa.*

Lacan was encouraged by Freud's discovery of the unconscious through his study of hysteria and theorised the subject as being divided (represented by '$\mathcal{S}$') and lacking an identity proper (see Lacan, 2011 in Stavrakakis, 2002, p. 15). As such, identity for Lacan is presumed impossible, for the mere idea of the subject can only be reached through identificatory processes. When searching for initial instances where this radical ex-centricity in the subject is first recognised, Lacan (1949) presents the 'mirror stage' as being an early form of imaginary identification. According to Lacan, an infant affirms its bodily unity from the sixth to the eighteenth month of its life, an affirmation that is first experienced when the infant recognises its image in the mirror for the first time, giving it a sense of wholeness from the distinctive presence of a protective figure thought of in terms of a 'significant other' (usually the mother or father) (Lacan, 1949, see also Fink, 1995, pxxx).

This jubilant imaginary integration of the body as *ego* appears, at first, as the enjoyment experienced through a sense of totality and closure. However, the infant's continuing experience of lack and precariousness through the actual body makes it clear that such a reified self-image is no other than an *alien* (see, for example, Lacan, 1991, p. 243). The ego, ascribed as a symmetric and coherent unity, is, in fact, an *alter*-representation of 'an inchoate collection of desires' expressed in a fragmented body that can never really 'erase the external and alienating character of its own foundation' (Lacan and Miller, 2013, p. 39). In linking the

16

'mirror stage' with the absence of full motor-neuronal development, Lacan renders intelligible the main conditions for the possibility of the appearance of the ego as earlier conceived by Freud (1914). The main points here are that Lacan associates the imaginary register with a stage in which images spur anticipated mastery, where identification is consolidated through the distinctive figure of a 'significant other'. However, the subject and the ego can never fully coincide, for the imminent threat of disintegration also traverses imaginary identification.

By references to condensation, displacement, dreams, jokes and much else besides, Freud (1899/2014) exhibited a strong sense of the importance of linguistic structures as a highway to the functioning of the mental apparatus. Drawing on structural linguistics, Lacan further explored the principles and operations in language to unravel conscious and unconscious processes as earlier explored by Freud.[3] One finds the passage from the imaginary to the symbolic form of identification through linguistic associations in Lacanian theory.

As seen, imaginary identification provides a precocious and profoundly unstable identity, incapable of being articulated in much more stable terms. Thus, 'the only option left for acquiring one seems to be the field of linguistic representation, [through] the symbolic register' (Stavrakakis, 2002, p. 17). The symbolic is already at work during the mirror stage, mainly by a linguistic network constructed by the parents and family, such as through the name given to the infant, for example (Stavrakakis, 2002, p. 18).

It is here, where specular images build a momentary and alienating illusion of identity, that language, through the symbolic register, can provide an identity capable of being structured in much more stable terms, as 'the symbolic provides a form into which the subject is inserted at the level of his being' (Lacan and Miller, 2013, p. 179). We are referring here to the passage from a 'constituted' to a 'constitutive' identification, as in the imaginary register, the ego is

---

[3] For example, where Freud thought of condensation and displacement in the interpretation of dreams, Lacan formulated the functions of metaphor and metonymy as being central in the structure of the unconscious.

presented as the spectacular image of what 'we would like to be' (mediated by a 'significant other'). Whereas symbolic identification structures (through the 'big Other', i.e. culture, language, law, and so on) 'the very place *from where* we are being observed, *from where* we look at ourselves so that we appear to ourselves likeable, worthy of love' (Žižek, 1989, p, 105, emphasis in original).

Contrary to the realist representationalism schema (in which signifiers represent actually existing things), the signified is taken in the Lacanian framework as an effect of transference, as it emerges by virtue of the structure of the signifier (Lacan and Miller, 2013, p. 226). As recognised by Žižek (1989, p. 191), for Lacan ''Truth' is an empty *place*, and the 'effect of Truth' is produced when, quite by chance, some piece of 'fiction' (of symbolically structured knowledge) finds itself occupying this place''. The implication of assuming 'Truth' as an *empty place* is nonother than the linking of the signified to what Lacan refers to as the register of the *real*, defined as an order which resists symbolisation in the strictest sense, being beyond the reaches of the imaginary and symbolic registers. Signification, as symbolically structured knowledge, 'is accepted only to be located at the limit of signification and not in its kernel' (Stavrakakis, 2002, p. 24).

Through the imaginary, symbolic and real registers, Lacan attempts to formulate a consistent framework to conceive the constitutive impossibility of the subject to reach existential fullness (Fink, 1997). Therefore, the idea of the subject as lack is necessarily attached to the subject's attempts to overcome this constitutive lack through the *desire* of reaching its positive identity, signalling the socio-symbolic dependency of subjectivity and the centrality of signification in such an endless pursuit. From this perspective, the subject experiences a prohibition of the enjoyment (*jouissance*) entailed in the reaching of a full identity, allowing desire to be structured around this constitutive lack (Glynos and Stavrakakis 2008, p. 260-261).

The lack in the subject is, in the strict sense, a lack of *jouissance*, as desire is sustained by the subject's 'limit-experiences to a jouissance of the body' and the construction of fantasies purporting to deliver the impossible task of reaching fullness (ibid. 263). As in the essential component sustaining the subject's fantasy, the object-cause of desire is represented under the guise of 'object *a*'. For Lacan, object *a* assumes the role of an excessive X which can be taken as the lack in the symbolic Other; in other words a utopian centrepiece that promises to deliver the fullness of *jouissance*. The fantasmatic narrative of object *a* ultimately supports reality, as it is by this object that the subject can access a partial-enjoyment, enduring the fact that enjoyment will never be entirely attained (Žižek, 1989, p. 162). Therefore, object *a* embodies a partiality that, as in an internal exclusion from the symbolic order, comes to represent the totality through a beatific narrative (when the object is raised to the dignity of the Thing). As will be seen, Laclau sees the logic of populism as overlapping with that of Lacan's object *a*. It is thus to Laclau we now turn to extrapolate this development.

1.1.3. *The discursive turn: populism as terrain of engagement*

In his early *Politics and Ideology in Marxist Theory: Capitalism, Fascism, Populism* (1977), some of the fundamental theoretical grounds for Ernesto Laclau's interpretation of populism were laid out for the first time. By abandoning 'the [Marxist] reductionist assumption' which afforded the economy primacy over the political domain, Laclau defines 'classes as the poles of antagonistic production relations which have no necessary form of existence at the ideological and political levels' (Laclau, 1977, p. 159). Therefore, rather than depending on and deriving from an objective economic base, class compositions are shaped by what appears in Laclau's seminal reflections as 'processes of articulation' (Laclau, 1977, p. 161).

Partly reflecting Antonio Gramsci's intellectual legacy, Laclau's early work takes *popular identities* and *social classes* as core societal structures of a double articulation in the conformation of populist political discourses. Populism, as such, 'starts at the point where popular-democratic elements are presented as an antagonistic option against the ideology of the dominant bloc' (Laclau, 1977, p. 173). Laclau's scope preserves at this point the core Marxist notion of class – which he would abandon together with the political theorist Chantal Mouffe in their pioneering *Hegemony and Socialist Strategy* (1985; from now on referred to as *HSS*). However, in focusing on *processes of articulation*, the kernel of Laclau's seminal approach is already afforded to the category of 'discourse' (Stavrakakis, 2004, p. 255).

Laclau and Mouffe had each explored non-reductionist horizons in Antonio Gramsci's intellectual edifice from the 1970s (Laclau, 1977; Mouffe, 1979). By that time, these two authors were exposed to and triggered by plebeian political struggles in Latin America – Laclau explicitly reflecting upon *Peronism* in his home country Argentina. At the same time, Mouffe's passage through the *Universidad Nacional* in Bogota, Colombia, coincided with widespread anti-elitist contestation and popular rebellion against the elitist regime instituted under the banner of *Frente Nacional*.

With the advent of new political ideas in the early-eighties in Europe, while envisioning some salient tensions building at the heart of the Socialist Bloc, Laclau and Mouffe saw in the prevailing notion of class – so central in the Marxist theory – a category that was ill-equipped to unfold and comprehend epochal changes, urging the composition instead of novel ontological grounds.

What is now in crisis is a whole conception of socialism which rests upon the ontological centrality of the working class, upon the role of Revolution, with a capital 'r', as the founding moment in the transition from one type of society to another, and upon the illusory prospect of a perfectly unitary and homogeneous collective will that will render pointless the moment of politics. The plural and multifarious character of contemporary social struggles has finally dissolved the last foundation for that political imaginary (Laclau and Mouffe, 2001, p. 2).

Drawing on structural linguistics, post-structuralism, psychoanalysis and Marxism, Laclau and Mouffe (1985) articulated a field of political analysis in its own right. This approach establishes, broadly speaking, that all objects and actions have a meaning, which is deliberated by particular systems of differences (see Howarth, 2000, p. 102). By breaking with the essentialist and totalising conception of social class in the Marxist theory and drawing, instead, on discourse, the post-Marxist label started to be applied to Laclau and Mouffe's work. They would finally appropriate this label, formally acknowledging it through *HSS*'s second edition (2001) preface as the formal foundation of a new ontological perspective.

As Stavrakakis (2017a, p. 537) states, through *HSS* Laclau and Mouffe stress the importance of representation as being the key 'in accounting for the construction and (partial/temporary) sedimentation of political subjectivity, social objectivity, and hegemonic orders'. Therefore, *HSS* elaborates a new theoretical articulation, forging, from a post-Gramscian approach to hegemony and the Lacanian notion of lack, a passage from *politics* (ontic) to *politics as such* (ontological).

Hegemony *a la* Laclau and Mouffe seeks to account for the articulation of new political representations (with their inherent and external limits) and their transient crystallisation (marked by the invariable impossibility of being fully constituted). As no social fullness is rendered possible, hegemony supposes the practices that continuously (re)negotiate the stability of its articulations, preventing the visibility of contingency and a subsequent dislocation from taking place.

The conception of discourse embeds a key ontological question for Laclau and Mouffe, as it formulates an understanding of how social meaning comes about, ultimately questioning the conditions of possibility for social existence. If identity, for Marxism, came about through a homogeneous social subject constituted by objectively pre-conceived social classes, post-Marxism would analytically engage with social identity from pluralist and contingent perspectives. For Laclau and Mouffe, identity is instituted politically, which means that its very condition depends on the work of the negative – that is, from *antagonism* (Marchart, 2018, p. 9).

By drawing on Lacanian theory, Laclau and Mouffe assume the social to be an always lacking realm as no symbolisation can render social reality complete. In turn, such a constitutive lack makes representation (identification) necessary (1985, p. 114). However, if any form of social representation supposes only a partial effort of constructing society, then *antagonism* functions as the expression of the excluded possibilities by the predominant social structure, through which the latter can come to be challenged (Biglieri and Perelló, 2019, p. 333). Within this perspective, discourse does 'not [entail] forms of thought that add a second sense to a primary, [...] instead, they are part of the primary terrain itself in which the social is constituted' (Laclau and Mouffe, 1985/2001, p. 110; see also Žižek, 1989, p. 142).

Reflecting upon the antagonistic process enabling hegemonic disputes, Laclau and Mouffe echo Gramsci's notion of crisis (Stavrakakis, 2017a). Gramsci drew on the idea of 'organic crisis' as an interregnum through which 'national-popular ideological elements' emerged unsatisfied. Gramsci attributed to these elements a privileged role in the articulation of a new collective will. Laclau and Mouffe's discursive turn would regard these national-popular elements as signifiers that assume a certain degree of independence by detaching them from the dominant social structures. Indeed, by exhibiting its inherent precariousness, the instability of a social structure provides an abundant amount of 'floating signifiers' whose meaning is suspended, opening the possibility for them being articulated by opposing discursive fields (Laclau and Mouffe, 2001, p. 123). The 'floating signifiers' thus relate to democratic demands which are not considered within the existing realm of social meaning, and, by being disputed by rival projects, they open, in turn, the possibility for articulating a novel hegemonic terrain (*ibid.*, 108).

However, signifying elements require *something* with the ability to formally articulate them into a discursive structure. This *something* is identified in the form of privileged discursive points, described by Laclau and Mouffe as 'nodal'. Drawing from the Lacanian terminology of *points-de-capiton* and *master-signifier*, the 'nodal points' convey a patchwork character that enables a partial fixation of meaning in a signifying chain (Laclau and Mouffe, 1985, p. 112). As laid out by De Cleen, *et al.* (2020) 'in liberalism the signifier 'freedom' or 'liberty' plays such a central role. Other signifiers, such as 'state', 'individual', and 'society', acquire meaning in relation to the nodal point 'freedom''.

In short, political struggles for Laclau and Mouffe constitute *practices of articulation*, entailing 'the construction of nodal points which partially fix meaning; and the partial character of this fixation proceeds from the openness of the social' (2001/1985, p. 113). As in the Lacanian symbolic register, the 'social' here relates to a structure that supports and regulates the discursive representations we use to describe the world and oneself. It always pre-exists and takes over the subject and, as in every structure of meaning, carries incompleteness, as in a gap (the Lacanian *real*) resisting subsumption under the socio-symbolic realm. This structure of meaning can have no other name than 'discourse' in the work of Laclau and Mouffe (Howarth, 2000).

By privileging the moment of political articulation, Laclau and Mouffe's approach provides the category of *hegemony* with an absolute centrality. *HSS* founded a pioneering contribution to political theory, configuring a new ontological perspective for analysing articulatory practices enacting in the (de)construction of political antagonism and the instalment (and contestation) of social identities. It draws from a deconstructed concept of discourse, incorporating the necessary 'undecidables' that permeate every terrain seen as governed by structural determination (Derrida); for every hegemonic articulation is contingent in nature. Such a formulation reveals how the post-Marxist approach is entrenched in the domain of post-structuralism, taken as a compelling turn for understanding the political instalment of social identity.

What creates and sustains the *identity* of a given ideological field beyond all possible variations of its positive content? *Hegemony and Socialist Strategy* delineates what is probably the definitive answer to this crucial question (Žižek, 1989, p. 95; italics in original).

Delving deeper into psychoanalytic perspectives on identity and subjectivity, Laclau's solo publication *On Populist Reason* (2005; hereafter referred to as *OPR*) further fleshed out some central analytical features of the post-Gramscian conception of hegemony. The concept of populism, however, would now be placed in the post-Marxist spotlight, presented through *OPR* in the form of a *political logic*.

While Laclau's seminal reflections drew on Argentinean politics as an ontic reference (Laclau, 1990, p. 200), *OPR* would find, in Latin America's so-called *pink tide,* a fertile social and political canvas for delineating and refining its theoretical contours. Moreover, like *HSS,* the analytical potential enclosed in *OPR* would remain underutilised for a few years before being seized. Indeed, *HSS* had a somewhat prophetic outlook, as it posed central problematic points in the leftist camp, which would become visible years after its publication – particularly at the dawn of the 1990s with the implosion of the socialist camp and the European leftist adherence to the neoliberal hegemony (Laclau and Mouffe, 2001/1985, p. vii-xix). Likewise,

Laclau's visionary and decidedly theoretical and analytic moves featuring *OPR* would strike a chord with a political era that was not yet obviously present.

When *OPR* finally came into print, the Anglo-Saxon and European world gave little attention to it, affording essentially peripheral and non-western concerns to populism and political emotions. Little did they know that less than five years later, Latin America's social upsurge and political discourses from the late 90s and early 2000s would find an echo in the popular effervescence taking over the European, North American and British streets and parliaments (see Gerbauldo, 2017; Eklund, 2019). *OPR* came to embody one of the most captivating and influential political theory pieces of the 21st century.

Since Saussure (2011), we have known that language comprises a system of differences between relational values (e.g. a glass is a glass, insofar as it is not a vase or a bottle). Therefore, differences shape identity and, through broader relational networks, a structure of meaning. However, in order to compose a meaning structure, these elements would have to be somehow equivalent to a certain level, only by opposition to an outside-system. In other words, the very condition of possibility for a glass, a vase, and a bottle to be made equivalent as recipients, is the existence of an outside linguistic system, as blankets or automobiles could be.

By wanting to better distil the role of 'nodal points' in structuring and fixing the meaning of a signifying chain, Laclau's *OPR* goes back to psychoanalytic theory – namely Lacan's axes of *metonymy* and *metaphor* – to introduce a secondary theoretical foundation: the logics of *difference* and *equivalence* (Laclau, 2005a, p. 67; see also Stavrakakis, 2004, p. 257). Thus far, two main formal anchors endow the conceptual articulation of populism as logic: the *nodal points*, vital for the apparent fixation of meaning in a structure that is always incomplete, and the logics of *difference* and *equivalence*, formulating a relational network-structure of signifying interactions.

Laclau introduces an additional element he had been working on since the early 90s. This was the 'empty signifier', a key factor in the predominance of the logics of equivalence in political representation (Laclau, 1996) and now assuming a critical component in the formal composition of populism. This concept accounts for the structuring of heterogeneous demands and grievances (such as 'free public transport', 'environmental rights' or 'better education'), articulated as general opposition to the system as a whole.

The deconstructed notion of the Saussurean sign by people like Derrida and Lacan not only stresses how structures of meaning are always unstable. Most importantly, it exhibits how signification derives from an empty place. Rather than linking a signifier (symbolic) to a signified (real), signification appears by the desire to order a constitutively lacking realm, as formulated by Lacan. This is to say, knowledge, as such, is impossible to reach as the conditions of possibility for the meaning-making process rely on differential operations we engage in within the socio-symbolic field structured by our very own limited historical attempts to reach knowledge with a capital 'k'.

The post-structuralist framework featuring *OPR* sees, as *HSS* did, identity as an endless chimeric search, highlighting how every structure of meaning is necessarily unstable. This is far from the classical structuralist presupposition in which structures appear stable. A post-structuralist framework is very much like Wittgenstein's 'language games' and states that as signifying elements within the discursive structure slide, the signification processes also slide – thus presenting a structural reconfiguration.

Paraphrasing Laclau, we could ask ourselves 'how may we signify something that is not a difference, but the radical exclusion which grounds all differences? (Laclau, 1996, p. 39). A subversion of all units of signification is then required, as in a split within them, emptying one side by its differential nature through an opposition with the system-represented side. The empty signifier, as 'a sequence of sounds deprived of any signifying function, through the subversion of the [*saussurean*] sign' (p. 36), embodies this radical contestation by articulating the heterogeneous demands that remain unsatisfied by the system (Laclau, 2005a, p. 73).

The role of the empty signifier assumes particular importance, and it draws attention to the seemingly ambivalent, however necessary, relationship between *particularity* and *universality* in social representation processes. Any form of composition of an equivalential discursive field supposes the investment on a partial object – which is *not* a *partiality* within the *totality* but a *partiality* that becomes the *totality*. As aptly stated by Balibar:

> The fact is that when one offers a criticism of universalism—religious or secular, political or scientific—in the name of defending cultures, idioms, beliefs, and their absolute right to particularity, this enunciation is immediately expressed *from the standpoint of the universal*, which means both in a rhetoric that is rigorously interchangeable and from the perspective of a totalisation of differences, thus of another universalism (Balibar, 2007, p. 51).

Put more fully, every community worthy of its name can only preserve its inherent plurality and be constituted as a unity insofar as a partial element embodies the total representation of this social universe (see Laclau 1996, p. 26). As already mentioned, every signification process is inherently relational, for the logics of equivalence and difference underlie every discursive mediation.

The construction of the 'us/them' opposition in populism often leads to a formal antagonism established between 'the people' and 'the elite'. De Cleen et al. (2018) do well to note, however, that, from a discourse analytical standpoint, 'populists can rely on a wide range of labels to posit themselves as the representatives of the underdog (the 'down-group') against the powerful (the 'up-group')'. Constructions of this core antagonism could perhaps pit 'the ordinary people' against 'the political caste' or formulate a boundary confronting 'the simple (wo)man' with 'the establishment'.

To spell it out explicitly, for Laclau, populism is a logic marked by the simplification of the antagonistic boundaries between an underdog ('the people') and its illegitimate 'other'. It entails establishing a 'chain of equivalence' by the articulation of various 'social demands', which had hitherto been displaced, by an 'empty signifier' (Laclau, 2005a, 181). The empty signifier relates to a signifier without signified, serving as means of representation of the 'absent fullness' within 'the precarious character of any positivity' by an ontologically lacking social reality (Laclau, 1990, p. 92).

Therefore, if discourse amounts to the structures through which one constructs and accesses social meaning (constituted by articulatory practices), discourse analysis should critically explain the concrete signifying elements and the main logics that make a specific (populist) discursive structure possible. However, as discourse theory deconstructed understandings of populism as derived from the formal logics enacted in any signifying operation (ontological), the formal principles which constitute *populism-as-logic* in turn enable political analysis on a much more concrete basis (ontic).

1.2. The Essex School

1.2.1. *Laclau and Mouffe and after*

A generation of scholars that was concerned about the narrow positivism encompassing social sciences and the determinist economistic scope of most Marxist analyses found much to like in Laclau's oeuvre. With the excitement of old and new fellow travellers, Laclau and Mouffe's joint and solo contributions gained momentum, encouraging a healthy and rapidly growing discourse theoretical tradition. The *University of Essex* which had been Mouffe's *alma mater* and Laclau's main centre of intellectual operations since the early 70s, quickly became an institutional reference to post-Marxism. As a result, the *Essex School* label expanded widely as a discursive blanket to shelter Laclau and Mouffe's school of thought, with *HSS* and *OPR* as crucial intellectual milestones.

With inventive linguistic turns and laborious conceptual crafting, various theoretical ideas were brought home by Laclau in *OPR*. The pointer in the 'lacanometer' – to borrow Stavrakakis and Glynos's (2004) terms –, already visible through his *New Reflections on the Revolution of our Time* and *Emancipation(s)* would reach its tipping point in the scale through *OPR*. As Laclau admitted himself (Laclau 1993, p. 58), Lacanian theory began assuming a much more prominent role in his writings and, for better or worse, intellectual exchanges demanded a more polished and integrated picture of psychoanalytic grammar into the post-Marxist frame (e.g. Žižek, 1989; Žižek, 1990; Butler, Laclau and Žižek, 2000; Stavrakakis and Glynos, 2004).[4]

As expected, however, the publication of *OPR* not only awakened lavish praise. Reactions to this book sparked heated debates. Some even abruptly dissolved provocative intellectual closeness which had long nourished post-Marxist thought. This was particularly

---

[4] Stavrakakis and Glynos (2004) describe a 'lacanometer' measuring the increasing presence of Lacanian influence in Laclau's texts.

the case with Slavoj Žižek, whose blistering discussions with Laclau after *OPR* gave their intellectual deliberations a more exasperating than beneficial culmination (for the Laclau and Žižek debate, see Žižek, 2006a; Laclau, 2006; Žižek, 2006b).

With earnest criticism and endorsement, moreover, some concerns arose at the heart of the *Essex School*. From the 1970s to the 80s, Laclau and Mouffe had been trying to break with the class essentialism in Marxist theory, initially finding through Gramsci's hegemony the key to unravelling the formation and sedimentation of political identities (Laclau and Mouffe, 2001/1985, p. 193; Thomassen, 2016, p. 164). With *OPR*, however, populism came to be seen as 'the royal road to understanding something about the ontological constitution of the political as such' (Laclau, 2005b, p. 67; see also in Moffit and Tormey, 2014, p. 386). As provokingly captured by Arditti (2010), this conceptual tension immediately raises the question: is 'Populism is Hegemony is Politics?'.

Voices within the *Essex School* have long drawn attention to the conceptual proximity and the relational difference of populism and hegemony, raising concern over the theoretical vagueness of such conceptual overlapping (Arditi 2010; Moffit and Tormey, 2014; Moffitt 2016; Katsambekis and Kioupkiolis 2019). While hegemony raises questions about norms, political institutions, dominant discourses and their potential disruption, taking issue with overriding cultural and civilisation features (see Howarth, 2004, p. 263), populism seems to engage with articulatory practices disputing common sense, contesting existing regime dominance and articulating new majorities in the area of civil society (see Mazzolini, 2020).

Indeed, populism and hegemony might not be directly interchangeable concepts. However, they are intrinsically inscribed within the same ontological post-Marxist horizon. As has been elaborated, such a horizon undertakes the primacy of politics in the dispute and instalment of society precisely because social meaning is relentlessly inscribed in a field dominated by radical contingency. Some might spot a flaw in relating either populism or hegemony to politics (e.g. Moffit and Tormey, 2014; Dean and Maiguashca, 2020). Nevertheless, this move might well disclose the theoretical consistency in post-Marxist thought.

As aptly noted by Eklundh (2020, p. 124), 'Laclau's argument that politics is hegemony is populism is in this case not a sign of lacking analytical utility, but should be seen as the way to circumvent the emotion-reason divide'. In line with Eklundh, I believe this has been spelt out explicitly by Laclau himself when asserting that the logics endowing populism and hegemony 'and that of the Lacanian *object a* largely overlap and refer to a fundamental ontological relation in which fullness can only be touched through a radical investment in a partial object' (Laclau, 2006, p. 651).

From a Laclauian perspective, the emotion-reason divide is obsolete precisely because meaning-making comes about through the affective construction of the social world by endlessly desiring the impossible mediation between concepts and things as such (Stavrakakis, 2007). To put it in a rather forthright way, in exposing the self-defeating enterprise of knowledge-reaching (positivism/Marxism), the *Essex School* sets an analytical and emotionally endowed framework for meaning-making (post-Marxism/post-structuralism).

1.2.2. *From concept to concept and signifier*

As seen, discourse theory approaches populism as a logic underlying the bottom-up *underdog-versus-elite* challenge to the totality of a real existing hegemonic form (Laclau, 2005a). This is useful since it invites an understanding of the composition of antagonistic actors, the forms and processes of articulatory practices at stake and the relational 'weight' of demands in the (performative) conformation of new forms of identity positions in a given field of analysis – not to mention the undetermined elements that might later resurface to structure new forms of political challenge to the dominant social order. In this sense, populism as a logic already provides a grammar to analytically engage with populist discourses in a situated fashion.

What is more, in considering populism as a 'vanishing mediator', discourse theory claims that the relevant analytical issues lie not in populism as such but rather in the strategical, ideological and normative social stakes (De Cleen and Glynos, 2021, p. 184). The purpose of populism as a concept is thus revealed as an analytical starting point, requiring a deeper immersion in the interaction of populist and non-populist elements, thus enabling the construction of a more integrated picture of political antagonism and social meaning-making (De Cleen, Glynos and Mondon, 2018, p. 653). The ontological principles embedded in the category of 'discourse' offer strategic venues to explore these dynamic interactions further.

Since 'all identity is constructed within this tension between the differential and the equivalential logics' (Laclau 2005a, p. 70), every new form of identity position, no matter the scale, relies to a certain degree on the logic of populism (Laclau, 2005b, p. 45). Thus, the distinction between the self and the other – or 'us' and 'them', to formulate it in more political terms – encloses a formal pattern which can 'provide important insights for the study not only of populism, but of politics in general' (Marchart, 2018, p.110). The principles of lack (Lacan) and undecidability (Derrida) are central here, as they denote, through the constant movement of actors and sliding of concepts, how human interactions constantly give way to new discursive articulations, thus resulting in new representations of social reality.

These key ontological features inevitably create a critical stance to concept-centred analyses, as formulating meaning-making processes comes about through mutual feedback relations. By mutual feedback, it should be understood that identificatory processes are relational, and thus the meaning of concepts is also dependent on articulatory practices (Laclau and Mouffe, 1985; Stavrakakis, 2014). Put less gnomically, when a signifier X features prominently everywhere, the discursive dynamics and signification processes regarding X are not restricted to X. In as much as X acquires a given meaning, all discursive elements within this given discursive universe reconstitute their identity in relation to the signifier X and thus to the other existing meaningful elements in the signifying chain. Let us now imagine signifier X refers to either 'populism' or 'populist'.

1.2.3. *Populism discourse studies*

By moving from 'concept' to 'concept and signifier', discourse theory has uncovered fresh analytical potential, moving the focus from populist discourses to studying discourses about populism, including pro-populist and anti-populist discourses (what I call in this thesis populism discourse studies). In so doing, the bulk of this research analyses the central discursive role populism as a signifier assumes in the antagonistic construction of contemporary political disputes and social meaning-making processes.

In an initial exploration of discourses on populism, Glynos and Mondon (2016) analyse the discursive uses of the words 'populism' and 'populist' by specific segments of the European press. In recognising how these two signifiers are employed in a rather exaggerated and dramatic fashion, the journalistic discourses analysed seem to emphasise populist elements at the expense of others, depicting, through the 'political logic of populist hype', the construction of a populist meteoric menace fuelled by journalistic liberal angst.

This provoking analytic turn has been welcomed (see De Cleen, Glynos and Mondon, 2018; Dean and Maiguashca, 2020; Eklundh, 2020; Goyvaerts and De Cleen 2020), inspiring further discursive studies about populism in the Greek (Nikisianis et al. 2019), British (Brown and Mondon, 2020) and Brazilian (Ronderos and Zicman de Barros, 2020) press. Interestingly enough, while most British and European media-centric studies solely identify anti-populist discourses, some pro-populist journalistic elements were found in the Brazilian case (p. 36).

Moreover, the media has assumed a leading role in structuring the public debate regarding discourses about populism and therefore also the centrality of populism discourse studies. However marginal, the role of academia is often hinted at in these studies, and, again, the Brazilian case seems somehow distinctive. While academics are said to impose influence over anti-populist journalism in the British (Brown and Mondon, 2020) and Greek (Nikisianis et al. 2019) contexts, the Brazilian case suggests opposite relational feedback, highlighting how journalistic and political debates about populism prompted the seminal academic conceptualisations of populism in Brazil. Notwithstanding the marginal role these mutual feedback processes assume in this research production, the reference to journalism and academic inter-sphere dynamics highly echoes Anthony Giddens' (1984) double hermeneutic.

Nearly 40 years ago, Giddens asserted that 'theories and findings of the social sciences cannot be kept wholly separate from the universe of meaning and action which they are about' (Giddens, 1984, p. xxxii-xxxiii). Following Giddens, Stavrakakis (2017b) embarked on the pursuit of the genealogy of anti-populist academic discourses in an attempt to show how the discoveries of *the sciences* often help the construction of the very context they intend to describe. In so doing, this study identifies Richard Hofstadter's Pulitzer winner *The Age of Reform* (1955) as a conspicuous root of the widespread derogative views of populism in the North American context and beyond (p. 17).

However, Giddens' appeal to double hermeneutics does not restrict itself to stressing the academic enunciation as the source of (social) meaning. In his view, 'theories in the social sciences have to be in some part based upon ideas which (although not necessarily discursively formulated by them) are already held by the agents to whom they refer' (Giddens, 1984, p. xxxiv). It follows that a double-hermeneutical discourse theory approach should regard lay actors as social theorists. As such, double hermeneutics prompts populism discourse studies to attend to the lively interactions between journalists, politicians and political and social theorists (see Goyvaerts and De Cleen 2020; Rydgen, 2017, p. 493). This implies tracing, genealogically, the first example of when the words 'populism' and 'populist' were enunciated, overdetermining the political debate (see Jäger, 2017, p. 13; De Cleen and Glynos, 2021, p. 188).

Highly resonating with a post-structuralist ontological stance, double hermeneutics struck a chord with discourse theory's deconstructed understanding of mutual feedback processes. It also featured a profound resemblance with Foucault's 'transcendental-empirical doublet', which takes a subject as being both an object of knowledge and a subject who knows (Foucault 1970, p. 312; see also Glynos & Howarth 2007, p. 156, 48, 210). Just as discourse theory does, Foucault's doublet highlights how processes of mutual feedback do not restrict themselves to the sciences but rather endow knowledge production within and across all social spheres.

The point I want to raise here is that, while the literature studying discourses on populism has highlighted the need to study populism as a concept *and* a signifier within and across politics, academia and the media (Glynos and Mondon, 2016; Stavrakakis, 2017b; De Cleen, Glynos and Mondon, 2018; 2021; Nikisianis, et al. 2019; Goyvaerts and De Cleen and Glynos, 2021), most studies have limited their scope to studying populism with a rather one-sided hermeneutic approach, so to speak. In so doing, these mutual feedback processes of the articulation of meaning surrounding populism as a signifier are often implied rather than formally explored.

1.2.4. *The fantasy in populist-centrism*

By moving from 'concept' to 'concept *and* signifier', discourse theory has unleashed new analytical potential with which to study populism. The bulk of these strands of literature pay close attention to how key enunciators formulate the meaning of the words 'populist' and 'populism' and how a more nuanced picture of political dispute can be presented (Glynos and Mondon, 2016; Stavrakakis, 2017b; De Cleen, Glynos and Mondon, 2018; 2021; Nikisianis, et al. 2019; Ronderos and Zicman de Barros, 2020; Goyvaerts and De Cleen, 2020). This intellectual enterprise is certainly timely and apposite, as populism (sacred at times, dirty at others) features prominently in most social, political, journalistic and scholarly communication.

However, it is true that the deployment of discourse theory in the study of populism as a nodal signifying element has been aimed mainly at grasping the derogatory uses of the signifiers 'populist' and 'populism'. Glynos and Mondon (2016), for instance, explore the discursive employment of these two words by journalists and pundits via the psychoanalytic category of fantasy. The scrutiny over the discursive uses of such signifiers has raised awareness of how specific segments of the European press, rather than aiming to productively shed light on the public sphere's actual developments, sound the alarm over an anti-democratic populist-menace, in order to enforce their influence over the political agenda. Similar efforts have been made to analyse other media segments, as are the Greek (Nikisianis et al. 2019) and British press (Brown and Mondon, 2020).

In these studies, populists assume the terrifying figure of a dangerous *other*, embodied by the psychoanalytically inflicted figure of the 'thief of enjoyment' (Žižek, 1993). Responsible for the anxiety and anguish of the down-group, populists would be constructed as 'others not merely enjoying themselves excessively, but enjoying themselves *at my expense*' – which is to say, at the expense of 'the people' (Glynos and Mondon, 2016, p. 7). In the words of Jacques-Alain Miller:

Why does the Other remain Other? What is the cause for our hatred of him, for our hatred of him in his very being? It is hatred of the enjoyment in the Other. This would be the most general formula for the modern racism we are witnessing today: a hatred of a particular way the Other enjoys... The question of tolerance or intolerance is... located on the level of tolerance or intolerance toward the enjoyment of the Other, the Other who essentially steals my own enjoyment (Miller, cited in Žižek, 1993, p. 203).

As we have seen, Laclau was following the psychoanalytic theory of Jacques Lacan for structuring coherent ontological grounds in his theory of populism. This is why we can read *populism-as-a-logic* as being precisely rooted in Lacan's object *a*, enclosing the (re)articulation of a fantasy of popular sovereignty (social fullness).

As seen, the understanding of the Lacanian object *a* presents itself within Laclau's writing in a sort of overdetermined mode, as a direct equivalence to a part which 'is not a partiality within the totality but a partiality which is the totality' (Laclau, 2006, p. 651). Indeed, object *a* assumes the role of an excessive X which can be taken as the lack in the symbolic Other, thus making of it the utopian centrepiece that can finally deliver the fullness of *jouissance*. Žižek (1989, p. 162) delves into the matter:

When, for example, in his speech at Lenin's funeral, Stalin proclaims, 'We, the Communists, are people of a special mould. We are made of special stuff,' it is quite easy to recognise the Lacanian name for this special stuff: *object petit a*, the sublime object in the interspace between the two deaths.

Therefore, object *a* embodies a partiality that, as in an internal exclusion from the symbolic order, becomes totality through an other worldly narrative (when the object is raised to the dignity of the Thing). What if, instead of 'the Communists', Stalin had referred to 'the

Populists'? Would we not encounter an other worldly logic enclosed in (pro)populist discourse?

In terms of a promise of restoring popular sovereignty, I believe that players or groups associated with populism can capture the political agenda. This is to say, 'populist' and 'populism' could indeed represent the promise to deliver the impossible task of reaching fullness, the unattainable promise of finally achieving an identity position through which popular sovereignty can be enjoyed fully. Thus, by identifying the composition of discursive structures that rely on 'populism' and 'populist' as nodal points, further studies are needed to understand how populist fantasmatic narratives articulate and habilitate distinctive modes of social enjoyment.

1.3. Thesis Aim and Research Questions

Against this background, the overriding aim of this thesis is to exploit discourse theory's potentialities enclosed in the reading of populism as a logic, by placing the analytical focus beyond populist phenomena, strictly speaking. As such, I develop research strategies to empirically explore the distinctive virtues of discourse theory in unravelling signifying processes and affective articulations conforming and sustaining forms of political antagonism and social identity. This is done so in a context-specific manner, taking Brazil as an ontic social surface of inscription. The intent here is to develop a relational paper-based study of political antagonism by critically drawing on issues related to populism, but which intend to provide a more complex and anchored picture of political articulation and fantasmatic grip. The overall aim is broken down into four inter-related research questions.

RQ1: (How) did the signifiers 'populism' and 'populist' first become central features of Brazil's political debate and in what ways have these discursive articulations impacted Brazilian society?

The first research question sets out a genealogical exploration of how discourses about populism were first introduced in Brazil, paying particular attention to the discursive turns, disputes, feedback dynamics and articulations that made 'populism' a central discursive feature. In following this line of inquiry, I intend to make intelligible the concrete signifying processes and logics that enabled populism, as a 'thing', to be thought within Brazilian social reality, thus adding flesh and colour to the context-specific significance of populist politics and discourses about populism in Brazil. My interest here lies not in coming to terms with an objective and stable socio-political account of populism in Brazil. Instead, I intend to construct a detailed and nuanced picture of the antagonistic and non-antagonistic discursive modes derived from the use of the signifier populism, paying close attention to discursive interactions in the spheres of academia, politics and the media. This will allow me to answer a secondary context-specific question, enabling a deeper understanding of the discursive disputes in Brazil related to populism and contributing as a research question for further analyses drawing on discourses about populism. Namely:

- Which sphere in the media-politics-academia matrix takes on a privileged discursive role, and how might this inter-sphere relational 'weight' affect the (feedback) dynamics influencing discourses about populism?

Through this secondary research question, I examine the conditions underlying the particular type of relationship between these spheres, the character of the processes that transmit ideas and people within and across the three spheres and the feedback dynamics that influence not only populist politics but also the politics of discourses about populism.

RQ2: (How) are the signifiers 'populism' and 'populist' articulated and constructed in Brazil's contemporary journalistic language, and (in which ways) do they invite forms of enjoyment and endow normative responses to perceived problems?

Having explored the genealogical foundations of discourses about populism in Brazil, my second research question takes issue with the affective role of populism-as-a-signifier as an active factor in contemporary forms of antagonism in Brazilian politics. This question aims to unravel the role journalists play in the politics of discourses about populism as the media has been highlighted in recent scholarship as a key factor in untangling logics underlying the ubiquity of the signifier populism in contemporary political debate (Nikisianis et al. 2019; Goyvaerts and De Cleen, 2020; Brown and Mondon, 2021). Equally this question seeks to capture the affective force underlying discourses related to populism and discourses surrounding populism (Glynos and Mondon, 2016). In taking fantasy as an analytical grid, particular attention is given to the way mainstream journalists have taken part in constructing a crisis in Brazilian politics, particularly related to the left-wing Workers' Party (PT) and its undisputed leader Luiz Inácio da Silva (Lula). I intend here to not simply show the signifying elements and logics enacted in the configuration of discursive modes of antagonism. My target is to draw out the normative significance and ideological content guiding the journalistic anti-populist discourses, inviting readers to partake in distinctive fantasmatic modes of enjoyment.

RQ3: Can the rationale endowed in populism-as-a-logic be employed analytically to explain the articulation of prefigurative forms of collective representation contesting personalism?

As highlighted by Glynos and Mondon (2016), exaggerated journalistic (and scholarly) discourses about populism tend to focus on charismatic figures in an over-the-top way at the expense of highly significant yet underplayed aspects of political and social reality. This, I believe, has been the main focus of analysts, scholars and commentators in terms of Jair Bolsonaro's presidential victory in Brazil's 2018 elections, which were depicted as yet another unequivocal sign of a rise in worldwide right-wing populism (Hunter and Power, 2019). In circumventing this main line of enquiry and moving beyond the study of populism, my third research question invites the critical exploration of non-populist phenomena drawing on the rationale of populism as a logic. In so doing, I intend to explore the productive analytic horizons enclosed in discourse theory, paying close attention to how its ontological presuppositions and analytical tools are useful to analyse and critically explain meaningful aspects of political antagonism and the articulation of new forms of democratic representation and social meaning-making processes beyond the reaches of strong personalist appeals.

RQ4: Can (dis)identification and meaning-making be conceived from a perspective of desire? With populism as my primary area of engagement, the questions above take issue with the articulatory practices and modes of antagonism affectively challenging, sustaining and co-forming distinctive structures of social meaning. As will be seen in my research strategy, the outlined objectives encompass signification processes (political logics) and the force and grip underlying them (fantasmatic logics) from critical and analytical points of view (Glynos and Howarth, 2007). These questions trigger a more profound ontological question about the very conditions of possibility for meaning-making processes beyond the reaches of formal signification. While populism has been widely seen as an over-emotional and dangerous form of politics, Laclau's insightful turn would draw precisely on populism to show how every form of political action and social meaning is inherently emotional. Like populism, the discursive appeal to emotions has chiefly followed exclusionary dynamics, as conforming antagonising modes with subjects seen as undesirable by dominant discourses considering them to be 'too emotional' – be they woman, non-western, non-white, and many others (Eklundh, 2020, p. 110). Hysteria has also been used discursively as a form of female and popular exclusion (see Krasny, 2020). In identifying hysteria as a promising scope in which to think of identificatory processes and the production of social knowledge, this question invites the exploration of further theoretical avenues to find in desire the very condition of possibility for meaning-making.

1.3.1. Contribution

In adopting a four-step approach, this research project aims to contribute to discourse theory at the frontier of populism studies. This is to say, by drawing on discussions derived from the study of populism, I move forward lines of analysis, often referenced by discourse theory academic circles but which remain underexplored, to critically explain political and social dynamics beyond the study of populist phenomena. These encompass, saliently, the study of populism as a concept and a signifier across academia, politics and the media; the deployment of fantasy as an analytical grid for the study of discourses about populism; the role of the media in the ubiquitous nature of discourses about populism; and the analytical exploration of discourse theory beyond charismatic figures. Notwithstanding the inter-relational character underlying these four papers, the contributions are distinct and bring into dialogue concrete strands of literature and related debates in each step of the overall approach.

Paper 1 makes a contribution to the study of populism as a concept and a signifier, bringing to bear feedback dynamics and interactions within and across social spheres (chiefly journalism, the academy and politics). I bring to dialogue strands of literature reflecting upon the logic of populism (Laclau 2005ab; Marchart, 2018; Stavrakakis, 2004; 2014; 2017a), literature exploring discourses about populism (Stavrakakis, 2017b; De Cleen, Glynos and Mondon, 2018; 2021; Nikisianis, et al. 2019; Ronderos and Zicman de Barros, 2020; Goyvaerts and De Cleen, 2020), and scholarly work concerned with the feedback dynamics and interactions that assume a nodal role in the political articulation of social meaning (Giddens, 1984; Foucault, 1970; Laclau, 1991; Stavrakakis, 2017b). As has been referenced, some studies have devoted productive efforts to exploring some of these aspects empirically, mainly focusing on the role populism plays as a signifier in journalistic discourses (Glynos and Mondon, 2016; Brown and Mondon, 2020). While most studies lean towards a rather one-sided hermeneutical approach, the interaction with academia and politics is often referenced as paramount in fully capturing the concrete dynamics underlying the ubiquity of the word populism and its discursive influence in the structuring of social reality (e.g. Stavrakakis, 2017b). As far as I know, no such study has been undertaken and certainly not in respect to concrete case studies to date. Therefore, in taking these strands of literature seriously, paper 1 develops a multi-sited framework to study populism as a concept and a signifier. This framework features a novel research strategy to study discourses about populism by unpacking discursive modes, feedback dynamics and synchronic and diachronic functions enacting in the structuring of meaning within and across social spheres. It also draws on ethnographic strategies in 'following the word' as a means to trace the interactive construction of social narrative (Marcus, 1995). In terms of methods and techniques, it contributes to discourse analysis by incorporating algorithms for database construction (via Python coding), allowing the gathering and handling of an extensive body of work across various sources and outlets (academic, journalistic or otherwise). In tracing the genealogical employment of the signifiers 'populism' and 'populist' in Brazil, this paper also brings new insights to this case. Delving into Brazil's fourth republican period (1946-1964), this article reconstructs the main political disputes and scrutinises the most prominent journalistic outlets of the time, something with no precedents in both Lusophone and Anglo-Saxon scholarship.

Moving on, while Glynos and Mondon (2016) helped set the scene for the study of populism as a signifier, the importance of their work to the exploration of fantasmatic narratives sustaining discursive structures and gripping subjects has been virtually set aside in subsequent research production (). What is more, most studies drawing on the signifiers 'populism' and 'populist' have broadly relied on the correlation of broad discursive trends via Corpus Linguistics (CL). In so doing, they have left out the concrete structuring of meaning, the formal signifying turns and the contextual tenor animating such discursive operations, which would allow a deeper and more anchored normative and ideological picture to be drawn (e.g. Brown and Mondon, 2020). As such, Paper 2 derives from and engages with literature exploring populism as a signifier (e.g. Glynos and Mondon, 2016), research drawing on the paramount role of the media in terms of the ubiquitous character of discourses about populism (e.g. Goyvaerts and De Cleen, 2020), and psychoanalytic strands drawing on fantasy as a distinctive category for political analysis (Žižek, 1989; Chang and Glynos, 2011; Glynos, 2001). Inspired by these repertoires, paper 2 contributes to the discourse theory tradition by further exploring insights into the affective force animating journalistic discourses about populism. This is done with reference to a prominent Brazilian news magazine (*Veja*). It also contributes to the intersection between psychoanalysis and discourse theory by engaging with orbiting psychoanalytic concepts, which play a central role in fantasmatic analysis, chiefly the tropes of 'thief of enjoyment' (Žižek, 1989; Glynos, 2008) and 'guarantor' (Chang and Glynos, 2011). Furthermore, while rhetorical analysis has been developed in exploring *Veja* (Benetti, 2016; Chicarino et al. 2021), no discursive analysis has been undertaken to untangle and explain the way this news magazine constructs the political debate through populist discursive elements, making additions to literature about Brazil.

Paper 3 engages with political science debates drawing on institutional crisis and personalism. In so doing, this paper contributes to extended strands of literature by proving discourse theory's analytic virtues in explaining meaningful aspects of political processes that appear as paradigmatic in terms of mainstream theories and models derived from political science debates. The contribution to these debates also relies on giving nuance to aspects of electoral politics that remain underexplored and which challenge the theoretical principles of mainstream literature drawing on institutional crisis and the personalist character of electoral politics. Specifically, the contribution to discourse theory by paper 3 is twofold. On the one hand, by distancing itself from the obvious line of inquiry in terms of populism in Brazil's 2018 election (Bolsonaro's victory), this paper deploys the analytic arsenal enclosed in populism-as-a-logic to explain the appearance of a strikingly new prefigurative electoral experience in Brazil's electoral scene (the *Bancada Ativista*). On the other, by mixing (and confronting) DT with analytic insights from Critical Discourse Analysis (CDA), this paper opens a space for applying mixed-strategies to macro-textual analysis. Not least, paper 3 contributes to the literature on Brazilian politics by analysing an electoral experience that, regardless of its electoral significance, bypassed most journalistic and scholarly radars. This is important since its significance raises a big problem in relation to analyses based on Brazil's 2018 elections, as they have prominently depicted 2018 as an electoral inflexion produced and taken over by the sole appeal of right-wing populism (Hunter and Power, 2019).

Finally, Paper 4 advocates a foregrounding of the psychoanalytic foundations of discourse theory, in order to cultivate further avenues for the exploration and fleshing out of the (dis)identification dynamics that are operative in the process of meaning-making. By putting the Brazilian case against a wider background of social disruption and political contestation, this last paper's contribution comes from the engagement of a lively discussion between the leading schools of thought encompassing populism studies, discourse theory debates and psychoanalytic insights on discourse and affect, attempting to formulate a theoretical contribution that places desire at the heart of meaning-making.

1.3.2. Structure of the thesis

The thesis encompasses this introductory chapter, four (stand-alone) research papers and a closing section that outlines the concluding remarks of this research. Through the preceding section 1, I have first sketched out the background and scope of the thesis by laying the post-Marxist and post-structuralist theoretical and conceptual grounds through which discourse theory came about as a field of research in its own right. Moreover, I have situated the logic of populism in this broader tradition, presenting such a theoretical turn as this thesis' primary area of engagement. I further constructed an overview of some critical debates within the discourse theoretical tradition of populism to point out open questions and promising analytic scopes, giving way to the rationale and research questions of this thesis. The introductory chapter proceeds with section 2, which outlines the practical aspects of carrying out this research, providing a description and reflecting upon the overall research approach and methodological strategy undertaken. This provides the basis for the four papers as discussed.

As outlined in the overview of the intended contributions, paper 1 deals with a set of theoretical and conceptual debates on the role the signifier populism plays in the formal structuring of social meaning and possible strategic avenues to explore related discursive dynamics. To address these questions in a context-specific manner, paper 1 proposes a distinctive conceptual framework that is grounded in the re-articulation of a set of three basic presuppositions highlighted through the literature (meaning comes about relationally; populism is a concept and a signifier; and the interactions within and between the media, politics and academia spheres are central in understanding the articulation of social meaning). Subsequently, paper 2 takes issue with the central role media players have in constructing the

46

discursive dynamics that inform the ubiquitous nature of populism-as-a-signifier in political debates and analyses. Here, the affective force animating and inviting the articulation of debates centred around populist discursive elements is explored through the psychoanalytic concept of fantasy. Moreover, paper 3 reintroduces some basic concepts and logics encompassing the discourse theory deconstructed conceptualisation of populism, animating an analytical enterprise to understand political disputes and collective articulations derived from a period of heated social disruption. The last chapter which makes up the main body of this thesis, paper 4, delves into a theoretical exploration of the conditions of possibility for social meaning beyond the reaches of formal signification, exploring the role of desire in knowledge production through the psychoanalytic idea of hysteria. Finally, the thesis presents each paper's conclusions.

1.4. Research Strategy and Theoretical Approach

1.4.1. *The application problem*

Gaining momentum through the incorporation of new PhD students, Laclau and Mouffe's *Essex School* bolstered research utilising their framework, and in doing so set the stage for debates and concerns about the horizons of applicability of the theoretical fusion of intellectual domains into the discourse theory tradition (Glynos et al. 2021). To a great extent, the challenges and exchanges brought about after the publication of *HSS* provided a refreshing vigour to the post-Marxist project (e.g. Žižek, 1989, 1990). Most were addressed and honed by Laclau through subsequent work culminating in the milestone publication of *OPR*.

However close the attention given by Laclau in his work to agonistic and antagonistic challenges, these developments continued to raise considerable concern and criticism (e.g. Critchley 1996; Critchley and Marchart 2004; Geras 1990; Mouzelis 1990; Tønder and Thomassen 2005). Broadly speaking, these related to methodological questions about non-positivist approaches to operationalising discourse theory so as to address empirical and theoretical investigation. Similarly, questions arose regarding ways to address differences and shared resemblances with other approaches such as hermeneutics or critical realism (Glynos et al., 2021, p. 63; see also Glynos et al., 2009).

Indeed, invoking Paul Feyerabend's famous (and infamous) opposition to method and Wittgenstein's rejection of the 'application' of a rule, Laclau's reflections often assumed a rather sceptical attitude towards formalising social-scientific methods as well-defined and value-free procedures narrowly construed (see Laclau, 2004). At heart, such a cavalier approach to methodological aspects was guided by an underlying conviction that no unified and orderly established system of procedures could ever replace the researcher's intuition (Laclau, 1991), and good reasons endowed and supported such claims through incisive and thorough ontological reflections (e.g. Laclau, 1991; 1996).

Pitched at a high level of abstraction, however, the ontological primacy in discourse theory came at the expense of epistemological and methodological aspects, inviting discussions with other traditions in a more practical fashion (Howarth, 2004). Could one reflect on methodological aspects of an articulatory practice while rebuffing the difficulties surrounding the mechanical application of 'formal-abstract' theory to 'real-concrete' events and processes? Are there ways discourse theory can render intelligible particular narratives so as to evaluate and criticise normative features of a practice or regime? How can discourse theory describe, explain, criticise and evaluate the institution and destitution of social practices and regimes in non-inductive or deductive manners?

1.4.2. *The retroductive cycle as a post-positivist discourse theory research strategy*
Set out to respond to mostly left unaddressed methodological questions, Glynos and Howarth (2007) *Logics of Critical Explanation* (hereinafter *Logics*) revisit Laclau's concept of a 'logic' (1996; 2005), elevating it as a central category in the discourse theory tradition to address the pressing challenges levelled by contemporary social sciences. In thinking beyond the causal law paradigm, Glynos and Howarth engage in conversation with hermeneutical approaches whose epistemological turn centred around *contextualised self-interpretations* (such as Winch, 1990; Taylor, 1985; Bevir and Rhodes, 2005), and *neo-positivist* and *critical realist* thinkers emphasising and seeking to delimit the role of causal mechanisms in scientific inquiry (such as Elster, 1989; Bhaskar et al. 1998; Shapiro, 2005). While the former overplay the particularity of historical context, the latter find themselves restrained in a domain governed by the causal law paradigm, presenting too limited a scope to fully engage in a post-positivist approach which, while admitting a certain degree of generality, respects the specificity of empirical and theoretical objects, while also granting critical space to the practitioner.

In its appeal to retroduction, the *Logics* therefore provides the conditions to elaborate critical explanations of problematised social phenomena beyond the restraints of mechanisms, laws or self-interpretations, by placing 'method' as a whole on a much wider horizon. This is performed by Glynos and Howarth, as they develop and articulate narratives that can render intelligible the rules structuring and governing a practice or regime, as well as the objects and conditions that make the operations of such rules possible. While taking into account the researchers' views, beliefs, and affects, the *Logics* is not confined to self-interpretations and invites engagement with a credible body of evidence that can be put to the consideration of other scholars. Glynos and Howarth thus present a cyclical, post-positivist, and retroductive mode of critical explanation, one which I take as the research approach of this thesis.

In assuming discourse as an articulatory practice that links together and modifies meaningful elements through and into relational (and always incomplete) systems, Glynos and Howarth engage in a 'middle-ranging theorization' (Laclau, 2004, p. 323, also in Glynos et al. 2021) by seeking to operationalise some core ontological discourse theory assumptions and concepts into the conduct of critical empirical research. This is done through a triad of 'logics' – social, political and fantasmatic – regarded as the core categories under which we can analyse and structure practices and regimes.

Social logics characterise practices and regimes in different contexts by revealing the rules, features and properties underlying them. While social logics serve to characterise such 'norms' and established social practices, *political* logics, specify the more dynamic aspects of a practice or regime. These logics invite the researcher to comprehend the dynamics and conditions sustaining the (de)institution of practices and regimes, thus focusing on how social logics are installed and contested (*ibid.* p. 141; see also Laclau, 2005a, p. 117). Finally, *fantasmatic* logics add a further explanatory layer that investigate the affective force in the (in)stability of determined signifying functions, thus accounting for the 'gripping' force linking subjects to discourses. In turn, they allow the analyst to describe and critically explain the idealised narratives underlying signifying constructions and the different modes of enjoyment subjects acquire through their identification with discursive structures (Glynos and Howarth, 2007, p. 145). As this thesis' main research concern relies on antagonistic discursive modes in moments of contestation and the affective force underlying political disputes and discursive constructions, an emphasis is given to the *political* and *fantasmatic* logics throughout this research project.

The retroductive style of reasoning conveyed by the *Logics* approach is distinctly at odds with the narrow positivist procedure of 'testing' falsifiable/verifiable predictions based on pre-established hypothetical criteria, which by-passes the construction and interpretation of research findings. Unlike more linear inductive and deductive methodological slants, the *Logics* retroductive character 'implies that the single most important criterion for admitting a hypothesis, however tentatively, is that it *accounts* for the phenomenon or problem at stake' (Glynos et al., 2009, p. 10). Put more fully, retroduction states that a hypothesis cannot be adequately inferred until its content is rendered visible in the construction of a pressing puzzling feature of a practice or regime, as no hypothetical account can be induced or inferred outside the problematisation and construction of the specified research problem.

Indeed, the instance of problematisation highlights the need for identifying a puzzle or concern in a social practice or theorisation, evidencing the *problem-driven* nature of the *Logics* in contrast to *method-* and *theory-oriented* research strategies (Glynos and Howarth, 2007, p. 167). Engaged by encountering a puzzling or paradigmatic theoretical or empirical feature, the research then goes into constructing the research problem (*explanandum*). In terms of this thesis, for example, by encountering the 'reification problematic' in populism studies (De Cleen and Glynos, 2021, p. 182), I point out problems in the strands of literature reflecting on populism beyond the ascription of inherent attributes to players and practices which invite populism to be thought of in terms of a 'thing as such'. Interestingly enough, through the process of problematisation, I have been able to construct paradigmatic theoretical features; for example, that while populism is thought of in terms of a category, its employment as a word seems to overdetermine non-academic discursive domains. So too I have encountered puzzling empirical attributes; such that, while European and Anglo-Saxon media discourses appear to limit their scope to anti-populist discursive inflexions, media discourses about populism in Brazil seem to convey positive and negative signifying turns. With these remarks, I make evident that this introductory chapter gives evidence of retroduction at work and already crosses some crucial ground in the construction of the overall research project.

In turning the *research puzzle* into a more intelligible *explanandum*, the researcher can then undertake an explanatory venture through a to-and-fro movement between empirical investigation and theoretical work. This back-and-forth movement prevents the empirical objects from being subsumed under theoretical standpoints, and *vice versa* (Glynos and Howarth, 2007, p. 180), for the 'reconstruction of discursive sequences [logics] governing the action of social actors… are at the same level as the discursive sequences that constitute the theoretical framework' (Laclau, 1991). Through this point, the *Logics* urges researchers to pay close attention to the contingent character underlying both empirical and theoretical objects of inquiry. This is to say, while pre-existing objects and concepts provide room for a problem-driven research engagement, a non-subsumptive process of linking empirical and theoretical elements may well (and should) introduce something different in kind, derived from the construction of a plausible and convincing *explanans*.

The moment of retroductive explanation in this thesis features the construction, problematisation and re-articulation of the concepts and grammar underlying recent discourse theory scholarship on populism in light of the empirical material assembled through readings, data gathering, interviews, and textual and image-based analyses. This process enables the construction of a putative explanation for the concerns identified in concrete practices or regimes. It also invites theoretical and methodological innovation by engaging with adjacent idioms to articulate new theoretical grammars and research strategies.

From within this to-and-fro movement between the problematisation and discovery contexts, the insights and findings configuring a plausible proto-explanation can then be submitted to the evaluation and critical scrutiny of other practitioners and put into consideration and debate in relevant scholarly fora (Glynos and Howarth, 2007, p. 38). I have presented all four research papers in this thesis at conferences and other academic gatherings, contrasting my explanations and discoveries with the work of peers that, from divergent standpoints, reflect upon meaning-making, affect and populism. On the basis of these exchanges, I have kept an attentive focus on the evolving research process, substantially revisiting and reconfiguring my research framework, methodological strategies and the interpretations of the findings. Resulting from this lively engagement and co-creation with peers and colleagues, I have exposed my work to peer-review processes, achieving academic peer-reviewed publication of papers 3 and 4 in well-positioned and related academic peer-reviewed journals, showing consistency and already making modest contributions to relevant fields of study.

1.4.3. *Case Selection*

In limiting the empirical scope of this thesis to the Brazilian setting, the case selection has been derived from the problematisation of the empirical and theoretical objects of inquiry. In concrete terms, the formal construction of each paper, as a step in the overall project, serves as a problematisation from where a new paradigmatic feature enables the construction of a new case selection. This point evidences how the retroductive cycle is systematically adopted in the development of this thesis and highlights the mutual feedback dynamics enacted in the inter-related construction of the four papers.

Following Foucault, Glynos and Howarth, I take the practice of problematisation as a synthesis of *genealogy* and *archaeology* (Glynos et al. 2009, p. 10). As such, paper 1 traces and uncovers the seminal references to populism in Brazil, finding in most Brazilian populism scholarship allusions regarding political events related to Brazil's Fourth Republican Period (1946-1964). In revising the Brazilian literature, two outstanding features appear. Firstly, I identify published scholarly work describing populism in derogatory terms even before Hofstadter (1955) published his Pulitzer-winner *The Age of Reform* (Jaguaribe, 1954),[5] showing Brazil as an amenable case of analysis in terms of the study of discourses about populism. Secondly, in reviewing literature drawing upon Brazilian politics from 1946 to 1964, the trope of *Populist Republic* appears as a frequent reference in academic and non-academic work,[6] featuring Brazil's Fourth Republican Period as a promising case of analysis of populism as a concept and a signifier. Thus, paper 1 draws on the political disputes taking place in Brazil's Fourth Republic as an indicative case of how the lively interaction of discourses and participants across spheres construct broader social narratives about populism.

Partly inspired by recent scholarship affording the media a central role in making populism a ubiquitous word in contemporary discursive dynamics (see Goyvaerts and De Cleen, 2020), and instigated by the findings constructed in paper 1, which captures an intense interplay of journalistic discourses about populism, paper 2 aims to construct contemporary journalistic discourses on populism in Brazil. As also found in the construction of paper 1, discussions regarding populism in Brazil's Fourth Republican Period later served as antagonising references directed at the Workers' Party (PT) founder and leader Lula (see, for example, *Folha de S. Paulo*. 2006). As Brazil's leading news magazine, and identified as a

---

[5] Work identified by Stavrakakis (2017) as to be the genealogy of anti-populist scholarship, extending from centre to periphery.

[6] Wikipedia, por example, describes Brazil's Fourth Republic in terms of *Período Populista* [Populist Period] showing how such label became widespread in and outside the academy. See: https://pt.wikipedia.org/wiki/Per%C3%ADodo_Populista [accessed 05/08/2021].

media group fiercely opposed to Lula and PT (see Chicarino et al. 2021), *Veja* magazine is selected as the case of analysis in paper 2. Supplementary factors uphold my selection of *Veja* as a case of study for paper 2. While I focus mainly on political logics in constructing the signifying operations and political disputes in Brazil's Fourth Republic (Paper 1), paper 2 commits to exploring fantasmatic logics in journalistic discourses. Often seen in tabloid-like narratives (see, for example, Chang and Glynos, 2011), the deployment of fantasy to analyse journalistic discourses with more technocratic narratives might evidence new ways of enjoyment, making *Veja* a valuable case selection for paper 2.

I have chosen to focus on the collective candidacy of the *Bancada Ativista* in the 2018 elections (Paper 3), as it features a highly controversial and novel political venture within an electoral process studied and undertaken as a political turning point in Brazil. Focusing on Bolsonaro's victory, studies have depicted the 2018 election as a fracture of the PT's hegemony and is taken as indicative of the rise of right-wing personalist appeals in Brazil. To some extent, these elements have been constructed in the development of paper 2. Intriguingly, however, no scholarly focus was given to the *Bancada Ativista* despite it becoming the 10th highest voted political force in Brazil's leading electoral college (Sao Paulo). As such, the *Bancada Ativista* presents itself as a thought-provoking case with which to problematise the disputes that framed the 2018 electoral scene, as well as allowing for an exploration of the analytical horizons of discourse theory in the study of non-populist phenomena.

Finally, paper 4 takes the theoretical work of Ernesto Laclau in *OPR* as its main focus, invoking a problematisation of the notion of 'demand' in Laclau's work, via the psychoanalytic conception of hysteria. Drawing upon political and fantasmatic logics, the exploration and construction of findings in the preceding papers unravelled underlying logics that speak to unusual ways of political antagonism. As such, these papers dealt with constructing meaningful elements in the dispute and conformation of practices and regimes from a post-foundational standpoint. While political and fantasmatic logics provided worthwhile analytic pathways with which to reflect about articulatory practices, a more formal engagement with negativity to reflect upon meaning-making processes seems missing from a discourse theory standpoint. From a psychoanalytic point of view, desire appears as the core element animating knowledge production, seen in the discovery of the unconscious through Freud's study of hysteria. For discourse theory, however, demands appear as minimal units of analysis for understanding meaning-making processes. With antagonism as an overarching background, paper 4 undertakes a theoretical inquiry of meaning-making processes from a perspective of desire.

1.5. A note on methods of data generation

This research focuses on analysing distinctive repertoires, stemming from journalistic articles and political discourses, to individual experiences and scholarly texts. It should be clear to the reader by now that this thesis' deconstructed approach to meaning-making assumes that the discursive logics governing the actions and speeches of social and political actors are at the same level as those underlying the articulation of academic documents (Laclau, 1991). As such, I engage in a deconstructive game by confronting empirical and theoretical objects, seeking to articulate plausible explanations to pressing questions, and, in so doing, introducing distinctive elements to both theoretical and empirical dimensions of the thesis (Glynos and Howarth, 2007).

I have framed the main puzzles of this thesis in relation to the analytic deadlock of 'populism studies' in its predominantly descriptive characterisation of players and practices as being populist (with little clarification of what such a character actually means). I have decided to focus on debates of discourse theorists as these have been most vocal in stressing the need to reflect upon populism beyond the study (and construction, I should add) of current populist elements. By placing the empirical objects of investigation in the Brazilian setting, I have also distinguished amenable cases to engage in this critical explanatory research venture.

In formulating a more focused account of the objects of inquiry, this thesis relies on publicly available journalistic texts and magazines, academic books and journal articles, dictionaries, as well as the self-interpretation of activists in their engagement with grassroots bodies and political articulations. Notably, the data collection, analysis and status derive from 'the *full* range of theoretical issues that arise... from the activities of describing, explaining, evaluating and criticizing' (Glynos and Howarth, 2007, p. 6). As such, the methodological techniques in collecting and generating primary sources are formulated in specific regards to each case. However, these stem from the combination of three main methodological techniques: *archival research*, *document analysis* and *semi-structured interview*.

1.5.1. *Archival research*

Archival research involves the study of documents and textual materials produced at some point in the relatively distant past. Thus, archival methods include a set of activities undertaken to access, retrieve and analyse events and practices involving organisations, individuals and events from an earlier time (Ventresca and Mohr, 2017). The tools employed to retrieve the main material of investigation may vary according to the field and objects of study, ranging from official institutional reports held in archive repositories to material artefacts stored in a museum (Mills and Mills, 2018). In this thesis' case, a Python algorithm was used as a tool to gather journalistic and scholarly documents from 1946 to 1964 stored in various virtual repositories in Brazil, such as the *Brazilian National Library* online repository (Paper 1). Using algorithms in archival research provides a valuable technique for retrieving an extensive corpus of data, as well as in organising (and making sense of) such data in diachronic terms.

1.5.2. *Document analysis*

In terms of the study of discursive repertoires associated with contemporary social players and practices, document analysis denotes an integrated and conceptually informed method for identifying and retrieving documents. This method is distinct from archival research's inquiry of past events, as it focuses on constructing evidence regarding contemporary dynamics (Bosi and Reiter, 2014). In political and social studies, document analysis includes as primary sources the production of (numeric and narrative) texts by the very same agents involved in the practice at stake in a given investigation (Altheide and Schneider, 2013, p. 5). However, in questioning the dominance of written texts as the key source of document analysis, non-written texts (such as images, drawings, pictures or recordings), as symbolic representations of a social event and practice can (and should) be included as prime sources of a document analysis investigation (see Carpentier, 2020, p. 2122). After all, the deconstructed notion of discourse which rests at the heart of this thesis takes all meaningful practices to be discursive, as any meaningful piece produced by the agents in a researched practice may be taken as a source of document analysis. In terms of this thesis, the data generated from document analysis is mainly built upon retrieved textual- and image-based material from scholarly and journalistic digital repositories (Paper 2).

1.5.3. *Semi-structured interview*

Interviewing, in broad terms, constitutes a key methodological tool in the social sciences and the humanities with which to generate 'first-hand' data about the motives and interpretations of the participants at stake in a researched social or political practice. While in the structured form of interview, 'the interviewer uses a preestablished schedule of questions, typically referred to a *questionnaire*, with a limited set of response categories', a semi-structured interview acts more as a *guide-like interview* of broad themes and questions, giving more expansive room to the interviewee to elaborate on such aspects (Blee and Taylor, 2002, p. 92).

Given the discourse-analytical nature of this problem-driven research and my interest in exploring underlying logics regarding discursive and rhetorical aspects in a set of practices or regimes, the semi-structured form of interview provides a more suitable methodological strategy for constructing analyses through thick descriptions. In concrete terms, I conducted a semi-structured interview as a means of gathering evidence and interpretations as given by Anne Rammi, one of the nine co-deputies of the *Bancada Ativista*, on the articulation of the *Bancada*'s campaign in 2018 (Paper 3). The aim here was to create an interaction between individual action and events at the macro-level, allowing me to construct and understand salient biographical aspects and conditions of possibility of political participation processes (p. 104). With all due ethical approval processes granted by the University of Essex prior to the conduction of the interview, the interview was conducted in Portuguese and transcribed from the original language to English.

Paper 1: Populism in the Making: A Multi-sited Discursive Approach to Brazil's Fourth

Republican Period (1946-1964)

Abstract

Political discourse scholars have identified a gap in the literature concerning the need to take more seriously discourses about populism, particularly the way they interact with and help constitute populist discourses themselves. I build on the concept/signifier opposition and the idea of the double-hermeneutic to develop an analytical framework within which to operationalise these ideas in a way that can bring out in greater detail the dynamic interplay within and across populism discourses. I illustrate the added value of this framework through a case-based study centred around Brazil's Fourth Republic (1946-1964), often referred to as the 'Populist Republic'. In doing so, I also supplement existing accounts of this period by showcasing in greater detail and nuance the significance of key moments in the Fourth Republic. Of particular interest here are the pro-populist discursive moves made by Adhemar de Barros, which have had non-trivial implications for the way I have come to understand later political developments in Brazil.

Introduction

It is hard to deny the power and significance associated with the signifier 'populism' today, as it provokes heated discussions throughout the media, ferocious discourses in political debate, and careful theoretical scrutiny in academia. Not only is 'populism' omnipresent in our daily language, but it has been taken as a common currency for depicting the kernel of our political age (Mudde, 2004; Mouffe, 2018). What is in a word that so persistently apprehends our attention?

A plethora of intellectual efforts have been made to make of populism a category for political analysis, and a wide span of theoretical constellations so insistently give way to novel conceptual compositions for reviling the peculiar unity entailed in populism. They range from ideological to stylistic, socio-cultural to strategic. While, at times, some of these efforts imply populism forecloses a menace to the enlightened forms of social organisation, others provide to it, in turn, the positive characteristics required for refreshing democracy in its form and spirit.

When confronted with the wide-raging debates on populism, one cannot but question the sources through which this centre-piece has acquired such diverse and conflicting academic and non-academic understandings, ultimately provoking the very question of how social meaning-making comes about.

While most scholars in the field of populism studies tend to neglect the role the signifier 'populism' plays in political debates, political discourse scholars have identified a gap in the literature concerning the need to take more seriously discourses about populism, particularly the way they interact with and help constitute populist discourses. This is to say, if on the one hand, populism may be understood as a political logic that simplifies the discursive field in opposing 'us' versus 'them', in political discourses, the signifier 'populism' itself can be mobilised to talk about populism, to evaluate populist discourses, to 'hype' populism, and to advance political agendas. This signals a need to study populism as both a concept *and* a signifier.

In this vein, the appeal to Anthony Giddens' double hermeneutics has been identified as a promising ide with which 'to think more broadly about how the ubiquity of the concept of populism itself' and how this 'feeds into and has become implicated in wider mediatic and political dynamics' (De Cleen and Glynos, 2020, p. 14; see also Stavrakakis, 2017). However, while discourse theory scholars have pointed to this promising arena of research (regarding discourses *about* populism), there have been very few case studies that examine the character of these discourses, particularly how their normative and ideological features and significance emerge and evolve. Treatment of discourses about populism still tend to be relatively brief, speculative, and open-ended, with scholars inviting further research rather than undertaking it themselves.

In this study, I affirm the utility of the concept/signifier pair and the double-hermeneutics perspective and seek to advance these insights further by developing an analytical framework within which to operationalise these ideas in a way that can bring out in greater detail the dynamic interplay between populism discourses in a variety of fora. (I use the term populism discourses to include both populist discourses and discourses about populism.)

I illustrate the added value of this framework through a case-based study centred around Brazil's Fourth Republic (1946-1964), a period referred to as the 'Populist Republic' (see Ronderos and Zicman de Barros, 2020). Through a detailed exploration of the interaction between political, mediatic and academic ideas and actors, I reveal some salient social and political dynamics in Brazil during this period. In so doing, I supplement existing accounts of the Fourth Republic by showcasing in greater detail and nuance the way the signifiers 'populism' and 'populist' circulated in Brazilian politics, provoked responses by political pundits in the media, and inflected the way scholars sought to theorise populism. In short, I argue that the political and journalistic uses of the term, coupled with the way actors travelled between the spheres of politics, the media, and academia, had a decisive impact upon the way actors sought to grasp the populist phenomenon.

A Discursive Approach to Populism Studies

When applied to populism, a discursive approach that takes the deconstruction of the sign seriously suggests that the concept (or meaning) of populism and its associated signifiers, such as 'populism' and 'populist' (hereinafter collectively referred to as 'populis*'), undergo a constant sliding as they are articulated or performed in different contexts, whether in politics, the media or academia. The theoretical presuppositions of the discursive approach to populism studies, therefore, already point to the need to supplement concept-centred analyses of populism with analyses that treat populism as a signifier, thereby opening up pathways for the study of discourses *about* populism.

It is true, of course, that in an academic context there is always an attempt to pin down a concept as much as possible, trying to establish sufficient definitional clarity and stability so as to permit analytical and critical insights to emerge from this. As a branch of discourse studies, for example, the Essex School of discourse theory suggests that the concept of populism is best understood in terms of a *populist political logic* that divides the discursive field vertically into two antagonistic groups: the 'people' as underdog versus the dominant, illegitimate 'elite' (Laclau, 2005). There are, however, other ways in which academics have sought to conceptualise populism, for example as a thin ideology, as style, or as strategy.

I do not intend to rehearse the debates between advocates of these different theoretical perspectives—instead, this paper focuses on efforts to move beyond debates about the best way to conceptualise populism. And yet I have chosen to situate my approach in relation to the work of discourse scholars because they have been most vocal in calling for an expansion in the field of populism studies to include the study of discourses *about* populism. Scholars have rightly pointed out that little attention has been paid thus far to the dynamics informing the way the signifiers 'populis*' travel between sites in the spheres of politics, media, and academia; and how these intra- and inter-sphere travels produce signifying effects with important normative and ideological significance (De Cleen & Glynos 2021; De Cleen, Glynos, and Mondon 2021, 2018; Mondon and Brown, 2021). Not only is the dynamic relationship between populist discourses and discourses about populism under-researched and under-theorised, so too is the character of the processes that underpin their dynamic interactions as they play themselves out within and across the three spheres of politics, media, and academia. Conducting in-depth studies may thus help us to answer interesting context-specific questions, such as: Which sites in the media-politics-academia complex take on privileged roles, and how might this affect the (feedback) dynamics animating populism discourses? How should we think about the character and status of the intra- and inter-sphere processes that constitute these feedback dynamics?

Scholars have already pointed to some promising ideas in terms of which to grasp these processes in the media-politics-academia complex (Stavrakakis, 2017; De Cleen, Glynos, Mondon 2021, 2018; Glynos & Mondon 2016; De Cleen & Glynos 2021; Goyvaerts and De Cleen 2020; Csigo 2016). While highly suggestive, these studies convey underdeveloped and underexplored ideas by lacking in-depth empirical explorations. I thus seek to contribute to the advancement of their work by conducting more in-depth case studies and, in so doing, shedding further light on the interactions that characterise populism discourses and their relevance for understanding complex political and social dynamics.

A multi-sited discursive approach to the study of populism discourses and their dynamic interactions

I have already noted how discourse theory's deconstructed distinction between concept and signifier is helpful because it enables us to think about the potentially complex and dynamic relationship between populist discourses and discourses about populism as they are performed across different contexts. However, such a distinction on its own is unable to address the challenge of elucidating this dynamic complexity. To overcome this shortcoming, therefore, discourse scholars have begun to enlist the help of other theoretical and analytical resources in order to make such an investigation possible. In this respect, Giddens's notion of double-hermeneutics stands out (see Stavrakakis, 2017; De Cleen and Glynos, 2021).

In developing the idea of a double hermeneutic, Giddens trains our attention on the way ideas used by social scientists to understand people's practices can be taken up by the people themselves to readjust their own self-understandings. A double hermeneutic perspective captures the way lay ideas and self-understandings can come to shape the concepts used by social scientists and *vice versa*.

As Glynos & Howarth note, however, the idea of a double hermeneutic resonates with, and can thus be further elucidated by, a number of other cognate terms, including Foucault's 'transcendental-empirical' doublet, 'which arises from the famous "doubling of [wo]man" in the modern episteme, where the figure of "[wo]man" appears in the "ambiguous position" of being both "an object of knowledge and . . . a subject that knows" (Foucault 1970: 312)' (Glynos & Howarth 2007: 156; see also 48, 210). The more abstract formulation of the transcendental-empirical doublet helps see that the idea of the double hermeneutic should not be restricted to describing the relationship between social science and the practices it studies. It can be applied to any attempt by anyone to make sense of any practice that is receptive to interpretations about itself. This describes for me a relation of *mutual discursive constitution*, whereby the ideas and meanings of a 2nd order discourse (discourses about populism) help to constitute a 1st order discourse (populist discourses), and *vice versa*.

Therefore, while it is true that the academic domain represents for some a privileged sphere in which discourses about other discourses abound, it is also true that the academic sphere has no monopoly on the production of 2nd order discourses, as they can be produced at

any site in any sphere. For this reason, I develop a multi-sited discursive framework comprising

three key spheres: academia, politics, and the media.

Figure 1. Dynamics of Inter-Sphere and Intra-Sphere Interaction

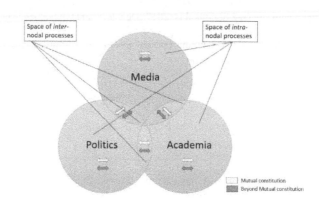

My multi-sited discursive framework is loosely based on what George Marcus calls a

multi-sited ethnography (Marcus, 1995), an approach that develops 'a strategy or design of

research that acknowledges macrotheoretical concepts and narratives of the world system but

does not rely on them for the contextual architecture framing a set of subjects.' Nor does it

remain 'focused on a single site of intensive investigation'. Instead, it traces discursive

formations by following such things as people and metaphors 'across and within multiple sites

of activity', examining 'the circulation of... meanings, objects, and identities in diffuse time-

space'. This enables the researcher to construct 'the lifeworlds of variously situated subjects',

as well as 'aspects of the system itself through the associations and connections it suggests

among sites.' (Marcus, 1995, p, 96). In a similar fashion, I suggest that the dynamic complexity

of discourses can be understood in terms of the processes that animate relationships within and across spheres, comprising both intra-sphere and inter-sphere processes, applying this analytical framework to elucidate the complexity and dynamics of populism discourses.

In terms of *inter-sphere* processes, the politics-media-academia complex can be unpacked by paying attention to the importance or 'weight' of some sites in one sphere compared to sites in other spheres, which can vary depending on the context. In some contexts, sites in the media sphere may be considered central and dominant. In other contexts, journalists and academics may be more deferential to politicians. In yet other contexts, academics may be held in high esteem and might thus have significant suasive force in influencing the discourses of other spheres. In terms of *intra-sphere* processes, the politics-media-academia complex can be nuanced by paying attention to the importance or 'weight' of particular sites compared to others *within* a given sphere: for example, specific media outlets in the media sphere; certain academics (or academic disciplines) within the sphere of academia; or particular politicians or political orientations within the sphere of politics. I suggest that tracing both inter- and intra-sphere processes is important in untangling the shifting relational 'weight' and influence of particular discourses, thus enabling the construction of a wider (and more anchored) picture of the dynamics underpinning the interaction among populism discourses.

So far, I have suggested that the significance of intra-sphere and inter-sphere processes that constitute and transmit discourses vary as a function of their location or site, and that their 'spheres of influence' are, in turn, a product of socio-historical context. However, the character of such processes has been described exclusively in terms of the idea of *mutual discursive constitution* which, as I recall, generalises the insights of the double-hermeneutic (i.e. where ideas/meanings in a discourse are parasitic upon the ideas and meanings of a meta-discourse, or/and vice versa). I would like now to anticipate some of my findings by pre-emptively adding greater analytical texture to my understanding of these processes, both in terms of their character and in terms of their enablers.

Character of discursive constitution. First, I would like to note that the character of mutual discursive constitution can be understood in both antagonistic and non-antagonistic terms. This serves well to illustrate the way Dutra constitutes his anti-populist discourse, as will be later seen. However, my understanding of the character of mutual constitution is not necessarily exhausted by an antagonistic conceptualisation: it can take on a different non-antagonistic inflexion regarding, for example, the relationship between populist and pro-populist discourses. This is clear to see in both Selgado's pro-populist right-wing discourses and Adhemar de Barros's pro-populist left-wing discourses, even as they maintain an antagonistic relationship with anti-populist discourses.

Enablers of discursive constitution. Second, I point to what I call 'enablers' of discursive constitution. By enablers, I aim to describe aspects of a practice that make possible the constitution of discourses, particularly those conditions that facilitate and amplify certain features of those discourses. Enablers of discursive constitution is a potentially expansive category that would include, for example, the enunciators or articulators of a discourse. In a multi-sited discursive approach, therefore, enablers of discursive constitution at different intra- and inter-sphere locations help me to offer a fuller account of the character and dynamics of discursive constitution.

Processes of discursive interaction: A typology

The above discussion points to my need to be rather more precise about the way I conceptualise processes by which discourses interact with one another. As has been seen, populism discourses can be understood to be in a relation of *mutual constitution* with each other. The process of mutual constitution emphasises the way elements in different discourses relate to one another. It takes these elements for granted and foregrounds the way that the meaning and significance of those elements emerges out of their relation to one another. It could thus be said I am now emphasising the synchronic dimension of the process of discursive interaction, or perhaps this type of discursive interaction could be simply qualified as a (synchronic) *process of mutual constitution* (corresponding to the yellow arrows in Figure 1). These processes aim to capture the way ideas relate to one another, the way ideas are articulated by politicians, journalists and academics to comment on or make a judgement about other ideas. Discourses about populism, for example, are 2nd order discourses that discuss, comment on, and often normatively judge 1st order populist discourses. As seen earlier, the mutual constitution of these discourses can take on an antagonistic form (e.g., anti-populism) or a non-antagonistic form (e.g., pro-populism). Such synchronic processes of mutual constitution thus have an important role to play in shaping the complexity and dynamics of populism discourses within and across spheres.

As has been shown, however, the idea of mutual constitution does not exhaust the processes that connect populism discourses to each other. These processes are related to what I earlier referred to as 'enablers'. The focus here is not so much on the conditions that make possible the meaning of discourses (their synchronic-relational character), but rather on the conditions that make the articulation of discourses possible. This aims at something Foucault called discursive conditions of existence: the rules that facilitated the production of particular discourses, including the logics that bestow authority on the articulators (journalists, politicians, and academics). I call these types of discursive interactions (diachronic) *processes of discursive mediation* (corresponding to the red arrows in Figure 1) – processes that mediate discourses or serve as the medium of discourses. What is distinctive about such processes is that they are not defined primarily by the explicit reference to or exchange of ideas and meanings associated with, in this case, populism discourses. They are 'adjacent' to them. Here, in other words, I identify processes that might promote or amplify aspects of populism discourses and their inter-relation that are not reducible to such explicit mutually constituting features. In this case study, I point to a salient aspect of such processes, in particular the movement of people through networks – whether professional, social, or other sorts of networks – showing how this movement of people can take place within and across spheres. In the sphere of politics, for example, I find politicians moving between different sites (political parties) or entering into unexpected alliances. However, I also find people moving between all three spheres of politics, media, and academia.

In what follows, therefore, I use the above framework to elucidate key aspects of my case study. In identifying the spheres, sites and processes of discursive interaction at stake, I trace, untangle and articulate the dynamic production and evolution of the populism discourses appearing in Brazil's Fourth Republic (1946-1964). In so doing, I demonstrate the added value of my multi-sited discursive framework while also showcasing in greater detail and nuance the significance of key moments in this period. I adopt Marcus's methodological postulate of following the word or, in our case, 'following the signifier', which serves as a useful way to access and build my empirical material.

Following the signifiers 'populis*' in the Fourth Republic

While the term 'Populist Republic' came about *after* the period that was described as such, this label is now widely used to refer to Brazil's Fourth Republic. The oldest reference to *Populist Republic* I could trace takes me to Celso Lafer's PhD thesis, written at Cornell University and published in 1970. That said, the exact origins of this designation have never been established. Lafer himself confesses that he does not know the term's true origins or whether he was really the first one to use it. It is worth pointing out, moreover, that the expression 'Populist Republic' in his work was not at all derogatory. Its employment aided the description of a new political era, after a fifteen-year dictatorship upheld by Getulio Vargas, marked by the expansion and emergence of popular classes in electoral politics.

Either way, this was a turbulent time. Although Brazil held four presidential elections in the eighteen-years of the 'Populist Republic', from 1946 to 1964, it had eight different presidents: Eurico Gaspar Dutra (1946-1951), Getulio Vargas (1951-1954), Café Filho (1954-1955), Carlos Luz (1955), Nereu Ramos (1955-1956), Juscelino Kubitschek (1956-1961), Jânio Quadros (1961) and João Goulart (1961-1964).

In a later book, Lafer (1975) described the 'Populist Republic' as a period when the Executive branch, supported by popular sections of society under a charismatic leadership, dominated through a tenuous balance backed by the 'organised coercion' of the Army, with the Congress working as a conservative mediator. As such, the fourth republic began with the promulgation of the 1946 Constitution, after the catastrophic collapse of Vargas' corporatist dictatorship (1937-1945), and ended in April 1964 when the military overthrew president João Goulart in a *coup d'état*, installing another dictatorship that lasted until Brazil's democratisation in 1985.

As will be seen, a 'populis*' descriptor was first adopted in Brazil by the pro-fascist Integralist movement led by Plinio Salgado during the 1940s. However, the main antagonistic frontier through which the signifiers 'populis*' assumed a key role in Brazilian politics would pivot around the discursive struggle between two main forces: the so-called 'democratic-conservative', elite forces, led by the military Euricio Gaspar Dutra (anti-populist bloc), and the pro-populist, progressive front forged between Getulio Vargas' Brazilian Labour Party (PTB) and Adhemar de Barros' Progressive Social Party (PSP). Dutra assumed as president of Brazil in 1946. While Vargas' PTB initially favoured his presidency, Dutra adopted a centre-right political stance through the course of his mandate, closely forging a strategical alliance between his Social Democratic Party (PSD) and the National Democratic Union (UDN), with Vargas progressively becoming his primary political foe. Not only is the fourth republic of paramount importance in shaping Brazilian politics by having adopted a 'populis*' descriptior,

71

but also because this was the first time popular layers in Brazil decisively participated in electoral politics. The struggles from therein still form the contours of contemporary Brazilian political disputed, for deploying my multi-sited matrix in the study of this period will provide substantial explanatory layers to the Brazilian case.

Building a database using the media sphere as an entry point

While the origins of the academic expression 'Populist Republic' remain unclear, it is nevertheless interesting to ask when and how the signifiers 'populis*' entered the academic sphere. One might wonder whether this was a term that was first appropriated from another sphere, before subjecting it to analytical and theoretical treatment. For example, could it be that the Brazilian people themselves considered their republic to be a 'populist' one? Were the signifiers 'populis*' present in their daily life?

My way to investigate this has been to create an algorithm to search for references to 'populis*' in Brazil's main media outlets from 1946 to 1964 available at the Brazilian National Library and the newspapers' digital repository. In fact, an in-depth media analysis of this period has not been done before, even though such a study promises to shed light on the complexity and dynamics of populism discourses in Brazil. The signifiers 'populis*' served as ideal search terms with which to identify the relevant discourses about populism, enabling us to construct a database of 12,580 occurrences present in eleven of the most influential newspapers of the time.[7] I thus used the media sphere as 'entry point' in exploring key moments in the evolution of the dynamics of the populism discourses, using these moments to structure a more in-depth analysis within and across spheres, elucidating the processes by which populist discourses relate to those second-order discourses about populism.

---

[7] If a word appears several times on a single page, they are counted as one occurrence. Therefore, we may say that the number of occurrences refers to the number of pages which include at least a single reference to *populis**.

Graph 1: Monthly occurrences of *populis** in selected newspapers (six-month moving average)

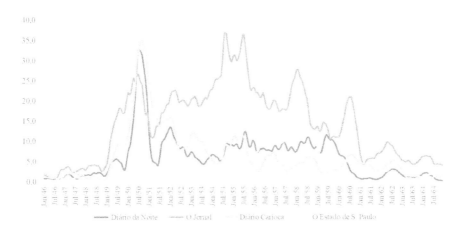

From the perspective of how to structure my analysis, it is of course not the overall number of occurrences *per se* that is important, but rather their temporal distribution. It is interesting to note, for example, that almost no occurrences appear in the press until the end of the 1940s (the few exceptions tend to refer to non-political topics such as the mention of the French Populist novel award [*Prix du roman populiste*]); yet, from March 1949 onwards, a massive surge in the use of the signifiers 'populis*' swept through the content of these media outputs. Notwithstanding the variations in each region and newspaper, the aggregate analysis shows peaks of the uses of the terms in electoral years, notably during the presidential election of 1950, the electoral races of 1955 and 1960, and the São Paulo local state elections of 1957 and 1958. Finally, it is worth noting that while I have carefully read all articles in my database from 1946 to 1964, in order to better grasp the discursive textures underlying patterns the graphs exhibit, I have structured my analysis around four of the most prominent newspapers of the time, taken as key sites of the media sphere (*Diario da Noite, O Journal, Diario Carioca* and *O Estado de S. Paulo*).

The Emergence of 'Populism' in the Political Sphere and the Rise of a Populist Republic (1946-1949)

From the beginning of 1946 to the end of 1948, the references of populism in the media are rather scarce, but already depict the dynamic interplay between the political and media spheres. One of the first groups to introduce the term populism in Brazil's public debate were the former integralists, led by Plínio Salgado. These extreme right-wing militants refounded the former Brazilian Integralist Action (AIB) in 1946 under the name of Party of Popular Representation (PRP). Salgado's forces started to refer to themselves as 'populists' or those who are 'on the side of the people' (*O Estado de S. Paulo*, 1946). Despite the lesser appeal of Salgado's ideas in the post-war period, it is worth noting that, in contrast to current use, the term *populist* was widely used in an approving manner and affirmed as such throughout the media outlets.

Putting aside the rather niche and peripheral appropriation of populism by the integralists, the term expanded as a signifier used to label other political forces. On December 20, 1946, a non-signed article accused Getulio Vargas and Hugo Borghi (one of Vargas' most eloquent allies in his Brazilian Labor Party, PTB) of 'populist demagoguery' (*O Jornal*, 1946). On January 10, 1947, in the same newspaper, the journalist Marcelo Coimbra Tavares described Vargas' cattle-raising policies as 'demagogic and populist' (*O Jornal*, 1947).

While underplayed until 1947, this discursive logic would gain prominence two years later. In the run-up to the pre-election campaign of 1949, prior to the 1950 presidential succession dispute, sectors of the press, pundits and leading politicians began to announce the alarming meteoric arrival of a populist menace. This was embodied in a likely – and virtually unbeatable – alliance between Vargas' PTB and Adhemar de Barros' Progressive Social Party

(PSP). Foreseeing this coalition, already in early 1949, the communication tycoon Francisco de Assis Chateaubriand and, more poignantly, the journalist Murilo Marroquim – undoubtedly the journalist who used the terms 'populis*' the most during the entire fourth republic, responsible for 18% of the overall occurrences in *O Jornal* –, started to glimpse in the horizon the risk of demagogic populism, or a 'pernicious' and 'exacerbated populism', not far from communist ideas (*O Jornal*, 1949b; 1949c). The Populist Republic itself, however, would formally start a few months later.

Fearing the return of Vargas to power, President Eurico Gaspar Dutra aimed to form an alliance between two conservative parties: the Social Democratic Party (PSD), whose force resided in the political leaders from the countryside, and the National Democratic Union (UDN), the historical party of the urban middle classes. At a meeting between Dutra and the governor of Minas Gerais, Milton Campos, on March 20, 1949, the former outlined what would come to be known as the 'Petropolis Scheme': a two-column table listing, on the one hand, the 'democratic-conservative' forces (PSD, UDN and a third small Republican Party, PR), and on the other the 'populist' groups (PTB, PSP and elements from the then-proscribed Brazilian Communist Party, PCB); the latter described as those which were 'hostile to the regime' (*Diário da Noite*, 1949a, p. 1). A few days later, former president Dutra gave an interview in which he described the 'populist' as a 'demagogic approach aimed at winning the support of the proletariat and with no other objectives than pure vote hunting' (*O Cruzeiro*, 1949, p. 13–19).

Dutra's efforts to build an alliance between the PSD and UDN came to nothing. Nevertheless, one could claim that the discursive frontier drawn between the conservative-democrats and demagogic-populists was a key milestone in the widespread use of the term 'populism' in Brazilian politics. Although Dutra did recognise some 'healthy elements' that could be recovered from populism, it was due to the 'Petrópolis Scheme' that the 'populists' were attacked as such and accused of being 'the shark that lives exploiting the misery of the wretched' (*A Manhã*, 1949, p. 9).

Recent studies have argued anti-populist discourse is often found to be in a relation of antagonistic mutual constitution with populist discourses (Nikisianis et al. 2019), and so there seems little doubt about this in my analysis of the Brazilian case. In a crafty move, São Paulo state governor de Barros decided to appropriate the term 'populist' for himself, giving it a positive connotation. He rejected the distinction between democrats and populists and described himself as a democrat precisely because he was a populist opposed to those 'politicians who make a living from politics', whose interests are served and sustained by 'artificially dividing the country'. In his weekly program on *Radio Bandeirantes*, on May 12, 1949, de Barros said:

> […] we are populists, which means being a democrat in the noblest and most modern sense of the word democrat. For us, being a populist means expanding the social function of the state which has been constantly absent until now. It is to govern by giving everyone an opportunity, seeking to elevate each one according to their potential and supporting each one according to their needs. For us, this denotes being a populist (*Diário da Noite*, 1949c, p. 1–2).

If the signifier 'democracy' had become a key element in the antagonistic frontier drawn by anti-populist discourses, associating 'populism' with 'dictatorship', 'extremism' and 'demagoguery' in the equivalential composition of an anti-democratic subject, de Barros' populist move was to reframe such terms. Like the anti-populists, de Barros drew on the signifiers 'democracy' and 'demagoguery' to construct an 'us'/'them' opposition. However, de Barros tried to attach the floating signifier 'democrat' to himself and sought to label as a demagogic the artificial discursive opposition forged by his greedy conservative-elitist detractors.

Adhemar de Barros' discursive strategy had an immediate and dramatic impact on the political agenda. In the 1950 elections, the PTB and PSP would march together triumphantly as a 'Populist Front'. This does not mean that de Barros' movement did not prevent his opponents from continuing to spread the derogatory uses of the term 'populism' and the danger 'populists' allegedly entailed in terms of democratic practices. Be that as it may, the important takeaway here is that the signifiers 'populis*' became a focal point in the production of political antagonisms in Brazil's fourth republican period.

The Rise to Prominence of the Media Sphere and its interplay with the Sphere of Politics (1949-1964)

The constant dispute over the meaning of populism was expressed in various newspapers analysed, with pejorative as well as positive references to the terms 'populis*' appearing throughout the fourth republican period. These second-order media discourses do not merely comment on political affairs; they often set out to shape the contours of inter-sphere dynamics occurring in politics.

What is clear from the media readings, though, is that the press had little interest in pinning down a clear definition of what populism actually was. The pejorative or positive uses of the terms relied less on the theoretical conceptualisation of 'populis*' and more on the author's view of the players at stake. Congressman Alberto Pasqualini, considered one of Vargas' PTB prominent ideologues, encapsulated nicely this definitional indifference in the early 1950s. Asked by a journalist about the opposition between conservatives and populists, Pasqualini claimed that it was quite clear 'what conservatism stood for'. The term 'populist' as employed by Dutra and the press, however, remained a mystery word for him. He described it as an artificial term to label adversaries, frequently acquiring a pejorative tone (*O Jornal*, 1949a).

Pasqualini's words vividly depict the volatility and dynamism at the intersection of the politics and media spheres regarding 'populis*', exhibiting a wide array of first- and second-order discourses feeding and erecting from and against each other. Allow me to untangle further these dynamics in a more formal way.

First order populist discourses in the sphere of politics (1949-50)

From a discourse theory standpoint, populist discourses have a political logic not only constituted by an antagonism (them) which in turn articulates a collective subject (us), but this antagonism takes an up-down form dividing the *illegitimate powerful elite* versus *the underdog people*.

As a seminal populist discourse in Brazilian politics, Salgado appears as a salient figure. While attracting scant attention by the public, the integralists' appeal to the people not only constituted a populist discourse from where other second-order discourses would feed from, but also brought to the fore a stiff pro-populist rhetoric by defending 'populis*' elements.

I have noted, however, that second-order discourses (discourses about populism) can enable the discursive constitution of populist discourses, and, indeed, I am not the first one to do so (Nikisianis et al. 2019). The 'Petropolis Scheme' drawn by Dutra helped to inform most second-order anti-populist discourses in both politics and the media spheres. However, it was also the source from where de Barros would articulate a pro-populist stance, feeding this into his populist discourse, claiming not only to represent 'the people' against 'the elite', but also affording to 'populis*' the capacity to overcome such a battle. Thus, Dutra's discursive articulation served as a discursive enabler of both antagonistic and non-antagonistic mutual constitution processes.

It is worth noting that, while de Barros' populist front running-mate, Vargas, clearly upheld an anti-elitist and people-centric first order discourse, his explicit defence of 'populis*' were rather rare. From the various disputes with the 'conservative-democrats', Vargas left the populist/anti-populist antagonistic frontier at bay, claiming to represent the people via a labour movement.

Second-order discourses about populism: from politics to the media and back again

Anti-populism (1949-1950)

On the anti-populist side of the core antagonistic boundary in Brazil's Fourth Republic, I find more conservative sectors, hegemonic in the mainstream press, which often reaffirmed Dutra's position and take it as a prime anti-populist discursive reference, forging a stiff opposition to the political forces headed by Vargas and de Barros. As such, the media reference to Dutra's 'Petropolis Scheme' depicts a centrality of politics, from which the media sphere tends to feed. As such, the anti-'populis*' predominance in Brazil's media ecology of the time enacts as a key enabling condition for anti-populism in both the media and politics spheres, highlighting the logic of media ownership as being key in these processes of mutual constitution.

Apart from a few exceptions when these outlets published articles defending Adhemar de Barros (*Gazeta de Notícias*, 1949), in general terms, media conglomerates such as *O Estado de S. Paulo* group and Assis Chateaubriand's *Diários Associados* emphatically supported the National Democratic Union (UDN), the main urban and elitist opposition party. In these conservative newspapers, the signifiers 'populis*' are constantly accompanied by depreciating adjectives, saliently described as 'low' and 'demagogic'. Another frequent trope was the association between 'populism' with 'extremism' and 'communism' (see, for example, *O Jornal*, 1949d).

However, the journalistic reference to 'populis*' discursive employment in the political sphere is not restricted to Dutra nor to anti-populism. At times, explicitly referencing Salgado's fascist forces served as discursive means to attach to populism a reactionary character. In this vein, the journalist A. R. Gama, from the *Diário de Notícias*, produced a series of two articles called *Theory and Practice of Demagogic Populism*. By claiming that de Barros had stolen the term from the extreme-right integralists, Gama upheld the view that populism was nothing but a by-product of dictatorship. In so doing, he formulated a differential logic between 'populist' and 'popular' – something deemed recurrent in both the media and politics nodes, linked to the idea that although populists claimed to represent the people, they never actually defended popular interests in practice. As the title suggests, the articles strongly associated populism with demagoguery and claimed that de Barros represented the ultimate '*demagogic-populist*' in Brazilian politics (*Diário de Notícias*, 1949a; 1949b).

Other more 'precise' definitions are in fact mere attacks, as in this article by Osvaldo Chateaubriand from November 14, 1950:

> [...] our populism, which is composed almost entirely of crooks, is a page of grotesque humour and unique blandness in the history of the republics, from this and the other hemisphere (*O Estado de S. Paulo*, 1950).

Consequently, populists were treated as 'cheats of the worst kind', and a 'new species of tireless rodents, eating their victims from the outside to the entrails, leaving them only the carcass' (*ibid.*).

Pro-populism (1951-1961)

Founded in June 1951 and edited by the journalist Samuel Wainer, the newspaper *Última Hora* had a more sympathetic view of populism. Closer to Vargas than to de Barros, Wainer's newspaper sometimes reproduced the mainstream hostility against 'populism' in the moments PTB and PSP were not close, yet usually sustaining a more pro-populist rhetoric. This reinforces the close intra-sphere link between media and political spheres, foreclosing a non-antagonistic character of mutual constitution of populist discourses from Vargas and de Barros' forces and pro-populist discourses in the media. After Vargas' suicide, however, the editorial line had a stiff change.

It is worth noticing that Wainer hired former congressman Danton Coelho as the *Última Hora*'s managing director for a few months in 1955. Coelho, who was Vargas' Labor Minister in 1951 and presided over the *Getulist* PTB for a few years, left his position in the newspaper to be de Barros' running mate in a renewed 'Populist Front' candidature for president and vice-president. As such, processes of discursive mediation can be identified through populist and pro-populism discourses in the media and political spheres, as not only an ideational interaction is identified but also the inter-sphere transit of players.

Despite the overall hostility towards populists among the big press conglomerates, however, many elements suggest that, at the first moment, Adhemar de Barros seemed to have temporarily won the dispute over the meaning of populism.

Already in July 1949, there were disputes involving all political parties to define which one was genuinely populist, as the term frequently appeared as a synonym of 'popular', assigning those who work for the people. In an illustrative case, while congressmen from the integralist PRP and de Barros' PSP disputed the ownership of the 'populist' label, a politician from the UDN intervened to point out that every party, including his, is somehow 'populist' because no party exists 'without the people' (*Diário da Noite*, 1949b).

Between Vargas' election and 1955, there is a normalisation of the signifiers 'populis*', which became the self-proclaimed label of de Barros' PSP and were mostly used by the press with neither positive nor negative connotations to refer to it. Simultaneously, the label was partly attributed to Vargas and the PTB (yet less frequently), also without pejorative connotations. Evidence of the victory of the saliently laudatory meaning of 'populis*' at the time was the fact that some vehicles even adopted the habit of writing 'populis*' within inverted commas, as to indicate that it was not intrinsically a eulogy.

Adhemar de Barros and his acolytes' initial victory over the signifiers 'populis*' was also a victory of populist politics. For years, the UDN had struggled with the signifier 'populism', and so set at the periphery of the political disputes. On various occasions, the 'conservative-democrats' tried to impose a differential logic between 'populis*' and 'popular', associating the former with demagoguery (*O Estado de S. Paulo*, 1958). Before the 1960 election, however, some factions of the party understood that their approach was fruitless (Benevides, 1981, p. 212-13).

As a result, I observe a growing concern among journalists such as Marroquim that the so-called 'centrist' parties would face difficulties to get to power only gathering the dwindling votes of the urban elites, without appealing to the 'populist sectors' of the electorate (*Última Hora*, 1957; *O Jornal*, 1958).

Jânio Quadros's name starts to gain traction as he embodied a figure capable of disputing 'populist' voters, generally identified with governor Adhemar de Barros and vice-president João Goulart, the leaders of traditional 'populist' parties (*O Jornal*, 1960, see also Benevides 1981, 215). Quadros was even accused of 'fake populism' by pro-populist pundits (*Última Hora*, 1958).

While Dutra's discourse is not considered to be first order (as articulating a discourse *about* populism rather than a populist discourse), it is considered to assume a central enabling function in the politics-media sphere interaction since fist order discourses (de Barros; Vargas) and second-order discourses, both pro- (Wainer; Coelho) and anti-populist (Chateaubriand; Marroquim), feed and constitute themselves from it.

Figure 2. First- and second-order discourse weight/interaction

As such, de Barros wins inter-sphere discursive battles in politics. His populist discourse was not only parasitical from the antagonistic line drew by Dutra in the 'Petropolis scheme', but de Barros' populist and pro-populism lines reconfigured the discursive contours within the political sphere. Yet, such an impact is not solely restricted to politics. The political disputes reconfigure the discursive contours within the media sphere, inflicting substantial changes in 2nd order discourses about populism. Such interaction not only discloses intra-sphere dynamics of mutual constitution, but also highlights the predominant weight of politics over the media in the sphere complex.

An Academic Interlude

It is worth noting here, if only briefly, how the academic sphere was evolving in relation to populism. Although the academic sphere had a rather negligible influence on the spheres of politics and the media at this stage, it is important to register its growing interest in the topic and how its theoretical investigations responded to the above described non-academic disputes and, in turn, how they later helped to give shape to those disputes.

If during the so-called 'Populist Republic' the terms 'populis*' did not have a clear negative connotation, being disputed and claimed by various actors in many ways, the academic formulations reinforced those who saw populism as a downgraded form of political organisation. The political context and the institutional authority of actors matter here. While the scholar Hélio Jaguaribe wrote his reflections in the early 1950s, when populism was on the rise, the reflections from the 1960s took place in a moment of growing political crisis that finally led to the military coup of 1964. In this context, left-leaning theorists such as Francisco Weffort were trying to grasp what had gone wrong in the fourth republic – and seemed to reach a consensus that its 'populist' status made it intrinsically limited (Cardoso, 2010, p. 44). To a large extent, these prestigious intellectuals targeted populism as an insufficient alternative to political emancipation, explaining the military regime's appearance through the Fourth Republic's inherent contradictions.

This general hostility against populism through second-order academic discourses would later lead to profound political consequences, as many of these intellectuals reflected on possible avenues for contesting the military regime and organize the opposition. As vividly stated by former president Fernando Henrique Cardoso (1977, p. 32) himself: 'we spent several years in a populist regime, and we know from experience that populist paternalism leads nowhere. It might immediately lead to an outburst, and then to a *coup*'. They all seem to imply that the democratic resistance against the dictatorship should resist not only the military but also the populist temptation.

A Cultural Interlude

The media-politics interaction so far highlights a terrain of relatively high volatility during this period, as things tended to be quite fluid, particularly at the intersections between spheres (be referred to figure 1). However, perhaps one can also say that this set of complex interactions is framed by a more diffuse cultural backdrop. This is merely to suggest that once discursive battles are won in the more dynamic quarters of our sphere complex, the results tend to be secreted as 'cultural sediment'. Moreover, dictionaries can be a good index of 'relative sedimentation' in the wider cultural arena and this applies no less to the meanings associated with populism.

By turning to the dictionaries, I find evidence of how the signifying dynamics coalescing around 'populis*' transformed the Brazilian political lexicon. The best example is probably the *Pequeno Dicionário Brasileiro da Língua Portuguesa*, one of the most influential dictionaries of the time. Its first edition was published in 1938, with a ninth edition in 1951, and a tenth edition a decade later in 1961. The comparison between these different versions is enlightening in terms of the relevance of 'populis*' in the Brazilian context. While the word 'populism' remains absent prior to the 1961 edition, the dictionary defines 'populist' as:

> *Populist.* Friend of the people; used to describe a kind of literature that describes the life of the common people sympathetically (*Pequeno Dicionário Brasileiro da Língua Portuguesa* 1951).

A slight change was made in the 1961 edition, and the definition of 'populist' acquires an important addendum:

> *Populist.* Friend of the people; used to describe a kind of literature that describes the life of the common people sympathetically; *(Brazil) related to populism; that which is or those who take part in populism* (*Pequeno Dicionário Brasileiro da Língua Portuguesa* 1961a).

And finally, in the 1961 edition, the definition of 'populism' enters the scene:

> *Populism.* (Brazil) Politics based on enlisting the lower classes of society (*Pequeno Dicionário Brasileiro da Língua Portuguesa* 1961b).

As will be later seen, the rationale for grasping this latter definition emerges more clearly once I examine in more detail the role played by the sphere of academia. For now, however, I continue to focus on the dynamic interplay between politics and the media.

Deflating pro-populism and populist discourses (1961-1964)

Despite the apparent triumph of populist politics, it is interesting to note that with Quadros' victory and his abrupt resignation seven months later (January to August 1961), de Barros took some distance from the term 'populism'. In a moment in which the new national government led by Joao Goulart (1961-1964) was fostering reforms considered as being too 'radical', producing endless political crises, de Barros decided to adhere to a new conservative discourse in vogue at the time (Sampaio, 1982, p. 154).

That might explain why, despite de Barros running and winning the São Paulo gubernatorial elections in 1962, there is no significant peak in occurrences of 'populis*' in the press that year and an overall decline in the uses of the term in general, exhibiting, once again, the dominant weight of the sphere of politics in relation to the media. It may also explain why populism became associated with reactionary politics. Adhemar de Barros started his electoral political career in an alliance with the Communist Party and presented himself in opposition to reactionary sectors. In 1962, however, he took a clear right-wing position, which may have alienated some part of progressives who used to see populism as a left-wing alternative.

In this context, there were even discussions in the press on whether populism was 'dead', with a new clear cleavage between left and right dominating the political landscape (*Última Hora*, 1963b). That being said, many outlets indicate that de Barros regretted this strategy soon after the 1962 state election and would resume to refer to himself as a populist and continue to do it until his last breath (*O Jornal*, 1963; *Última Hora*, 1963a).

The Rise of Academia and its Role in the Three-sphere Complex (1954-1970)

If the Brazilian Populist Republic led the words 'populis*' to be dictionarised for the first time, it also significantly impacted academia. In fact, I argue that it is no accident that the advent of the first theorisation about populism in Brazil flourished a few years after the beginning of the so-called Populist Republic. Jaguaribe's essential work on the subject, published in 1954, sought to give a detailed account of the phenomenon of 'ademarism'. The influence of non-academic discourses within the scholarly theoretical formulations of populism becomes clear when Jaguaribe states that 'the classification that suits [ademarism] has already been used countless times in everyday language' (Jaguaribe, 1954, p. 291). He stated that 'ademarism is [indeed] a populism', and of a reactionary kind (Jaguaribe, 1954, p. 291).

Moving from political and mediatic discourses to an academic theorisation of populism, Jaguaribe regarded this type of movement as one that would emerge in the presence of three *sine qua non* conditions. These were: 1) a *mass* of unorganised workers; 2) a *ruling class* that has lost 'its aptitude to direct the social process with a minimum of efficiency'; and 3) the subsequent emergence of a charismatic leader 'gifted with a special appeal to the masses, able to mobilise them politically for the conquest of power' (Jaguaribe, 1954, p. 294–295).

When drawing on the Brazilian context, Jaguaribe believed that the formation of a mass came about by a spontaneous process of urban migration. Large migratory inflows from the countryside brought unorganised workers in precarious conditions to concentrate and settle in the urban peripheries. Simultaneously, the reorganisation of the dominant groups by the replacement of the landowners was not assumed by organised industrial capital but by diverse and conflicting speculative groups seeking to establish influence and authority (Jaguaribe, 1954, p. 298–299). This double composition in the demographic reorganization that the unstable modernisation process brought in Brazil, created room for a strong personality to intermediate between them – a role that de Barros would assume. Yet, Jaguaribe saw de Barros' leadership as somewhat conditional since other figures – such as Hugo Borghi – could have also exercised the similar commanding role Brazilian populism would require (Jaguaribe, 1954, p. 301–302).

Jaguaribe's work was highly influential. In 1962, for instance, the prominent sociologist Fernando Henrique Cardoso would repeat his claim that the Brazilian proletariat composed by migratory inflows from the countryside was disorganised, being manipulated by a paternalist populist leader (Cardoso, 1962, p. 152). Yet, while Jaguaribe embarked on a persistent criticism of the 'Marxists' by regarding their theoretical tenets as unfit for educing populism as a phenomenon (Jaguaribe, 1954, p. 291; 298), the works from the early 1960s have aimed to flesh out his work further and make explicit its compatibility with Marx's tradition. In this effort, the name of Francisco Weffort, a student, contributor and friend of Cardoso, stands out. Weffort would show how the key concepts for understanding populism are found in Antonio Gramsci's comments on Caesarism – which, on their turn, were based on a particular reading of Karl Marx's critique of Bonapartism presented in *The Eighteenth Brumaire of Louis Napoleon* (1852).

For Gramsci, the axial concept to understand Caesarism is the notion of subalternity (Gramsci 1971, Q13 [1932-1934] §27). The Italian thinker articulated this term from a notion present in Marx since his youthful texts: the notion of mass (Marx, 1847, p. 159). Both Gramsci's subaltern groups and Marx's mass are progressively opposed to the notion of *class*. Unlike the class – which is assumed to organise itself independently – the subaltern mass is seen as an intrinsically disorganised collective body, regarded as a multitudinous conglomerate of individuals rather than a social unit proper.

In his reading of Marx, Gramsci outlined the conditions for the emergence of Caesarism – or Bonapartism – through a rather paradoxical claim. As Gramsci reads it, Bonapartism emerges when the French proletariat found itself as a long-suffering, weakened class following a series of successive defeats. At the same time, the bourgeoisie's mode of domination had found its limits (Marx, 1852, p. 34-35; 62). Therefore, Gramsci understands that Caesarism emerges in a moment of equilibrium of forces between the two fundamental organic classes of capitalism (i.e. the *proletariat* and the *bourgeoisie*). In this context, the Bonapartist leader would achieve relative independence within the political sphere in relation to the intrinsic economic interests by arbitrating between them (Weffort, 1965a, p. 55).

In so doing, the command of the charismatic Bonapartist leader would lean on an 'inorganic' social group: the peasantry (Marx, 1852, p. 12; see also Laclau, 2005a, p. 145). The inorganic condition would relate to a dispersed social group with no conditions to organize as a 'class for itself' (Marx, 1852, p. 142-143). As the peasantry lacked class-consciousness, it would therefore be expressed in terms of a subaltern mass (Weffort, 1965b, p. 29). This means that the peasants, without organising themselves independently 'from below', would find the Bonapartist leader 'from above', suitable to their taste and judgement (Weffort, 1967, p. 74).

Weffort was well aware that the Brazil of the fourth republic was not quite the Bonapartist France, as it had a highly dependent economy, and the relative weakness of the bourgeoisie was closely linked to the crisis caused by the transition from an agricultural to an industrial economy (Weffort, 1965a, p. 58-59). Consequently, the mass could not be constituted by the same social groups on both sides of the Atlantic. However, the general picture is still somewhat analogous. To that end, Weffort invites us to mirror the way the Bonapartist manipulates the peasant masses to that of a populist leader – be it de Barros, Vargas or any other – finding in the new-formed urban masses an electoral base with no intermediaries other than the Bonapartist leader (Weffort, 1965b, p. 28-29; 1967, p. 79).

It is worth noticing that, in all its expressions, the distinction between mass and class rests predominantly on a concept of manipulation. It is true that Cardoso and Weffort – unlike Jaguaribe – do recognise a small emancipatory potential in populism (Cardoso, 1962, p. 122; 1976, p. 37; Weffort, 1967, p. 71; 84-85). In his more refined account, Weffort believed the mass would not only be passive (Weffort, 1967, p. 75) as it would carry alongside a remnant of class in order to exert some pressure on the leader (Weffort, 1965a, p. 60-61). Therefore, if the populist leader manipulates the workers, on the one hand, he gives them something back on the other in the shape of tangible achievements. In so doing, he becomes 'the main form of political expression' of the various popular demands (Weffort, 1967, p. 71).

Nevertheless, as in Caesarism (Gramsci, 1996, Q3 [1930], §48), in Weffort's work a deceptive character impregnates populism in its form and intention. To a certain extent, the workers' achievements are nothing but crumbs given to sustain those in power. For this reason,

Cardoso would point out that Weffort 'had a horror to populism', expressing a general trend among their peers (Cardoso, 1985, p. 31-32).

From academia to politics: enabling and mediation

Scholarship production and publication dynamics have delayed inter- and intra-sphere interactions. Academic discourses feed on first- and second-order extra-sphere interactions, silently yet steadily building antagonistic and non-antagonistic intra-sphere mutual-constitution processes. Indeed, editorial and peer-reviewed processes foreclose distinctive intra-sphere logics, conveying diachronic discursive interactions and articulations. For such specific discursive production processes, while adjourning its inter-sphere dynamic feedback, the academic sphere conveys a distinctive power of discursive sedimentation in our multi-sited framework. This is quite clear when studying the discursive dynamics deriving from the fourth republic.

While underplayed in the inter- and intra-sphere dynamics and disputes of populism discourses throughout the 1950s, the academic sphere assumes a dominant role in mediating and enabling discursive processes of mutual constitution, particularly from the 70s onwards. As mentioned in the academic interlude, the scholarship production deriving from Bonapartism, by drawing the emancipatory constraints of populism, identified in the self-organisation of workers truly emancipatory potential, serving as theoretical footprints for the democratic resistance against the military. However, not only did academic players act as discursive enablers, for they directly mediated mutual constitution processes in the political sphere.

Beyond their academic work, figures such as Weffort and Cardoso had critical militant engagements throughout the 1970s and 1980s, first taking part in reorganising the national democratic opposition as it coalesced in the Brazilian Democratic Movement (MDB, the main party opposing the military regime). Cardoso was even referred to as 'the most famous "organic intellectual"' of the party (Benevides, 1986, p. 23), assuming such an important role that would lead this sociologist to be elected president of Brazil in 1995 and then re-elected 2003.

It is worth noting that the intra-sphere dynamics in politics favoured the prominence of these academic figures in the Brazilian opposition. Even though many PTB deputies went to the MDB, the more ideological cadres were impeached, if not eliminated after the 1964 coup. Thus, Vargas' legacy fractures in favour of another way of organising opposition to the military (Motta, 1993, p. 109), showing that the crisis of hegemonic intra-sphere discourses enables a more fluid inter-sphere interaction, also facilitating the mediating transit of players and the enabling power of extra-sphere ideational content.

The political trajectory of Weffort is particularly interesting for, after taking part in the MDB, he would participate in the formation of the Workers' Party (PT), becoming a salient intellectual cadre of the party. Again, we find here the echoes of scholarship anti-populism and its mediating role in politics, as the PT came about at the dawn of the 1980s after widespread unionist unrest contesting the military and also Vargas' corporativist legacy, which constitutionally subjected union activity to the taste of the executive command (Singer, 2010, p. 101-102). As the anti-populist intellectual he was, it is no wonder that Weffort would later part ways with PT, arguing that after the election of its undisputed leader, Luiz Inácio Lula da Silva, to the presidency, the latter had become 'the Adhemar de Barros of these new times' (*Folha de S. Paulo*, 2006).

After the fall of the fourth republic, considered the truly seminal democratic bracketing in Brazilian politics by the participation of broad sectors of civil society, the academic sphere assumed a heavier weight in the sphere-complex, setting important contours for political and journalistic anti-populism. Furthermore, the theoretical and analytic contributions of the time have had a long-lasting impact on Brazilian scholarship.

Although more than half a century has passed since the seminal contributions of Jaguaribe and Weffort were first laid, their influence is still dominant in the Brazilian canonical literature as an analytic scope to the study of contemporary social and political developments. In this respect, André Singer's important work on *Lulismo* stands out (Singer, 2012, p. 33; 42), and via Bonapartism would Lafer formally conceived in the 1970s Brazil's fourth republican period as the Populist Republic.

Conclusion

Discourse theory scholarship has been highlighting the ubiquitous reference to 'populism' and 'populist' across various fora, training our attention to the need to study populism as both a concept and a signifier. They have also emphasised how the interaction of actors across social spheres articulate our views on the meanings we afford to populism. By taking these studies seriously, this paper has formally conveyed a multi-sited framework to study the dynamic interplay of what we have named as populism discourses, showing how, through discursive constitution and mediation processes, these interactions enact in the construction of social reality.

The distinctive virtues of this framework have been probed with reference to a concrete case study. Following the seminal references to 'populis*' in the Brazilian context, I have delved into the Fourth Republic (1946-1964), considered the first instance in which popular layers in Brazil actively participated in electoral politics. In identifying the spheres, sites and processes of discursive interaction at stake, I traced, untangled and articulated the dynamic production and evolution of populism discourses. In so doing, I demonstrate the added value of my multi-sited discursive framework, while also showcasing in greater detail and nuance the significance of key moments in this period.

Paper 2: From Lula to Bolsonaro: unravelling *Veja* Magazine's (anti)populist fantasies.

Abstract

In using the concept of fantasy to develop an analytical grid for the study of *Veja* magazine's discursive anti-populism, this study explores the distinctive virtues of adopting a psychoanalytically-inflected discourse theory approach to the study of political antagonism and the critique of ideology. By studying *Veja* Magazine's treatment of the words 'populis*', this paper intends to bring fantasy back to the core of the discursive study of populism as a signifier. It draws our attention to how, from an elitist policymaking perspective, the discursive disputes against the Workers' Party (PT) and the alliances for electing Jair Bolsonaro as president of Brazil in 2018 were normatively endowed and ideologically constructed.

I never understood the position, except a posteriori, of the richest classes in Brazil in relation to interest rates. Nor did I understand the extent of their aversion to paying for any part of the crisis.

- Dilma Rousseff, 2017[8]

Introduction

'Following the backlash against left-wing populism from the Lula-Chavez era, it is now the right that needs, as celebrities harassed by a foolish scandal, to reinvent itself' (Gryzinsky, 2021, p. 53). In its *2726* edition, *Veja* Magazine highlights the need for a non-populist movement that, complicit with 'the rules of the establishment', will be capable of appealing to those angry sections of the population that are still 'sensitive to right-wing populism'. The crucial question for the magazine is: 'Who will speak to these layers whose rise in Brazil was seen in [Bolsonaro's] 2018 election?' (*ibid.*). By denouncing the evil of left-wing populism and the inconvenience of its right-wing equivalent, *Veja* Magazine gives its assessment of the battered state of world politics at the dawn of the year 2021.

Although *Veja*'s journalistic use of the term populism focuses on Brazilian politics, its approach seems to embody a common use in today's political language. Populism is featured prominently everywhere – in headlines, opinion pieces and in many scientific discussion circles – and seems to capture the gist of our political era. Because of populism, we advocate *for* and *against* different social players and political movements. Today we even love and hate in the name of populism.

It is because we cannot stop talking about it that this little word, populism, draws our attention towards less perceptible analytical layers within the field of discursivity. The pervasive use of this term in the public sphere compels us to be *pre*occupied not only in describing what we say about populism. Perhaps, most importantly, we should aim to analyse

[8] Interview with Dilma Russeff, In: https://www.jornaldonassif.com.br/page/noticia/entrevista-exclusiva-dilma-rousseff-sem-censura-ou-quase-por-pagina-13-pt-parte-2- [accessed 05/05/2020].

how what we say about populism tells us *something* meaningful about our understanding of ourselves and the social world we are part of.

Interestingly enough, the most recent turn to populism within academic circles has meant not only 'a turn towards populist politics as an object of enquiry but also a turn towards populism as a [discursive] framework of analysis' (De Cleen and Glynos, 2020). The growing use of the word populism has triggered a sharp analytical focus on the various connotations given to this peculiar signifier.

Critical fantasy studies (CFS) has been formally presented as an analytical frontier deriving from discourse theory, drawing attention to the affective power coursing through social and political life (Glynos, 2020). By appealing to the psychoanalytic notion of fantasy, CFS aims to analyse *how* and *why* subjects invest in certain norms, ideas and identities. This approach can enrich the field of populism studies by providing theoretical and critical tools to analyse identificatory investments in discourses about populism and the normative, ideological and politico-strategic valences attached to them.

By focusing on *Veja* Magazine, this paper aims to construct the mainstream media's role within the current turmoil in Brazilian politics. In this article, I will investigate *Veja*'s treatment of so-called left-wing populism – in this case, Luiz Ignacio Lula da Silva (Lula) and the Workers' Party (PT) – and how the systematic attack on these political forces conveys a vital logic in the mainstream's support for an alt-right discursive composition organised around the figure of Jair Bolsonaro in the 2018 elections. In so doing, I will deploy a psychoanalytically-inflected discourse theory, arguing that the category of fantasy harbours acute ideological significance in the construction and analysis of political antagonism.

Discourse theory and media discourses about populism

For long, the media landscape has been subject to scrutiny and research by academic circles. So too, has the study of populism. Interestingly enough, the cross-section between media and populism studies is now gaining progressive traction, as scholars perceive a vibrant and necessary relation between the phenomenon of populism and the communication dynamics in the media. As succinctly referenced by Moffitt (2016, p. 94), 'media can no longer be treated as a 'side issue' when it comes to understanding contemporary populism'.

In this vein, mainstream populism scholarship has afforded media vehicles and social networks a privileged status. Through antagonistic and cooperative dynamics, the relationship between the media and populist actors is seen as pivotal in the latter's political success or failure (Mudde, 2007, p. 67). In constituting a complex array of heterogeneous institutions, the media offers a broad range of communicative networks for political interactions. Partly attributed to the populists' unmediated relationship with 'the people', the media may assume the role of a fecund arena where charismatic populist leaders can, without party-mediation, skew and take over the public agenda (Weyland, 2001, p. 16).

The media is also perceived by political communication scholarship as an amplifying source of populist politics (Cammaerts, 2018). While some point to the digital affinity between populists and social media (Gerbaudo, 2018), others highlight the hyperpartisan character of the press to be the key when situating populist players in the field of political communication (Rae, 2020). From their part, Wells et al. (2020) believe that interactions between candidate communications, social-, partisan-, and news-media all help shape the attention given to populist politics, for such interaction should be studied with all due seriousness.

Undeniably, many populism and media scholars give close attention to how (actually existing) populist elements travel and amplify their reach through a vast network of communicative fora. Surprisingly, however, the study of journalistic discourses *about* populism appears to be rather uncommon despite the ubiquity of the reference to populism and populists in the press (jointly referred to as 'populis*' from now on). Perhaps, from these few academic circles, discourse scholars stand out by stressing the need to study how the references to 'populis*' are discursively articulated in complex political and social interactions and how such references, in turn, interact in constructing the political perception of social reality.

Discourse theory scholars assume meaning-making processes in terms of an articulatory practice. This approach is based on the view that, as the social context shifts, the meaning of the words we use (and the identities we assume) to describe the world and oneself also shifts. The notion of 'articulatory practice' raises profound questions over concept-centred analyses, placing the focus instead on processes of meaning construction.

Deriving from within discourse theory (DT) academic circles, the appeal to the study of populism as a signifier has refreshed the core analytical focus for the contemporary study of populism (Glynos and Mondon, 2016; De Cleen, Glynos and Mondon, 2017; Stavrakakis, 2017; Nikos, Siomos, Stavrakakis, Markou, and Dimitroulia, 2017). In a bid to untangle central logics in the overinvestment key players place on the words 'populis*', Glynos and Mondon (2016) were among the first to highlight how these terms have been increasingly used by European media outlets.

The call to study discourses *about* populism has stimulated compelling empirical analyses over journalistic discourses in Europe (Nikisianis et al. 2018) and the United Kingdom (Brown and Mondon, 2020). These studies, relying largely on corpus linguistics (CL) to formulate macro-(con)textual analyses of broad discursive patterns, have explored the broad antagonistic constructions fostered by segments of the press. While the media employs the terms 'populis*' to refer to a wide array of heterogeneous political players, these media-centric studies identify journalistic anti-populist discursive tendencies, generally depicting populist players as a menace to liberal democracy.

While Glynos and Mondon helped set the scene for the study of discourses *about* 'populis'*, some of the main theoretical and analytical elements they use in their critical construction of the underlying logics of these discursive dynamics are anything but present in subsequent research production. This is particularly true when referring to the affective force underlying ideological discourses about populism, analysed by Glynos and Mondon through the psychoanalytically informed notion of fantasy (which will be introduced in the next section).

By relying on the broad correlation of discursive trends via CL, the bulk of scholarly production on discourses about 'populis*' ignore the energising power underlying these discursive constructs on populism. This is rather surprising, as recent research on populism arising from within DT academic circles has systematically stressed the importance of studying emotions for moving both populism studies and discourse theory forward (Eklundh, 2019; Ronderos, 2020; Zicman de Barros, 2020; Dean and Maiguashca 2020; De Cleen et al. 2020; Glynos, 2020).

I do not underestimate the value derived from combining DT and CL in recognising this gap. Instead, I highlight a relevant dimension on the discursive study of populism discourses in the media as worthy of further empirical exploration. After all, journalists have long assumed a privileged role in public discussions and opinion formation (Mccombs and Valenzuela, 2021) and a more in-depth media-centric analysis may offer valuable insights into broader discursive constructions and ideological articulations. As aptly put by Goyvaerts and De Cleen (2020, 100), 'Media are but one player in this house of mirrors, but in a mediatised society like ours, they are central to understanding the nature as well as the ubiquity of discourse about populism'.

By studying *Veja* Magazine's treatment of the words 'populis*', this paper intends to bring fantasy back to the core of the discursive study of populism as a signifier. In what follows,

I will show that identifying the composition of discursive structures which rely on 'populis*' as nodal points in the media can reveal how populist-centric discourses articulate social meaning and, through fantasmatic constructions, invite its readers to partake in experiences of enjoyment and thus articulate ideological content. I should add, moreover, that a discourse theory approach to ideology contends it as an open-ended affective construction. Still, and in line with this thesis' theoretical framework, I understand affective, ideological constructions as always rooted in preceding libidinal articulations constructed historically. As will be seen through this study, these historically-endowed libidinal structures play a rather significant part in the way 'populis*', as signifiers, are employed through media outlets. In particular, anti-populist sentiment in Brazil shares a rather stiff anti-leftist character, as will be rendered visible while analysing the discursive employment of the words 'populis*' by *Veja* magazine.

Overinvestment and *enjoyment*: core layers for approaching (anti)populist fantasies

Populism has long been studied as a concept as it is useful in capturing a relevant aspect of political reality. This line of argument has sparked long-lasting debate about the significance of populism as a category in its own right. However, the sheer volume of publications endlessly assessing and reassessing the conceptual foundations of populism has been met with increasing fatigue and frustration by many scholars (e.g. Dean and Maiguashca, 2020). Regardless of the impatience and unease encompassing populism studies as a field that has been done to death, we continue to reflect, write and speak in the name of populism.

Needless to say, this article does not propose to delimit or further flesh out the conceptual significance of populism. Given the ongoing interest and investment in populism inside and outside academia, I am interested in excavating and constructing – to borrow Wittgenstein's (1963, p. 23) words – the 'language games' involving 'populis*' as central signifying elements and explaining how these language games assume vital discursive functions in the ideational construction of social reality. This reflective stance directly follows the core principles of DT.

DT is associated with a post-Marxist and poststructuralist tradition, initially set by Ernesto Laclau and Chantal Mouffe (1985). Unlike other approaches that take discourse as a purely linguistic phenomenon, DT sees it as a structure that sustains all meaningful practices, ideas and identities. Discursivity, for DT, therefore encompasses the generalised field of (social) meaning.

The core ontological principles of DT derive from psychoanalytically informed perspectives on identity and subjectivity. By discovering the unconscious, Freud recognised a splitting (*Spaltung*) agency in the subject, which called into question the centrality of the conscious ego in social knowledge production. Inspired by Freud's discovery, Jacques Lacan subverted the cartesian idea of the subject as *cogito* and conceived it in his work as a subject of *lack* (Fink, 1997, p. 43).

Through the notion of lack, Lacan endeavours to comprehend the constitutive impossibility of the subject to reach an absolute existential fullness by the irreconcilable relation between the concrete phenomenality of being with the abstract ideal Being. So, as advanced by Glynos and Stavrakakis (2008, p. 260), the idea of the subject as lack is necessarily attached to the subject's attempts to overcome this constitutive lack through the affirmation of its positive identity. Such affirmation would require identifying with meaningful elements that provisionally provide a pleasant image in which the subject can *enjoy* by appearing likeable to him/herself. However, the more vigorously the subject (*over*)invests in meaningful pieces to attain a jubilant image of the self, its constitutive lack invariably resurfaces, exhibiting the precariousness in every socio-symbolic representation.

From this perspective, the subject experiences a prohibition of the enjoyment (*jouissance*) a full identity would provide, allowing desire to be structured around the attempts to overcome such a constitutive lack. Put less gnomically, the subject is taken as a subject of desire by the prohibition of the full enjoyment a positive identity would convey, thus making the lack in the subject a lack of *jouissance*.

The usefulness of the Lacanian framework for political analysis lies in the fact that desire is sustained not only by the subject's limit-experiences to a *jouissance* of the body but also by the fantasy in the intellectual construction of political projects purporting to overcome a lacking state.

Psychoanalytic theory is often presented as dense and obscure – claims which weight heavily on Lacan's oeuvre. When objectivist perspectives have failed to establish general laws governing social and political life, however, psychoanalytically informed standpoints have inspired new analytical turns. In this respect, the crossroad between discourse theory and psychoanalysis has proved to be enormously productive.

Inspired by the Lacanian notion of subjectivity, DT articulates a radically anti-objectivist and anti-essentialist social and political theory. In this vein, Laclau and Mouffe believe that, as any form of social representation supposes a partial effort to construct society, antagonism functions as the expression of the excluded possibilities by the predominant social structure (1985, p. 114). In other words, if the subject, as such, does not exist within a Lacanian framework, society appears as being impossible in the work of Laclau and Mouffe (Žižek, 1989, p. 142).

From a DT perspective, there is no post-ideological terrain precisely because every ideological representation of society cannot fully register social experience. Therefore, a fantasmatic analysis would seek to comprehend the structuring of narratives that purport to overcome a lacking-state and how these representations depict and account for a limit (or *loss*) of social enjoyment.

As fantasy is structured around the lack in symbolic representation (and the desire of its overcoming), one could say that 'the logic of fantasy names a narrative structure involving some reference to an idealised scenario promising an imaginary fullness or wholeness (the beatific side of fantasy) and, by implication, a disaster scenario (the horrific side of fantasy)' (Glynos, 2008, p. 283).

Both beatific and horrific narratives require central meaningful pieces through which the social subject explains this loss of its enjoyment. In this vein, CFS seeks to unravel the way subjects overinvest in certain discursive elements which are ultimately sustained by the desire to overcome the (social) lack of *jouissance*.

In analysing the underlying logics in *Veja*'s discursive mobilisation of the words 'popilis*', this study intends to help show how CFS can be analytically deployed for the critique of ideology, further operationalising underdeveloped and underexplored orbiting concepts that may serve as virtuous analytical devices. To advance this strategy, I rely on three figures that allow us to grasp affective constructions resting 'between the lines', so to speak, ultimately sustaining the gripping force underlying ideational-discursive articulations:

Thief of enjoyment (*thief*): individual, organisational or institutional representation of a parasitical agent which, in enjoying excessively, sustains or promotes regimes of social lack. Depending on the ideational narrative, these figures embody obstacles to distinct sources of enjoyment (whether political, economic, moral, affective/sexual or materialistic). Thieves are often seen as attaining or enjoying excessive and unearned pleasure and/or as bearers of a catastrophic horror. They tend to be portrayed or constructed in negative aesthetic terms (ugly, horrible, dirty, undesirable, and so on; for other accounts of 'thief of enjoyment see Žižek, 1989; Glynos, 2001).

Guarantor: individual, organisational or institutional representation of authority, safeguarding or promoting regimes of social enjoyment (these may encompass political, economic or moral guarantors). Guarantors are often constructed in opposition to *thief* representations (if one were to analyse a discursive construct opposing, for example, a *corrupt thief*, a *moral guarantor* is expected to play an important fantasmatic role or have a heavier 'weight' in relation to other guarantors). Guarantors are portrayed or constructed in positive aesthetic terms (beautiful, pretty, clean, sexy, and so on; for other accounts on 'guarantor' see Chang and Glynos, 2011).

Grammar enabling enjoyment: discursive elements sustaining the concrete representations of social enjoyment. These are seen as partial manifestations of an attainable and foreseeable beatific stage, inscribing abstract desires in a horizon of plausible plausibility.

Research Strategy

Justification

Although there is no doubt that the general public is reading fewer print newspaper and magazines which have been overtaken by Instagramers, YouTubers and bloggers, the traditional media's influence over policymakers and strategic financial and economic players is still up and running. This has been *Veja* Magazine's traditional purpose.

Veja, since the 1980s, has targeted the Brazilian elite in a trickle-down strategy, aiming to exercise general influence by appealing to decision-makers and discussion forums. Although it targets an elite readership, *Veja* has also managed, within a highly concentrated media environment, to position itself as Brazil's most influential news magazine.

Graph 2 - Circulation 1985 to 2019[9]

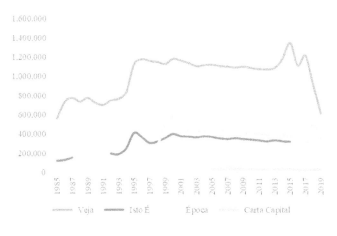

Source: IVC - Circulation Verification Institute

As a leading journalistic publication, *Veja*'s front cover appears in newsstands and bus stops across the country and it addresses its regular readers in everyday political language.

Interestingly enough, *Veja*'s circulation attained historic peaks between 2014 and 2017, a period of intense social activity in which Dilma Rousseff's government and the Workers' Party (PT) influence over Brazilian politics was challenged. As noted by Chicarino, Lula and the PT have been the magazine's main foe since the early 1980s, striking a chord with the anti-PT social anger (Chicarino, 2020).

---

[9] According to IVC Brasil, the circulation of a publication is the gross number of printed copies, while circulation effectively represents the number of copies that reached the hands of readers, whether through subscriptions, separate sales or targeted distribution. IstoÉ magazine has not been affiliated to the IVC since mid-2015, for there is no data from 2016 onwards.

Moreover, the mainstream media assumed a more prominent role in laying the groundwork for public debate from 2014 until 2018. Inspired by the Italian *mani pulite* anti-corruption operation and echoing the mass-mobilisation protests, the Car-wash operation headed by judge Sergio Moro forged a direct communication channel between the judiciary and the media as a means of winning over public opinion and taking down heavyweight public figures involved in corruption scandals. This alliance has been seen as a key strategic coordination link, via the congress, in Rousseff's impeachment, and justifying the judicial imprisonment of former president Lula (Almeida, 2019).

The ubiquity of the signifiers 'populis*' have been evident in the Brazilian press since the early 1950s (Ronderos and De Barros, 2020). In the following article, I show that constructing a detailed narrative of *Veja*'s discursive employment of the words 'populis*' allows us to grasp salient underlying discursive logics in the mainstream's ideological foundations. It will also draw attention to how, from an elitist policymaking perspective, the discursive disputes against the PT and the alliances for electing Jair Bolsonaro as president of Brazil in 2018 were normatively endowed and ideologically constructed.

Methods and sources

As mentioned earlier, while some prolific scholarly effort has been devoted to studying the discursive employment of the words 'populis*' in the press, these studies chiefly rely on the broad correlation of discursive patterns. Conducting a more in-depth discourse analysis to grasp underlying logics sustaining textual articulations (rather than depicting the formal structuring of the text itself) requires constructing a detailed narrative drawing attention to a more comprehensive picture of the context and tone (Glynos and Howarth, 2017, p. 55).

Furthermore, the analytical employment of DT is taken as a macro-textual approach, as it provides the grammar to study the way social identity comes about (Jørgensen and Phillips,

2002). That is to say, it overflows textual meaning production, constructing broader interactions of social meaning-making. Visual rhetoric, 'with its layers, images, and, without a doubt, pervasive affectivity' offers profoundly emotionally directed content articulating affectively oriented narratives.

As such, this study will encompass a multi-modal analysis of written- and image-based journalistic communication content. In constructing a database of all occurrences of 'populis*' through *Veja* Magazine's archives, I have read and familiarised myself with all relevant editorial content and commentary columns from 2015 to the end of 2019. For my narrative construction of a macro(con)textual analysis, I have limited my research scope from the third quarter of 2015 to the end of 2018. This allowed me to construct the discursive articulations surrounding four main events: a) the pro-impeachment demonstrations; b) Rousseff's impeachment; c) Lula's imprisonment; and d) Bolsonaro's 2018 election (and its immediate aftermath). Therefore, this study encompasses a database of 248 'populis*' occurrences[10], amounting to 113 issues from 01/08/2015 to 31/12/2018, enabling me to construct the disputes and discursive articulations formed therein. This study will also rely on magazine covers with higher occurrences as means of descriptive illustration.

Constructing *Veja*'s *populis*-centric narrative

Veja's anti-PT foundations

Dilma Vana Rousseff was the first Brazilian woman to reach the command of the executive branch. She was first elected president in 2010 then re-elected in 2014 and subsequently removed from the presidency on August 31, 2016, through an impeachment process.

---

[10] If a word appears several times on a single page, they are counted as one occurrence. Therefore, we may say that the number of occurrences refers to the number of pages which include at least a single reference to 'populis*'.

She succeeded her party leader and most prominent popular figure in Brazilian politics, Luiz Inácio Lula da Silva (hereinafter referred to as Lula) and her first presidential mandate lacked the stability forged by her predecessor.

Lula's stature grew rapidly throughout the first decade of the 2000s as he made a favourable impression on the international public and media. 'That is my man right here,' former U.S. president Obama said while approaching the Brazilian head of state who was surrounded by cheerful world leaders during the 2009 G20 summit. 'Love this guy, he is the most popular politician on earth. It is because of his good looks'.

Months later an image of the Christ the Redeemer statue rocketing into space appeared on *The Economist* cover under the title 'Brazil takes off'. In announcing the emergence of the 'Lula era', *The Economist* gratifyingly saluted Lula's social-distribution economic strategy. It said 'Lula is right to say that his country deserves respect, just as he deserves much of the adulation he enjoys' (*The Economist*, 2009).

Once a humble press operator in an automobile factory, Lula achieved an approval rating of 87%, setting a presidential popularity record and placing his Workers' Party (PT) at the heart of Brazilian politics. He also proved to be a successful political coordinator. By appointing Rousseff and forging an alliance with Brazil's strongest political party, the Brazilian Democratic Movement (MDB), the Lulist project seemed to enjoy good health.

Although Lula was exalted by Obama for his 'good looks', he was once branded the undesired 'bearded frog' of Brazilian politics (*Veja*, 1992, p. 39). Indeed, while applauded by prominent figures from across the ideological spectrum and cheered on by leading sectors of the international press for meeting the interests of both employers and employees, Lula had been challenged for a long time domestically. Nevertheless, the historical adversities forged by sections of the Brazilian press in antagonising Lula have not been restricted to his personal figure but extended to a discursive assault against the PT since the beginning of the democratisation process. This has been the traditional journalistic mark of *Veja* Magazine.

Lulopetism as a left populis* thief

Seen as a 'rickety' political force in 1980 (*Veja*, 1980, 27), the PT was described in 2015 by *Veja* as the 'Brazilian people's foremost enemy' (*Veja*, 2015a. p. 42 and 43), vividly portrayed on the Issue 2438 cover under the headline 'Brazil calls out for help'. In displaying social unrest through the famous *panelaços* [banging on pots and pans], *Veja* reported such events as the unambiguous sign of the end of the PT political cycle and qualified it as 'corrupt' and 'populist'.

Figure 3: issue 2438. 12/08/2015

Source: *Veja* archive

The magazine claimed both Lula and Rousseff's mandates rested on unlimited 'State interventionism', encouraging unsustainable desires of 'consumption and public spending'. By carrying out unhealthy economic practices and ignoring core market principles, the PT had plunged the country into chaos (Nobrega, 2015, p. 24).

A statement by Rousseff's vice-president, Michel Temer, highlighted in this 'special coverage' of the PT's pitfall appeared in which he distanced himself from his government position, further fracturing the coalition forged between the PT and MDB. In Temer's words, 'Brazil needs someone with the capacity to reunify everyone', an ability considered beyond Rousseff's skills by both Temer and the magazine (Pereira, 2015a, p. 46). Warning of the governments' lack of credibility, *Veja* alerted its readers that the *Lava Jato* ('carwash') operation would bring extraordinary incriminating evidence in the upcoming days and pointed to 'the beginning of the end of a cycle of populism and corruption that devastated Brazil' (Pereira, 2015b, p. 51).

The carwash task force was based in Curitiba and headed by judge Sergio Moro. It had featured prominently in the press since March 17, 2014 for its anti-corruption efforts. *Veja* was no exception. Depositions, recordings and pictures were published and amounted to what became an avalanche of weekly leaks from the operation to the media. These leaks provided 'solid and sufficient evidence' to believe that both Lula and Rousseff were well aware of the systemic scheme of corruption eroding the country throughout their governments (*Veja*, 2014). Moro has been hailed as a 'popstar' and a 'hero' ever since (*Veja*, 2015b, p. 40).

In a nine-page special report, the magazine paid tribute to Moro's audacious career against corruption and crime, listing the 300 sentences that made this young judge a 'national celebrity' (Petry, 2015, p. 50). As such, issue 2458, the last printed edition of 2015, was dedicated to the prodigious figure of judge Moro under the hyped headline: 'He saved the year!'.

Figure 4: issue 2458 30/12/2015

Source: *Veja* archive

Part of the good fortune forecast by *Veja* for 2016 was not only based on the fact that 'Lula ends 2015 in the flesh of a cornered mortal, surrounded by suspects' (*Veja*, 2015c, p. 64), but also on Latin America's gratifying turn against 'populism' and towards more orthodox economic views on market freedom. This was a specific reference to Mauricio Macri's aim for the presidency in Argentina and the majority won by the Venezuelan right in the parliamentary elections against the Chavista regime. As a result, Argentineans and Venezuelans had brought 'light to darkness', for they had awakened 'from the populist sorrow, giving their votes to political forces contrary to the measures that have destroyed their economy' (*Veja*, 2015c, p. 85).

The rhetorical reference to 'populis*' in *Veja*'s pages is often displayed in an additive semantic relation with the signifier 'corrupt[tion]'. In so doing, the 'populis*' reference serves as a means of describing how the common wealth is placed at the service of personal interests. The mixed-capital company *Petrobras* was in the spotlight of the carwash operation and its management of oil reserves was seen as the primary terrain for wide-scale corruption.

Oil, as such, was depicted by *Veja* as being a source of social wellbeing, as its (mis)management can result in a 'blessing or a curse'. Examples of the latter are given by *Veja* and described as 'deepening populism' processes, directly referring to Venezuela and Brazil. In the Brazilian case, the direct state interference in oil reserves by what the magazine called 'Lulopetismo' – as a reference to the PT project under Lula's leadership – 'took corruption to levels never seen in history' (*Veja*, 2016a, p. 10).

Like the oil industry, other segments of the energy sector were described as being on the verge of tragedy as a result of state interventionism. By interfering with the market dynamics, 'the populism of Dilma's government has disastrous consequences for the electricity sector and the consumer' (Alvarenga, 2016, p. 78). Lula had based his 'distributive populism' on the commodity boom but Rousseff would have to make use of different means to keep her 'foolish [interventionist] measures' and 'the Lulopetist model' afloat (*Veja*, 2016b, p. 10).

According to the magazine, disguised as a heterodox economic strategy, Rousseff and the PT had only one intention which was to get their 'hands on popular savings' and use the 'workers' money' to try and 'reactivate the economy they have for long ruined'. Not only did these measures go against the laws governing the 'creation of wealth', but they proved that 'populist regimes last only as long as the money of others' (*ibid.*).

As for Lula, 'the messiah, the new father of the poor', public prosecutors now had a 'high degree of suspicion' that the former president was the direct beneficiary of a luxury apartment renovation made with public funds. With a series of criminal indictments pointing towards Lula, 'the time has arrived for the carwash [investigations] to reach the *petista* [PT member]' (Prerira, Rangel and Bonin, 2016, p. 41).

Figure 5: issue 2468, 09/03/2016   **Figure 6**: issue 2469, 16/03/2016

Source: *Veja* archive

Under the headline 'Lula and the law', special issue 2468 detailed the many scandals haunting Lula, Rousseff and the PT. The main event was carwash's 24th phase, embodied by the so-called federal police operation *Aletheia*. This involved 200 personnel and was headed by judge Moro. It led to Lula being detained on March 4, 2016, at 8:40 am, and taken from his home in São Bernardo do Campo to be questioned by the Federal Police. Raids on Lula's apartment, the home of his son Fábio Luís, the *Lula Institute*, and addresses in Bahia and Rio de Janeiro were made in an attempt by *Lava Jato* to gather evidence of kickbacks and bribes channelled from inflated *Petrobras* contracts favouring the dodgy and weary PT leader (figure 5).

In a public speech, Lula savaged the operation, denouncing the media's involvement, coordinated by the judicial task force to make a live broadcast of the early raids. In a provocative tone, alluding to Moro's taskforce, Lula stated: 'If they wanted to kill the *jararaca* [pit viper], they didn't hit the head but its tail'. Echoing Lula's defiant closing statements against Lava Jato, *Veja*'s 2469 issue ran a headline 'The desperation of the *jararaca*', portraying Lula as an enraged, dangerous and frantic Medusa figure (figure 6). In so doing, the magazine claimed that those who followed 'simplistic and populist measures' could only end up cornered by history's judgment (Guandalini, 2016, p. 60).

For *Veja*, Lula's allegations were nothing but a populist sham, used in a despicable attempt to place himself above the law. As Alcantara vividly put it, 'like any other populist, Lula is a defender of egalitarianism as long as he is more equal than others' (Alcantara, 2016, p. 36). However, attention should be given to Lula's next moves for the 'PT's despair awakened by Lava Jato' only feeds its greed for power. Like other 'populist experiences creating consumption bubbles', the PT's 'disdain for the rich can only be explained by profound economic ignorance and unusual political autism'. If Lula prevails, the 'social chaos [in Brazil] will be enormous' (da Nobrega, 2016b, p. 24).

The Brazilian 'populis*' thief, now chiefly embodied by Lula's dreadful figure (as well as Rousseff and the PT), forges a parasitic and corrupt agent, feeding on sources of economic wealth through state interventionism, thereby sustaining a regime of social lack. A moral guarantor appears to challenge this corrupt and populist thief of economic enjoyment in the form of judge Sergio Moro. *Veja* portrays Moro as a stoic, handsome and tenacious righter of wrongs, opposing widespread corruption and heroically defending the interests of the Brazilian people against the left-populist menace.

Left populism as thief of economic enjoyment

The leaking by Moro of a 'revealing' phone call between Lula and Rousseff erupted in the media with the move to appoint Lula as the new chief of staff. The news had a striking impact and was splashed across *Veja*'s pages. Alarming its readers with the significance of such a government move, the magazine announced the unfortunate beginning of 'Lula's third presidential mandate'. With Rousseff 'obstructing justice' and 'placing the presidential sash on a *sub judice* minister', it is now the 'real country, the one that wakes up early and works all day, which is drifting miserably' (*Veja*, 2016d, p. 49).

Source: *Veja* archive

Lula's public reappearance was the comeback of 'left populism' and it could not but 'awaken profound fears over the populist mismanagement of the public machine'. Strictly speaking, it is not the voice of *Veja* that should be heard but rather the 'growing number of businessman saying there is no way out for the economy with Rousseff in the *Planoalto* [government palace]' (Sakate, 2016a, p. 75). Therefore, Rousseff's impeachment was necessary to stop the 'return of populist politics' (p. 76), now awakened by Lula's desperate return. He was portrayed as a despicable and deceptive figure who, according to reliable sources, had 'commanded a scheme[himself]' to side track the anti-corruption investigation (figure 7).

Lulavs nomination was seen as an obstruction to Lava Jato and only lasted a couple of days as it was overturned by the Supreme Court (STF) on the March 17, 2016. Worried entrepreneurs and economists now appeared in *Veja*'s pages, claiming that 'Rousseff is flirting with populism in order to survive'. As Rousseff's interventionism was disrupting the market, it was only through impeachment that the Brazilian economy could move forward (Sakate, 2016b, p. 71-72).

Figure 8: issue 2474, 20/04/2016

Source: *Veja* archive

While the horrific prospect enhanced *Veja*'s strong defence of an impeachment process, the outlook without Rousseff would not in itself save Brazil from the populist menace of *Lulopetismo*. *Veja* depicted the fall of populist forces as the beginning of a new prosperous economic cycle, whose benefits would be seen in due course. Though 'populism with oil prizes ruined the ethanol industry, now, without direct political interference at *Petrobras*, the sector is starting to rebuild itself' (Sakate, 2016c, p. 92). Such a principle is well known within financial sectors. Armed with this prospect, brokers and investment firms made deals to profit from Rousseff's downfall.

> The strategy has shown to be promising - and highly profitable at least until last week. Since its lowest point this year, the Ibovespa, the main index of the São Paulo Stock Exchange, has increased by 42%. There is a direct dependence. The weaker Rousseff's government is, the more valuable Brazilian shares become, especially those in state-owned companies, as they are most affected by populist interventionism (Rangel and Bronzatto, 2016, p. 67).

In a newly added special issue (2474), *Veja* festively celebrated the impeachment vote in the plenary session of the Chamber of Deputies. She was accused of breaking the budgetary law through so-called 'tax pedaling' and the process moved up to the Senate. With or without impeachment, one thing was certain: by lacking allies and losing the private sector's confidence, 'Dilma no longer commands Brazil' as her deceiving smile has been wiped from her face and she has been sent off from the game of politics (figure 8).

Figure 9: issue 2494, 07/09/2016

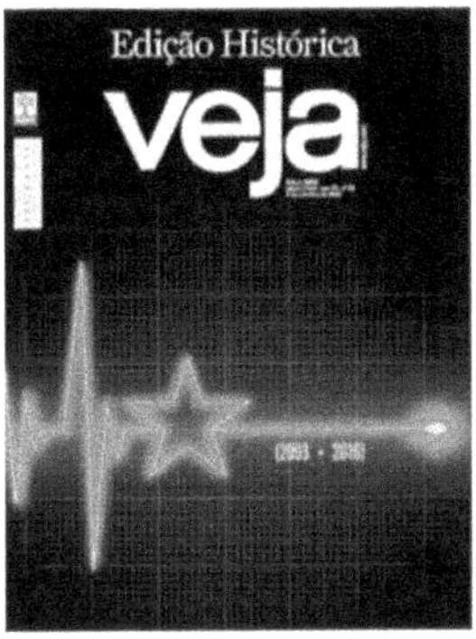

Source: *Veja* archive

Under the headline 'Historic Issue', *Veja* magazine depicted the PT's flatlined electrogram announcing, through Rousseff's recent impeachment, the Workers' Party irretrievable demise from Brazilian politics (figure 9). In a nutshell, 'Rousseff's impeachment puts an end to a cycle of the PT in power, the longest since the re-democratisation, and places populism and corruption at the centre of the nation's worries' (Pereira and Bronzatto, 2016, p. 49).

The populis* revival

While Rousseff's impeachment seemed to guarantee a transparent process granted by the market's good graces, political developments continue to upset the economy. Not only was left-wing populism in full swing, with Lula's popularity growing and making him the favourite candidate for the 2018 elections but a 'populist revival' had started to advance in the electoral race, embodied in the radical right-wing figure of Jair Bolsonaro. The populist menace, assumed dead, was still alive and kicking.

As recent polls had shown, the only two politicians whose popularity was growing were Lula and Bolsonaro. If the latter's popularity was seen as a striking novelty, it also embodied an ill-fated populist symptom that, as Lula does, feeds parasitically on democracy's crisis.

The rise of populists and radicals in moments of crisis or vacuum of political representation is a classic tragedy in the history of democracies, and this could not be better represented than by the figure of Bolsonaro (Rangel and Bronzatto, 2016, p. 67)

While Bolsonaro's tempting appeal is depicted as being unique in Brazilian politics, it foreshadows a menace extending elsewhere by the crumbling and battered state of the Washington consensus. As Gryzinski wrote, 'the basic principles of economic freedom and globalisation, which peaked at the turn of the millennium, are now challenged by the new populist, nationalist and protectionist right[-wing forces]' (Gryzinsky, 2016b, p. 46).

A series of articles and analyses assessed the weight of the economic losers from the previous years vis-à-vis the growing appeal of right-wing populism. Indeed, in globalisation, some 'missed the bus and know that they will not enjoy their parents' good life' (*Veja*, 2016g, p. 67). It was quite clear, however, how 'populist protectionism' would not 'appease the anguish of the excluded' by any means (Guandalini, 2017a, p. 71). By 'threatening tolerance among peoples and extending trade protectionism', the rise of right-wing populism could only assure further chaos (Teixeira, 2017, p. 58).

In the Brazilian case, Bolsonaro was favoured by the consequences 'of the overwhelming imbalances bequeathed by Dilma Rousseff and her populist revenue from draining public finances' (Alvarenga, 2017, p. 61). The economic collapse derived from left-populist interventionism and corruption favoured right-wing protectionist populism, sustaining an imperishable nightmare of polarisation and social anger. If liberals were to blame for Bolsonaro's rise, however, it was only insofar as they had not sufficiently challenged the PT's radicalism since the beginning (see, for example, Wolf, 2016, p. 72).

Nevertheless, with Dilma's replacement by her vice-president, Michael Temer, a window of opportunity was now wide open. Although 'there is still a bit of populism in the air', the investment prospects improved (Alvarenga, 2017, 62). And indeed, Temer was 'distancing himself from the PT's radical agenda', assuming a well-thought out and steady reformism, thereby emerging as a political guarantor of future social enjoyment. In Temer's own words: 'I want to go down in history as a reformist president... I am not a populist' (Junior, 2017, p. 65).

Us versus Them: reformism against populism

As elections approached, *Veja* went on the offensive. To offset the very real populist danger of Lula's credible chance of winning the 2018 elections (Guandalini, 2017c, p. 67), reforms were called to the fore to bring fiscal order and prevent further chaos.

Without reforms, there will be no confidence in the economy, and public finances will fail, putting the state's own control apparatus at risk and making room for populist leaders who sell illusions (and benefits) in exchange for support. We already know how that all ends (Sakate, 2017, p. 56).

Calls for austerity measures and responsible fiscal control were made throughout 2016 and these points were hammered home in *Veja*'s pages. In the end, without limiting the public spending, those who will suffer the most through the blow of an economic crisis are the poorest – 'a lesson populists don't make much effort to learn' (Guandalini, 2017b, p. 69).

Figure 10: issue 2555 8/11/2017

Source: *Veja* archive

By formally exposing the main populist antagonists to be challenged as representing an electoral menace, the magazine displayed Lula and Bolsonaro's morose faces with the headline 'The politics that frightens' (figure 10). Moreover, in recognising its populist opponent, *Veja* placed its bets on centre-reformism and said politics that should arouse enthusiasm. Henrique Meirelles appeared on the cover and was hailed as a promising figure. *Veja* presented him as a noble reformer with a great anti-populist calling.

Interestingly enough, in an article on the different kinds of right-wing figures, Meirelles had been branded by the magazine earlier as the neoliberal prototype (see *Veja*, 2016f, p. 42) but had now become the correct figure to beat the populists and achieve victory (Mirelles, 2017b, p. 48). In Meirelles' words: 'I am prepared to face populist speeches. This will be the main focus of the centre candidate' (Mirelles, 2017a, p. 42). At stake in the next presidential elections was the decision for 'a better or worse future' and such a battle 'will not be divided between left and right, but between reformism and populism' (Padua, 2017, p. 72-73).

Figure 11: issue 2571 28/01/2018

Source: *Veja* archive

So strong would the division between reformists and populists become and so seriously would *Veja* assume this antagonistic boundary that any slight move towards state interventionism could turn the most enlightened figure of centre-reformism into yet another despicable populist. The decree signed by Temer allowing federal intervention in the security area of Rio de Janeiro was regarded by *Veja* 'the greatest turnaround of a government in the democratic era' (Fernandes, 2017, p. 42) and earned a cover story headlined 'Temer's populist shift' (figure 11).

Figure 12: issue 2577 11/04/2018

Source: *Veja* archive

While the electoral dispute was in full swing, a special issue, which had been expected and announced by *Veja* since 2014 (*Veja*, 2014), was published (figure 12). On April 7, 2018, Lula was sentenced by judge Moro to prison for twelve years and one month. *Veja* Magazine gleefully dug up some of the 144 issues dedicated entirely to denouncing Lula's anti-democratic tendencies (in about 6% of the overall number of issues, Bronzatto, 2018, p. 93-94).

Unlike Obama, few now 'considered Lula to be 'the man' of any sort'. With Brazil's biggest populist out of the political arena, a Trump-like figure with opposite ideological tendencies (Teixeira, 2018, p. 59), it was now time to think carefully about the political prospects for the upcoming elections. Moreover, for those wishful thinkers who still had the idea that this 'white-collar criminal' was the father of the poor, *Veja*'s sole wish was that 'Lula's melancholic fate transforms into democratic strength' (Molica, 2018, p. 71).

Giving in to the (right) populist temptation

All of a sudden, Bolsonaro was talking 'about privatisation and even defends a Social Security reform, which he was against' (*Veja*, 2018, p. 27). Sympathetic to trade protectionism and wary of foreign capital, Bolsonaro's economic stance had changed quickly under the guidance of his Chicago School economic adviser, Paulo Guedes who Bolsonaro said would be his future Minister of Finance given an electoral victory.

Figure 13: issue 2604 17/10/2018

Source: *Veja* archive

With Lula playing an electoral role through his proxy candidate and was absent in the first person from the public debate, and Bolsonaro's more orthodox market stance safeguarded by the economic guarantor, Paulo Guedes, *Veja*'s reference to 'populis*' in terms of Brazilian political players or forces dropped dramatically. Not only were there fewer references but they became somewhat circumstantial and vague. While the populist menace was still something to be resisted, with Lula's presence at bay, the reformist*/populist* antagonism seemed far less important. Whether the winner was a populist or a reformer, what mattered the most was a responsible stance towards the economy.

The solution to Brazil's problems is not simple, and the temptation of populist promises grows in the final stretch of campaigns. However, regardless of who wins, the next occupant of the *Palacio do Planoalto* is expected to be responsible with the economy (Alvarenga, 2018, p. 47)

As Bolsonaro was the likely victor and had appointed reliable ministers, the utter fear has turned into vigilant expectation. Now, Bolsonaro needed to 'show he is capable of governing' (figure 14). After all, his rise symbolised nothing but the people's 'rejection of the PT's populism and reign of corruption (Costa, 2018, p. 46).

[Bolsonaro's] commitments to reduce the fiscal deficit and the public debt itself are hopeful, and explain the euphoric joy of the market in recent weeks given the growing chances that the right-wing candidate will receive the presidential sash (Alvarenga, 2018, p. 44)

The protectionist menace had dissolved amidst 'ultraliberal' prospects for the upcoming presidential mandate, safeguarded by minister Guedes, the main economic guarantor from the Bolsonaro government. This boosted the *Real* (Brazilian currency) and heralded a festive era for the Brazilian market (Figure 15).

Figure 14: issue 2607 07/11/2018   **Figure 15**: issue 2610 28/11/2018

Source: *Veja* archive

Amidst Bolsonaro's victory, *Veja* assessed Brazil's prospects with a more prodigious tone. After all, although Bolsonaro's figure might 'resemble that of Silvio Berlusconi, a right-wing populist', the Italian and Brazilian conditions were completely different. According to *Veja*, the *mani pulite* operation failed to punish corrupt politicians in Italy, favouring populism and allowing it to strengthen and grow. *Lava Jato*, instead, had 'elevated Brazil to a phase of higher moral civility', thus guaranteeing a market-oriented democratic cycle (Borges, 2018, p. 45).

[While] Sergio Moro took inspiration in the Maos Limpas [*mani pulite*] operation... carwash has fulfilled its duty. The corruption scheme in *Petrobras* has been unveiled, corruptors and corrupts have been all identified, sentenced and imprisoned (Borges, 2018, p. 43).

However, not everything was different in the Italian and Brazilian case. Just as the Italian prosecutor of *mani pulite*, Antonio di Pietro, went into politics, Sergio Moro now made a bold move (figure 14). With Moro as the new Justice Minister, 'Bolsonaro formed an 'absolutely unique' government by betting on superministers', bringing credibility to his anti-corruption mandate (Borges, 2018, p. 47).

Unsurprisingly, it is at this point that we find the only positive valence afforded to the signifiers 'populis*' in *Veja*'s pages. In an interview with The New School professor James Miller, *Veja* produced an article dedicated to populism. Following the headline 'Light at the end of the tunnel', the piece drew on how populist actors could often invigorate liberal democracy (Paduani, 2018, p. 17-19).

Unpacking *Veja*'s (anti)populism fantasies

So far, I have not simply drawn attention to the ubiquitous character of the words 'populis*' in the journalistic corpus of this study. In constructing my detailed narrative, I have also demonstrated the pivotal role these signifiers play in *Veja*'s construction of political antagonism. By focusing on lack/loss, I will now bring to bear how these key references to 'populis*' fantasmatically direct normative responses to perceived problems and invite distinctive forms of enjoyment.

From a psychoanalytic perspective, the swift blame over a threatening other, conceptually embodied by the trope of *thief*, usually serves as a means to avoid talking about loss (Glynos and Voutyras, 2016). While *Lulopetosmo* surges forth as a populist thief in *Veja*'s narrative, assuming a morally deprived social subject, Lula serves as the core horrific reference, giving Rousseff and the PT a more subordinate status. Even when referencing Rousseff's interventionism as a univocal populist characteristic, the primordial source of *Veja*'s anti-populist anguish remains Lula (see, for example, *Veja*, 2016c).

The pervasive references to *crisis* through Rousseff's mandate are endowed too by her predecessor. According to *Veja*, Lula's virtuous presidencies relied on the commodity boom triggered by China's commercial expansion. The government could have done nothing and the same economic virtues would still have been enjoyed. In meddling with the public machine through senseless redistributive (populist) policies, however, Lula disrupted market dynamics, compromising Brazil's future creation of wealth.

Lula was described as a lazy worker attaining unearned political power and was presented by *Veja* not only as an immoral thief of economic enjoyment but as a depraved and overspending subject enjoying excessively at the expense of others.

He fits perfectly into the definition of *bon-vivant*: a person who does not work, lives on privileges and perks... not being of rich origin, these types acquire access to luxuries through profitable contracts and power of a total absence of the values that enable the acceptable and the undesirable to be distinguished (Kramer, 2017, p. 63)

Redistributive mechanisms and public spending, assumed by *Veja* as core forms of populist politics, rest at the heart of market and economic failure, inflicting shortages and hyperinflation (usually making a comparison with Venezuela as depicting Brazil's future under the rule of *Lulopetismo*). In recognising this horrific construction, we can now focus on less perceptible discursive valences.

Veja's blind opposition to state interventionism and overall political mediation of social dynamics unveils a normative presupposition that favours the primace of market economy. It also foregrounds the fantasy of a depoliticised consensus democratic forged through dispassionate elitist expertise, leading the magazine, at times, to even question whether democracy is far too precious to be left in the hands of lay voters (e.g. Gryzinski, 2016a, p. 73).

Our point here is that the analytic value of the trope of *thief* is not restricted to account for lack/loss. It also renders visible normative elements in the articulation of broader fantasmatic narratives of social enjoyment. In other words, 'fantasy is the narrative of this primordial loss, since it stages the process of this renunciation... [by] the emergence of the Law'(Žižek, 1997, p. 43).

Given the economic primacy sustaining *Veja*'s technocratic fantasy, the PT's redistributive policy radically challenges the magazine's normative interest. That is to say, while the PT advocates political regulation of the economy to guarantee social enjoyment, *Veja* upholds the view that the general interest can only be met through unmediated financial freedom and market-rule.

Such opposing ideological principles meant that no economic guarantor could appease this ideological discrepancy. In fact, when Rousseff appointed the Chicago school market-oriented economist Joaquim Levy as finance minister in her second mandate, the magazine's anti-PT rhetoric seemed to have been stepped up. As such, only an extra-economic moral guarantor could face up to the interventionist and corrupt horrors brought about by left populism by limiting its reaches in the political arena. Sergio Moro assumed the role of guarantor, elevated to a figure gifted with profound moral sensitivity.

Moreover, *Veja* initially assumed Bolsonaro's appearance on the electoral scene as a new right-wing populist thief, endangering free financial dynamics and threatening democratic principles. However, not everything here was antithetical. Bolsonaro was already challenging PT's public spending, matching *Veja*'s rhetoric that public meddling over the private sector (i.e. 'the market') can only awaken unseen forms of systemic corruption. He had also stressed that he knew nothing about the economy and said such a matter should be left to the experts.

The overinvestment in the market economy's primacy depicts how pluralist values, attached to the magazine's defence of globalisation against the right-populist thief, are rather left at the periphery of *Veja*'s fantasmatic narrative. And indeed, an economic guarantor was deemed sufficient to transform this populist threat into an anti-PT (anti-interventionist/distributive) political strength.

Veja used a distinctive grammar to make economic enjoyment discursively accessible through its pages. In assuming its readers' desires within a realisable horizon of *expected real interest rates*, *loan returns*, *fiscal order*, *stock exchange rates*, and so on, the magazine imagined a kind of joy that was never fully attained no matter how grandiose and repetitive its message was.

While under Rousseff's crisis 'the market' (constructed as a coherent social unity attached to the general interest) experienced a random sense of modest happiness (Bronzatto, 2016, p. 67), Bolsonaro and Guedes' triumph captivated it with euphoric joy (Alvarenga, 2018, p. 44). However, such profound enjoyment brought about by the aftermath of the 2018 elections crumbled amid the new return of right-populist tendencies.

Figure 16: issue 2369 19/06/2019   **Figure 17**: issue 2727 03/03/2021

Source: *Veja* archive

Eventually, Moro's figure crumbled (Figure 16) and Bolsonaro's liberal mask, held up by minister Guedes' facade, fell off (Figure 17), exhibiting the true underlying populist menace.

As in the Lacanian notion of *jouissance*, *Veja*'s market-centred mode of economic enjoyment is only partly experienced, as in a form of *pleasure* in *pain*, always discursively limited by the return of a populist nightmare[11].

Conclusions

In using the concept fantasy to develop an analytical grid for the study of *Veja* magazine's discursive anti-populism, this study has explored the distinctive virtues of adopting a psychoanalytically-inflected discourse theory approach to the study of political antagonism and the critique of ideology. It has also contributed to CFS as a field of research, by fleshing out underdeveloped and underexplored fantasmatic orbiting concepts, such as *thief of enjoyment* and the *guarantor*. The main objective here has been to make the critical analysis of fantasy a core part of the discursive study of populism as a signifier.

While discourse theory scholarship has placed the focus on constructing broad correlations in the formal structuring of discourses *about* populism, this study suggests that in order to grasp the discursive logics underlying textual trends, the construction of a detailed narrative is a paramount hermeneutic endeavour. Only by attaining a degree of descriptive mastery of a contextually-specific social surface of inscription can the analyst further unravel the emotional and ideological logics sustaining discursive patterns and articulations.

This article has showcased not only how market-centred narratives and logics normatively sustain and strategically direct *Veja*'s anti-populist elite discourse, but also how key enjoyments linked to horrific thief constructions and joyful bets on guarantors sustain it ideologically. In concrete terms, these main normative and ideological valences sustain antagonistic discursive modes associated with left-wing populism and explain antagonistic and

---

[11] It is worth noting that, on March 23, 2021, the STF suspended judge Moro for his handling of Car-wash's treatment of Lula's case as being partial and politicized, prescribing all investigations against the PT leader and enabling him to run as presidential candidate in the 2022 elections.

non-antagonistic discursive modes of right-wing populism. In so doing, I have shown how enjoyment is embedded in elite narratives and how its fantasmatic exploration helps us further elucidate the logics sustaining the ubiquitous reference to 'populis*'.

Paper 3: Collectivising political mandates: A discursive approach to the Brazilian *Bancada Ativista*'s campaign in the 2018 elections

Abstract

This article analyses the political campaign of the rather under-researched *Bancada Ativista*, a prefigurative progressive experience comprised of nine co-candidates running for a single seat in the State Chamber of Sao Paulo during the 2018 Brazilian elections. The political experience brought about by the *Bancada Ativista* stands as a prolific effort in its aim to transform legislative action, responding to the challenges posed by the contemporary crisis of representative democracy. By taking the Essex School's discourse theory standpoint, this article critically explores the discursive composition of the *Bancada*'s political campaign and the significance of its electoral success in light of crisis-driven Brazilian politics.

Introduction

Brazilian politics have been subject to much attention lately. Scholars, pundits, and commentators have devoted ample interest to the rise of what they consider to be a conspicuous menace to democracy. As vividly described by Anderson (2019), '[t]he teratology of the contemporary political imagination – plentiful enough: Trump, Le Pen, Salvini, Orbán, Kaczyński, ogres galore – has acquired a new monster'. This monster is none other than Brazil's Jair Bolsonaro.

Bolsonaro's homophobic, misogynist, and racist allegations, his peremptory disavowal of the COVID pandemic and the ongoing ecocide in the Amazon rainforest have been effusively picked up by the national and international public and media. For its part, the academic realm has widely depicted Bolsonaro's electoral success as a conclusive seizure of power by conservative forces that made use of the social discontent to take over the presidency.

This article does not disregard the fact that Bolsonaro's former Social Liberal Party (PSL)[1] expresses a notorious break with Brazil's electoral trends or that its irruption onto the political scene is worthy of attention. Instead, it considers that an over-deterministic image of Brazil's political and social conjuncture, which focuses solely on its strong personalistic nature rather than critically engaging with its overarching aspects, neglects highly significant elements which problematise Brazil's social and political milieu beyond Bolsonaro himself.

Indeed, the previous elections in Brazil presented many significant changes, seeing the proliferation of new and stimulating political phenomena, most of which have been subject to weak journalistic repercussions and obtained virtually no scholarly attention. I consider the *Bancada Ativista*'s irruption in the electoral scene as the most compelling of these under-researched ventures.

The *Bancada Ativista* was publicly launched in the 2018 elections as a common platform constituted by nine co-candidates to a single seat in the State Chamber of Sao Paulo.

As members of the Socialism and Freedom Party (PSOL), the *Bancada Ativista* obtained a total amount of 149,844 votes, becoming the 10th highest voted position in the Sao Paulo State Elections – the largest electoral college in Brazil. Never a collective mandate had reached office in Brazilian politics.

For its novel and intriguing characters, this collective electoral experience compels researchers to delve deep into processes of social signification, and the discourse theory approach allows for a more involved analysis of this pioneering initiative.

This article aims to comprehend how the protests of June 2013 in Brazil generated new forms of political identification, ushering in unique discursive formations and social practices that can account for the articulation of the *Bancada Ativista*. As such, I seek to problematise the objects of enquiry through their genealogical construction, making it possible to critically engage in an analysis of the predominant discursive logics enclosed in this collective campaign (Glynos and Howarth, 2007 p. 41–46).

Furthermore, I believe that the study of this experience can provide productive insights not only in the Brazilian context but also to the study of politics. Strands of literature from the fields of political institutions and social movements have signalled a crisis in current forms of democratic representation. By problematising the prominent 'personalised hypothesis' in political science (Garzia, 2019), this case study will approach institutional crisis and political representation from a perspective of meaning-making.

Institutions, crisis, and personalisation

The existing literature on political institutions addresses crucial aspects for understanding electoral structures in moments of disruption (Dalton and Wattenberg, 2000; Mair et al., 2004). Through a broad diagnosis of the existence of a worldwide crisis in political institutions and forms of democratic representation (Mair, 2013; Streeck, 2014), compelling scholastic efforts have been addressing the personalistic character of elections and its adverse effects on the accountability of democratic institutions and political mandates (Berz, 2020; Mughan, 2000; Thomassen, 2005).

The increasing weight of a (single) political actor over the role played by parties, coalitions, and even institutions depicts a pervasive tension between persuasive personalistic appeals, electoral disruption, and lack of institutional accountability (Garzia, 2019). It is precisely this tension which has over-determined the current academic analysis of the Brazilian 2018 elections, solely focusing on Bolsonaro's victory and the threat it supposes to Brazilian democracy (see, for example, Cravo, 2019; Hunter and Power, 2019).

As a long-standing measure for assessing the propensity towards personalistic elections, scholars have relied on the nature of the institutional framework (McAllister, 2007). The Brazilian electoral system, for instance, with plebiscitary majoritarian elections and an open-list *d'Hondt* proportional representation system, is taken as one which indeed highly favours personalism (Nicolau, 2011, p. 56). Yet, as the growing appeal of strong (individual) personalities is observed in both parliamentary and presidential systems, personalisation is allegedly becoming a salient condition of the democratic process proper (Garzia, 2019).

Critical strands of literature draw attention over a 'hyped' logic in the way key enunciators and scholars have been over-investing in the irruption of individual personalities in the political arena. As Glynos and Mondon (2016, p. 3) have noted, 'This logic tends to marginalize meaningful debate about the way democracy tends to operate, that is, as an electoral democracy that installs and reinforces alienating tendencies'. Furthermore, excessive attention to individual personalities might distract us from comprehending other vital dimensions in a moment of electoral and social disruption. While there is no doubt that personalisation constitutes a crucial factor in contemporary politics, an analysis of the *Bancada*

Ativista might argue for the need to carefully reflect on whether personalism is as central as we assume it to be.

The literature related to social movements, on the contrary, has offered productive advances towards a broader analysis, by interconnecting questions of collective action and new forms of political participation, and stressing the creative political character enclosed within social agencies and grassroots communing in contexts of crises (Della Porta and Diani, 1999; Flesher, 2014; Prentoulis and Thomassen, 2013). These advances are particularly insightful when approaching collective organisations arising from social mobilisation in a crisis-driven context, as is the case of the *Bancada Ativista*. Nevertheless, there is room to expand academic understandings of experiences that attempted to innovate, through social movements, forms of formal democratic representation.

The emergence of a collective candidacy provides grounds for analysing vital elements at stake in a moment of political and social crisis. It can also offer valuable insights into the recomposition processes of political institutions, as well as their interconnection with social collective action.

Approaching the *Bancada*

Mainstream literature addressing institutional crises has focussed on the relationship between institutional systems and their propensity towards personalisation when assessing moments of institutional- and party-system disruption. However, analyses that focus mainly on the salient influence of political personalities reach a limit at the point in which this characteristic itself overflows and redetermines institutional arrangements and party-system structures (Garzia, 2019). The limitations of these models become more evident when one aims to tackle the electoral success of a collective candidacy that seeks to challenge the personalization of democratic representation from within an electoral system that mainly favours individual personalities.

We believe that mainstream models of institutional crises do not adequately address the fundamental relationship between power and meaning, as they tend to assume that institutions constitute objective and stable structures, which produce coherent and observable outputs. One might have to immerse oneself on the peculiar dynamics of political disputes to extract meaningful practices in a moment when institutional representation seems rather devious.

As Panizza and Miorelli (2013) have noted, 'politics plays a more autonomous role when institutional systems are in crisis and human agency can usually (but not always) more easily free itself from institutional constraints'. The Essex School of Discourse Analysis – hereinafter referred to as discourse theory – argues that institutions contain a plurality of repressed and contested meanings and practices. The fact that 'these practices can be reactivated to disrupt the institutional order is an important insight into processes of change in highly institutionalized societies' (Panizza and Miorelli, 2013: 315). Thus, discourse theory offers an insightful strategy for analysing the electoral success of the *Bancada Ativista*.

Research Strategy

The discourse theory approach to politics

Discourse theory has laid robust theoretical foundations to constitute a field in its own right. As formulated by the Essex School of Discourse Analysis, discourse theory has shifted its attention from the categories which delimit social objects as materially (pre)existing ones, rather focusing on the underlying logics and conditions which make their existence possible (Glynos and Howarth, 2007).

As grounded on the ontological assumption that meaning is constitutive to human existence, the Essex School postulates that any form of meaning depends on contingent relations of articulation with 'no necessary correspondence' (Laclau, 1990, p. 35). Glynos and Howarth (2007, p. 2–4) have aptly noted that discourse theory deviates from the causal law paradigm, constituting a truly post-positivist style of reasoning to the study of politics. This is to say, discourse theory, rather than empirically test, seeks to critically explain (Glynos and Howarth, 2007, p. 49).

By discourse, I refer to 'a social and political construction that establishes a system of relations between different objects and practices, while providing positions with which social agents can identify' (Howarth and Stavrakakis, 2000, p. 3). Put differently, *discursivity* denotes 'a horizon of meaningful practices and significant differences' which enable subjects to provisionally reach an understanding of themselves and the social world which they are part (Howarth, 2000, p. 9).

Yet, if social reality is said to be a discursive construct, one can certainly speak about a plurality of discourses and study them in less abstract terms. Not only does the Essex School foreground a novel theoretical standpoint, but it provides the grammar to engage with social and political developments in an analytically productive way.

As one can only reach an image of the self by identifying with some elements while marking a rigid boundary with others, difference and equivalence constitute vital functions in the formation of any discursive structure.

The fixation of these relational structures results from the privileging of signifiers, which give order to the signifying chain. Laclau and Mouffe (1985, p. 112) refer to these central discursive elements as *nodal points*. So nodal analysis consists of identifying the central signifying elements, which, through *differential* and *equivalential* logics, manage to structure signifying chains.

However, if social representation supposes a partial effort to construct the society, then every social discourse is always susceptible to being challenged. So antagonism, as a challenge to the imperative (hegemonic) understandings of social reality, is 'the ultimate source of social dislocation' (Marchart, 2018, p. 25). In a strict sense, subjects become political agents when they dis-identify with the governing structures, articulating, from pre-existing meaningful elements, new discursive formations from where they can feel, once again, represented (Howarth, 2013, p. 161). *Antagonism* and *dislocation* thus render the critical relation between crisis and (re)politicisation.

Discourse theory provides a conceptual toolbox consistent with its theoretical foundations (Glynos and Howarth, 2007). Our strategy will aim to identify, by analysing the campaign of the *Bancada Ativista*, discursive *nodal points* and understand how, through them, signifying chains of political representation are established, offering novel *subject positions* therein. The functions of *difference* and *equivalence* will be central to understanding how the *Bancada Ativista* particularly articulates signifying chains. This initial comprehension will provide a formal discursive structure to comprehend how *antagonism* (as a concrete structuring of a discursive difference) is here conveyed in light of a process of social *displacement*.

By analysing the campaign process of the *Bancada Ativista*, I seek to understand how this collective formation successfully articulated new discursive venues for political representation in the 2018 elections. Furthermore, I aim to explore the significance of the *Bancada Ativista* phenomenon in light of a widely noted crisis of institutional representation.

In a nutshell, my conceptual toolbox is chiefly constituted by *nodal points, difference, equivalence, subject positions, antagonism*, and *dislocation*. As of the analysis, the following questions will guide its conduction: What are the *nodal points* of the *Bancada Ativista*'s discourse? What *subject positions* does this discursive structure provide to its followers? Does the *Bancada* offer *something* new to its constituents? Who appears as the *Bancada*'s opponent? How is this opponent preventing that *something* that the *Bancada* offers from happening?

Materials and method

Since discourse theory takes the articulation of meaning as the primary terrain in which the social is constituted, it is said to be a macro-linguistic approach to the study of politics (Carpentier and De Cleen, 2007). It certainly shares various elements with other productive approaches to macro-textual analysis, as is Critical Discourse Analysis (CDA). The acknowledgement on the functions of 'genre chains' and 'equivalence and difference' by CDA profoundly resonates with some elements of our conceptual toolbox (Fairclough, 2003). Yet, CDA takes discourse as a field restricted to (mainly textual and written) language, on constrained settings (Carpentier and De Cleen, 2007, p. 277). This assumes limitations from micro-linguistic approaches for considering discursive implications in the structuring of (political) identities *tout court* (Jørgensen and Phillips, 2002, p. 146), whereas discourse theory provides a framework of discursivity to 'describe the way in which social identity is constructed' (Marchart, 2018, p. 19).

The endeavours of the present article encompass a macro-contextual setting, and my analysis will predominantly pursue a macro-textual one, for which the discourse theory approach displays a good fit. This is not to say the CDA has no productive strategies to offer. By relying on written and spoken sources, I will focus on how vocabulary is used to articulate descriptions in specific ways, helping me to further analyse how the functions of 'difference and equivalence' are rhetorically employed in *contrastive* and *additive* semantic relations (Fairclough, 2003, p. 88). This more constrained micro-contextual setting will refer to a semi-structured interview conducted at the end of the electoral campaign to one of the nine co-deputies of the *Bancada Ativista*: Anne Rammi.

Applying discourse theory initially 'involves constructing theoretical and empirical objects of investigation', as only then can the analyst (*de*)construct the discursive functions, which sustain the phenomenon under scrutiny (Glynos and Howarth, 2007, p. 11). For this purpose, I will broadly rely on the Brazilian canonical literature on political parties and social movements, together with the semi-structured interview, for constructing the campaign of the *Bancada Ativista*. Through it, I will analyse the discursive construction of the campaign from a discourse theory approach (discourse-as-representation), relying on a macro-contextual analysis altogether with my conceptual toolbox. Jointly, I will rely on a micro-textual analysis of open coding (discourse-as-language), identifying contrastive (i.e. 'but', 'however', 'yet') and additive textual patterns (i.e. 'and', 'with', 'also') taken as a critical layer in the overall analysis. The global analysis of the *Bancada Ativista*'s discourse will allow me to further assess the significance of this study in light of the broader fields of political representation and institutional crisis.

The aftermath of the 2018 elections

The 2018 Brazilian elections brought significant changes to the politico-partisan configuration of the Federal legislative houses and the State Legislatures – this was mostly the case in the election to the Legislative Assembly of the State of Sao Paulo (ALESEP). The first change that should be acknowledged is the reduction of the number of parliamentarians elected by the mainstream Brazilian Social Democratic Party (PSDB), falling from 19 to 8 state representatives in office. In the opposite direction, PSL became the dominant political force therein.

It is worth mentioning that, until the 2018 elections, PSL had no significant national representation, virtually absent in the State of Sao Paulo. Still, while having no territorial capillarity or party structure, it managed to increase the number of legislative seats by chiefly relying on the figure of Bolsonaro. PSDB, on the contrary, is one of Brazil's leading parties, having disputed the second presidential rounds with the Workers' Party (PT) since 1994 with two victories and four defeats. Both parties emerged in the wake of the re-democratisation of

Brazil, PSDB being a typical party of cadres and PT a party of masses (Limongi and Guarnieri, 2014).

In the state context, PSDB (centre-right in the ideological spectrum) has governed the State of Sao Paulo since 1994, leading the state's government with an outstanding base support that assists it for approving its bills. Even though they managed to elect João Dória (PSDB) as governor of Sao Paulo, PSDB now lacks its usual legislative strength. Considering the electoral results in relation to the state legislature and the office of governor, the *right-wing* candidate João Doria (PSDB) obtained 31.77% of the valid votes; Márcio França from the Brazilian Socialist Party (PSB), in the centre of the ideological spectrum, obtained 21.53%; and, in the centre-right, Paulo Skaf from the Brazilian Democratic Movement (MDB), 21.09%. Therefore, Doria and França disputed the second round, where Doria won with 51.75% of the valid votes.

As Fleischer (2007: 312) explains, since 1998, Brazil has lived through what can be called a bi-polarized pluri-partisanship, which profoundly resonates with the nature of Brazil's proportional elections. However, the existing bipolar opposition between PT and PSDB, which had been characteristic of the Brazilian political system at the national level since 1989, gained different contours after 2018 with the rise of the PSL and the victory of Jair Bolsonaro to the presidency – a candidate identified with the extreme-right in the party spectrum. PSL also won a historic victory in the State of Sao Paulo, becoming the leading political force after 2018, by electing 15 representatives.

While PT lost five parliamentarians when compared with the previous elections (15 representatives in 2014), they still managed to obtain the second largest number of seats (10 representatives), followed by PSB and then PSDB with eight representatives each. The Socialism and Liberty Party (PSOL) bench doubled in number, from two to four seats, one of which is held by the *Bancada Ativista*. Interestingly enough, the two poles within the ideological spectrum of the Brazilian political party constellation were the only ones that managed to grow (where PSL is at the 'far-right' and PSOL is in the 'radical left').

These were the two poles that influenced the discursive operations during the second round of the elections. França sought to distance himself from PT, specifically, but also from the ideological spectrum of the left generally speaking. However, Doria adopted a much more radical discourse: he systematically attacked PT, criminalised the left for its positions and policies, and developed a strategy of rapprochement with future president Bolsonaro (as evidenced by the 'Bolso-Doria' catchphrase that soon sprung up). Neither PSL nor PT participated directly in the second round of the elections for governor of Sao Paulo. Yet, they were fundamental for understanding the disputes that took place, and the coalitions formed therein.

Democracy and the lack of representation

The so-called collective mandates in Brazil present prefigurative electoral alternatives for the renewal of party cadres, broadening the permeability of the political system to the demands of its constituents, falling within the scope of the disruptive mass mobilizations whose turning point can be found in June 2013.

In 2013, social tides arose in Brazil. The June Days began with demonstrations initially mobilized by the Free Fees Movement (MPL) in the city of Sao Paulo, opposing the sudden increase in the public transportation fees from R$ 3.00 to R$ 3.20. In one of the protests (13 June), the police were violently unleashed against the demonstrators, leaving around 150 people injured and igniting the fuse of social resentment. From that day onwards, the mobilizations expanded and gained the support of thousands of people, who were outraged by the brutal repression undertaken by the police (Alonso, 2017).

Protests began to take place in other states of the country, composing the biggest social mobilizations in Brazil's democracy. The diversity of patterns and the growth of the participation of demonstrators were accompanied by a plethora of identity expressions as the protests grew and ushered in the arrival of heterogeneous social groups. Although the increase in public transportation fees had initially triggered the social movements, these had quickly spread out, starting to transform themselves and channel a series of broader dissatisfactions with the federal government. Indeed, the protesters initially forged an antagonistic frontier with Rousseff's administration, even if the federal administration had no agency in relation to the municipal and state public transportation fees (which are set at state and municipal levels).

While the protests had been initiated by an 'autonomist' left-wing cluster (which assumed an equivalence initially through the slogan, 'It is not only for 20 cents [of the transportation fees]!'), from 2014 onwards they diffused into a tremendous flow of popular energy, with many apparent and often contradicting facets (Singer, 2013).

While Chauí (2013) foresaw a symbiosis between the demonstrations and the mainstream media's conservative ideological language, stressing an equivalential link between the dispersed demands and a peculiar understanding of 'corruption', Souza (2016), through a much bolder assertion, pointed towards 2013 as the formal point after which the articulation, by the elites, of the parliamentary coup against Rousseff was possible (through the disciplined judicial and political persecution of the PT and its undisputed leader, Luiz Inácio Lula da Silva).

The dispersed and isolated demands of June started, from 2014 onwards, to outline two *antagonizing* poles of immediate identification: the *petismo* – of those represented by PT's overall political project – and the *anti-petismo* – which mainly identified the Workers' Party as the core nucleus of a systemic corruption scheme (Almeida, 2018). In 2016, Dilma Rousseff was impeached, and, in 2018, Lula – the most prominent popular figure in Brazilian politics and the favourite candidate for the 2018 presidential elections – was imprisoned.

The political action groups and social movements that emerged from this crisis-driven context were characterised by a radical critique of the predominant forms of leadership, political organisations, and existing democratic institutions such as parliament and the executive branch. This was cumulated with popular opposition against systemic forms of corruption.

Such a miscellany of indignities relates to the broader problem of representative democracy, seen by these groups as being incapable of meeting the demands of social movements and broadening the forms of political participation. Prentoulis and Thomassen (2013) aptly recognise how new communal identities and forms of organization articulate themselves through collective action in moments of crisis. As expressed by Laclau and Mouffe (1985), social structures are always incomplete, enclosing a multiplicity of *repressed* possibilities. It is in times of crisis (dislocation) that repressed forms of meaning are reactivated (see Laclau, 1990). This condition is of pivotal importance in the shift from social engagement to politico-institutional activism, as the systemic displacement of the political structures open venues of novel forms of social identification. In the Brazilian context, an imperative necessity for the creation of new forms of representation with the critical capacity to impact the activities of formal institutions was deemed palpable. In Anne Rammi's words:

What would the impact of people that have been effectively participating in street-politics be within the political-institutional field if they are leading such disputes within that field instead of traditional politicians with formal mandates?

The *petism*/anti-*petism* polarisation structured, throughout the mass mobilisations, a broad left–right antagonist frontier, thus expressed in terms of a horizontal discursive mode. This presented a key structure for Bolsonaro's PSL electoral strategy, as it was formulated as a severe reaction to the PT legacy (interpreted as the core nucleus of the mainstream left-wing party spectrum). However, the appeal to collectivise political mandates as a form of revitalising the prominent forms of political representation dealt with such a broad differential logic in quite a particular way. While, as Anne stresses, the *Bancada Ativista* located itself 'within the progressive field', its members comprehended 'the risk in the macro scenario of assuming the "leftist" slogan, which spent the last 15 years receiving an occupation in the popular imagination of being a bad thing, a threat'.

Thus, the composition of the *Bancada Ativista* appears discursively as a form to escape the predominant antagonistic frontiers stressed by the PT/anti-PT differential structure. The establishment of an equivalential camp by heterogeneous underrepresented subjects – as will be further noted – structures itself around the node 'collective'. Discursively, equivalence is reached by two main differential functions: horizontally, in opposition (antagonism) to 'conservatives and people who dominate power within a more patriarchal camp', and vertically, differentiating themselves from 'political leaders who make politics for themselves'. Within Anne's interview, the term 'collective' keeps its distance in relation to the signifier 'left'. Correspondingly, other signifiers associated with the *leftist camp* in Brazilian politics (as 'PT' or 'PSOL') assume, rhetorically, a subsidiary – at times even antagonising – role. On the contrary, 'collective' adopts a tight equivalential relation with signifiers such as 'new', 'feminine', and 'minorities'. Let me explore this discursive structure further.

The nine members of the *Bancada Ativista*

As seen, one of PSOL's seats in the Sao Paulo State legislature was organised around the *Bancada Ativista* in the 2018 elections. The *Bancada* is composed of nine members, stemming from a series of social movements in Brazil. One of its members is Anne Rammi, a 'woman with no direct party affiliations' and 'a mother of four' children. As she described, 'motherhood is at the core' of her activism and encompasses the struggle for humanised childbirth and for breastfeeding, all of which were fostered by an early experience of obstetric violence from which she suffered. Anne incorporates into her intersectional vindication as a 'mother' and a 'woman' 'the condition of being a child in the world', which, in her terms, are constrained by 'a model of domination'.

In addition to Anne, Jesus dos Santos is the second member of the *Bancada*. He is the Municipal Councillor of *Vila Maria* and a 'militant in the black movement'. As a representative of the Afro-Brazilian community from the Northeast of Brazil, Jesus has obtained vast experience in the current discussions around the public budget of the State of Sao Paulo. Another member of the *Bancada*, who is also from the most impoverished region of Brazil (the Northeast), is Chirley Pankará. As 'an indigenous woman' formally affiliated to the PSOL, she has been actively involved in the struggle for the demarcation of indigenous lands and historic reparations to her people. Likewise, Chirley serves as the director of the 'Ceci Jaraguá' School – a pedagogic facility that works with the indigenous community – where she has 'striven to make indigenous culture a pivotal part of the scholastic curriculum', integrating knowledge from traditional communities with the formal educational frameworks of Brazilian public schools.

From those officially affiliated to the PSOL, Erika Hilton is the member of the *Bancada* who is more directly associated with the LGBTQI movement. She is 'a black and trans woman' from the countryside of Sao Paulo. Her gender transition a key biographical event in the articulation of her political identity. In addition to Erika, Monica Seixas is also a 'black, female member' of the *Bancada*, who also came from Sao Paulo's countryside and is an actively engaged member of PSOL. She identifies her political identity through the signifier 'eco-socialism', a political (subject) position she took on through her resistance against the water crisis in the city of *Itu* in 2016.

Paula Aparecida, also from Sao Paulo, is another member of the *Bancada* collective. She is a public school teacher and leader of the Public School Teachers' Union of the State of Sao Paulo. As a member of PSOL, she 'holds Marxist/Trotskyist ideological affiliations' and has experience organising 'working-class' movements and vindicating the rights of public school workers.

Another member of the *Bancada* is Raquel Marques. She is a 'woman', a 'mother', and – together with Chirley, Erika, Monica, and Paula – an affiliated member of PSOL. Raquel is also an activist for humanised childbirth and the director of Artemis, a nongovernmental organisation (NGO) where she acts as a legal advocate committed to the 'struggle for gender equality'. In addition to Raquel, Cláudia Visoni is the eighth member of the *Bancada*: she is 'essentially an anarchist woman' affiliated to the political party Rede. In Anne's words, Cláudia is 'deeply involved in the occupation of urban spaces and in turning waste into useful things, absolutely committed to the environmental causes'. Finally, the last member of the *Bancada* is Fernando Ferrari, a 'black man active in peripheral cultural movements'. In Anne's words, Fernando, since he comes from precarious ecclesial communities, 'has a long trajectory resisting against the ongoing genocide of black, poor and peripheral populations in Brazil'.

Anne's own description is here taken literally to introduce the members of the *Bancada*, and this is not fortuitous. It is worth remembering a principle recurrently stressed by the discourse theory standpoint: identity formation is constructed within relational structures, which are shaped by political struggles. The dislocation of pre-existing identity structures – as, for instance, those generated by the water crisis in the city of *Itu* in 2016 or Anne's experience of obstetric violence – creates the need to redefine those identity positions, making it possible to deal with the new situations. As Howarth (2013, p. 252) stresses, 'it is precisely in this context that new forms of political agency are likely to arise, as subjects construct and identify newly constructed and available discourses'. The identities of every member of the *Bancada*, as conceived by them, are traversed by a series of critical biographical cleavages, emerging precisely in moments of crisis, through which they have all found new ways to identify politically. Hence, their (re)politicisation and the articulation of their demands find common grounds in a broader crisis-driven context of political representation – dislocation serving as a means for articulating new affective subject positions.

The specific way in which each one of the members of the *Bancada* identifies with – as will be further examined – is preserved within their electoral discursive structure. Yet, the 'collective' springs as a common signifier through which the plurality of demands expressed by each one of the members are *articulated* through an *equivalential chain* (Laclau and Mouffe, 1985). Indeed, discourse theory has widely noted how the structuring of meaning relies on *nodal points* – which, prima facie, we identify the 'collective' to be such a privileged signifier within the *Bancada*'s discursive structure.

Yet, the relational component in the production of meaning presumes that *equivalence* can only be articulated in as far as *difference* is established (Laclau, 1996, p. 43). This is to say, without properly identifying the limits of *who we are* (through the construction of an *other*), an idea of *us* as a political subject can never be reached, as 'equivalence is only effectuated vis-à-vis a common negative outside' (Marchart, 2018, p. 115). Here, the implicit antagonism with *personalism* (frequently assuming a metonymic function for 'political parties' in Anne's interview) as a 'pervasive form of politics' brings to the fore an initial binary distinction between 'personalism' (them) and 'collectivity' (us). Such a general opposition provides a wide-ranging structure for where I seek further to instigate the electoral discursive articulation of the *Bancada Ativista*.

Articulating the campaign

The choice for articulating a platform of nine co-representatives made use, since 2016, of the strategies of politically curating and mapping by grassroots-activists scattered in informal spaces. At first, 60 names were included in the *Bancada*'s preliminary list based on activism around three core pillars: reduction of inequalities, human rights, and radical democracy.

The loss of centrality of the party in the collective candidacy relates to the desire of fostering an independent platform, as a means of elaborating an alternative for political renewal. Anne, who participated of this process at an early stage, stresses how 'the *Bancada* came to be related to the Party [PSOL] only as means to formalize its candidacy', but was genuinely forged since the beginning as 'a multi-party movement, independent of Party lines, with multiple worldviews'.

Two central legal and normative issues arose during the composition of the *Bancada*: the impossibility of launching candidates without formal party affiliations and the need to choose a single individual to appear on the ballot box. As to the latter, the *Bancada* was quite critical, identifying the Brazilian electoral system as a 'hegemony of [traditional] parties which favour personalism', leaving little space for 'ordinary citizens'. Thus, by trying to maintain their multi-party character, the *Bancada*, after numerous 'sociocratic' processes (a tool for 'seeking progressive consensus' through 'a series of quasi-exhaustive dialogues'), finally delimited the spectrum of the party affiliation of their members to two political parties: PSOL and Rede.

Regarding the second normative issue, while there is a bill that intends to regulate collective mandates for legislative positions under discussion in the Federal Chamber of Deputies, there are still no legal provisions that could (1) officially include the names of all members of a collective candidacy in the ballot box, (2) grant collective candidates express access to the local legislature, nor (3) ensure parliamentary accountability to more than a single candidate.

Putting the lack of formal-legal provisions for symmetric enrolment and accountability of the mandate aside, the members of the *Bancada Ativista* understand that obtaining 'absolute consensus-reaching is impossible'. Yet, they commit to 'the idea of confluence [equivalence] as an engine, as the generator of this movement towards political renewal' as explained by Anne.

Note that the signifier 'independent' enters into the scene as means of representing opposition to the 'present forms of politics', which are here to be directly associated with the formal party structure and politicians. Thus, the differential discursive logic of the *Bancada* relies on the nodal point 'personalism', which provides an order to the *signifying chain* of the *opposing* camp, highly associated with the traditional parties, seen as those who promote politics in *dependent* terms. One can thus say that the *Bancada Ativista* encloses an anti-personalist discourse.

Yet, the nodal signifier 'collective' is discursively a much more central one, since it displays the predominance of equivalential logics within the campaigning discourse of the *Bancada*. The signifiers 'feminine', 'activist', 'new', 'diversity', 'multiplicity', 'particularity', and 'confluence' are often identified in additive relation to 'collective' in Anne's description of the *Bancada*'s campaign. I have previously elaborated that the core antagonism in the discursive composition of the *Bancada* rests on the differential function between 'personalism' and 'collectivity'. Interestingly enough, 'personalism' is discursively structured in opposition/antagonism to 'particularity'. Whereas the former encloses an additive relationality with political parties and politicians (deficient passive-representation), the latter assumes a vital signifying function in the *Bancada*'s composition (efficient active-representation).

Thus, the nodal signifier 'collective' is referred to as an expression which results from a sort of unity (confluence) out of a difference (particularity), rather than the mere aggregation of homogeneous elements or the homogenisation of individual subjects. Indeed, '[i]f it is

151

asserted that all particular groups have the right to respect of their own particularity, this means that they are equal to each other in some ways' (Laclau, 1996, p. 49). This is the sort of bond that the *Bancada Ativista*'s campaign brought about.

The apprehension of *confluence* as the key engine for political *renewal* from the *Bancada*'s perspective can be reached via 'sociocracy'. As Anne further explains, it was after a series of 'sociocratic' discussions that the head of the *Bancada* in parliament was elected:

[Monica], as a person, has a little bit of each one of us in her. She is a mother and a black woman from the periphery. She is an environmentalist and participates in that struggle as well. She is, therefore, a right image of the representative who takes into account and embraces all the core elements [of the *Bancada*].

The election of Monica to formally representing the *Bancada* in parliament is assumed as the equivalence of the core identities which the composition seeks to represent. Thus, the subject positions of 'motherhood', 'black', 'woman', and 'environmentalist', as 'peripheral' (excluded) ones, are presumed not only to be underrepresented but also that the explicit striving for their (collective/common) representation embeds the promise of political renewal. As Anne explicitly posits:

[The collective campaign] is self-regulating, as in a wall, preventing us from becoming [. . .] a tale of ourselves; it prevents power from rising to our heads. This collective desire occupies a much more privileged place than that of a [single] political leader.

In the course of a 'Vote for 1, Take 9 [representatives]' campaign, the members of the *Bancada* sought to combine traditional political communication with street activism.

Pamphleting, lengthy public collective deliberations and digital communication aimed at producing a decentralised and network-oriented campaign. On the face of it, the communicative strategy of the campaign maintained a double focus, through the use of digital networks, in which the nine co-representatives already had a presence through their political/social activism and street mobilisation. Face-to-face communication (key in so-called grassroots communing) is taken as a return to the essence of the organisation of social movements and is used for constructing an electoral platform from different segments of the population.

The close link shared with grassroots-communing strategies sought to bridge the streets and the institutions, 'actively constructing the campaign' with 'normal citizens'. Activism thus encloses an embrace of the public spaces as where politics can be adequately rehabilitated:

The activist is that person who is on the street floor. Ordinary. I can speak for myself: I am a user of all public systems. I do not have a car, I use public transportation, [. . .] public schools, public health care. That is the difference [an activist shares] with a deputy, with a political leader.

From the discursive composition of their communication strategy, a salient signifier assumed a strong equivalential relation with the node 'collective', as its use, when referring to the campaign, enforces the form of representation that the collective presumably embeds: 'feminine'.

The *Bancada Ativista* shows the way towards another means of doing politics, linked to the values of collaboration, solidarity and communal care. In a dichotomous world, these elements would most expectedly be found in the feminine field.

For Anne, the success of the *Bancada* is based on the ability to present 'solutions linked to that which is proper of unity, such as affection, solidarity and caring for each other, including all the values enclosed in the concept of motherhood'.

It is clear that, discursively, the rhetorical constructions in the description of the *Bancada*'s campaign are strongly related to Anne's own individual form of identifying, and how that subjective identification resonates with a broader political subject (i.e. the *Bancada Ativista* as a collective composition). If 'feminine' is to be found as a salient signifier in the campaigning strategy of the *Bancada*, it assumes a much more predominant role through Anne's words. Nevertheless, from the identity positions the *Bancada Ativista* offers to its followers, 'female representation' is a key one, accompanied by 'black' and 'people who identify with diverse gender roles'.

Thus, the *Bancada* provides the promise of a political renewal by the equivalence of excluded singularities. The core opposition with political parties presumes that such a renewal derives from the underrepresented ordinary citizens, scattered informally and independently articulated to challenge the passive form of politics the formal parliamentary protocols convey. The collective articulation of the *Bancada Ativista* sought to offer a series of subject positions, derived from the identities in crisis that the PT/anti-PT opposition failed to represent. The *Bancada Ativista*, laying its composition within the progressive field, has assumed a noticeable distance with the Workers' Party, managing to articulate diverse identity expressions that have assumed an antagonistic relation with Bolsonaro's PSL and a differential one with Lula's PT.

Conclusion

By constructing and problematising a complex crisis-driven Brazilian context, this article has showcased the most meaningful elements from the June 2013 social mobilisations and how their articulation resulted in the formal composition of the *Bancada Ativista*. The underlying logics which have given way to the electoral success of this collective venture display a set of repressed identities from the pre-existing representational party structure.

The study of the campaign process of the *Bancada Ativista* has provided novel insights for assessing the electoral disruption of the Brazilian 2018 State Elections from a meaning-making perspective. Yet, this case study not only offers valuable elements to the study of Brazilian politics.

Institutional crisis presupposes a displacement in the imperative forms of social representation, where the interconnection between social movements and political institutions is presented here as a fundamental one. The bridging of these two fields embeds promising advances for comprehending the party structures in moments of crisis, as of problematising the substantial elements at stake in a setting where persuasive personal appeals tend to take over the political (*and* scholar) agenda.

Furthermore, the discourse analysis conducted to the articulation of the *Bancada Ativista*'s campaign draws attention to the prominent role assumed by the local/regional elections for comprehending party-system changes. Brazil forecloses a system of representation which highly favours mainstream parties and prominent personalist figures. Yet, even in such a scenario, the local state electoral dynamics provide substantial critical elements for comprehending macro-contextual electoral disruptions. Thus, detailed case studies of novel local-electoral phenomena enclose significant inputs for problematising macro-contextual changes.

Finally, the interconnection presented between social movements and institutional (electoral) politics signals the contingent nature that embeds any social structure, as is the case with a political institution or party system. As such, *change* must be recognised as a constitutive feature of any form of institution or organisation, expressed by a failure in the predominant forms of representation. This compels researchers in the field of political institutions to instigate the conditions that enable a particular type of political organisation to operate, and academics in the field of social movements to question the implications that arise from social mobilisations to the changes that are complicit with formal forms of institutional representation.

A note of caution is in order here, as the success of a collective campaign cannot be directly translated into the merits of a collective mandate. I have conducted a discursive analysis to understand the political significance of the *Bancada*'s campaign in the light of the crisis of representation and a substantial shift in the party-system structure. Yet, further investigation is required to assess the proper prospects of novel forms of political representation within parliamentary action and their impacts regarding social representation and political accountability.

Paper 4: Hysteria in the squares: Approaching populism from a perspective of desire

Abstract

This paper explores the productive potential in the psychoanalytic concept of hysteria in terms of the study of populism. A Lacanian framework is adopted to broaden our understanding of the (dis)identification structures at stake in a populist logic, stressing the constitutive role of desire bears in social meaning-making processes. Against a background of public discontent – the 'square protests' – this paper exploits the emancipatory potential within the discourse of the hysteric as a crucial radical investment in the displacement of predominant socio-symbolic boundaries, leading to the production of social knowledge.

Introduction

After the implosion of the Socialist Bloc in the early 1990s, a worldwide scepticism arose over the utopian march of the 'singing tomorrows' which had called throughout the 20th century for the construction of a new subject and the imperative forging of a novel society through revolution. Revolting masses flooded cities and occupied parliaments, from Cuba and China to Tanzania and France. This astounding idea that revolution was inevitable suddenly seemed hopelessly inadequate and was abruptly replaced in 1992 by Fukuyama's memorable claim about the 'end of History.' Liberal democracy and the capitalist free market were to be seen as the ultimate milestones of human sociocultural evolution – with a stable expansion of the capitalist-financial world order and a strong aegis of neoliberalism from the early 1980s. Less than a decade later, however, such claims could be seen to have been premature, as uprisings reappeared throughout Latin America. These revolts were brought about not only by dissatisfaction caused by neoliberal reforms, but also by an additional lack of political representation within the institutional confines of liberal democracy. The anti-neoliberal backlash was triggered by the systematic privatisation of public assets (Bolivia, Argentina, Chile, Brazil), corruption scandals (Venezuela, Ecuador, Argentina), and ruthless institutional repression (Venezuela, Bolivia, Ecuador, Argentina, Chile). The social effervescence challenged the legitimacy of the prevailing order and opened a breathing space for the articulation of striking new political discourses. Popular leaders arose – with Hugo Chavez's election in Venezuela a first formal rupture in 1999 – and established left-wing governments that forcefully opposed the dominance of the United States' interests in the Latin American region.

These leaders, charismatic as they were, adopted new narratives opposing a 'them' – often called *oligarcas* [oligarchs], *roba-patrias* [homeland-stealers], *pitiyankees* [US-imitators], or *golpistas* [usurpers]. This conceptual opposition stressed a distinction, simplifying the antagonistic political frontiers, transposing the construction of new forms of identification from a 'left–right' to a 'bottom-up' spectrum, and forging a common-grounded main political agent of transformation: "the people." The world was gripped by this bewildering and exciting turn to the left, which coincided with the emergency of the Welfare State in Europe and growing global disenchantment with the authoritative understanding of (formal) democracy and its institutions. Intellectuals, academics, and social leaders throughout the world became enthusiastic, studying, getting to know, and even supporting the changes that were rapidly reshaping the world's most unequal region. The Western world was no exception, as the impulse for a European movement with the ability to restore popular sovereignty, like those which sprang up so intensely throughout Latin America, seemed possible at an early stage. As Balibar (2010) wrote:

[W]e need something like a European populism, a simultaneous movement or a peaceful insurrection of popular masses who will be voicing their anger as victims of the crisis against its authors and beneficiaries, and calling for a control "from below" over the secret bargainings and occult deals made by markets, banks, and States. (p. 70, emphasis in original)

This impulse would soon find an echo in a spontaneous social outburst taking over public places. After the financial meltdown of 2008, a wave of revolts began to emerge. These started in Greece and Iceland and later spread to Tunisia and Egypt, before returning to the West in 2011, mainly affecting the United States, the United Kingdom, Greece, and Spain. As this tide seemed to subside, protests arose in Turkey and Brazil in 2013, subsequently followed by France in 2016 and 2018–2020. There was a significant resurgence throughout Latin America in 2019–2020, particularly in Chile, Bolivia, Ecuador, Haiti, and Colombia. After the

159

movement of 'the squares' (Gerbaudo, 2017), left- and right-wing actors emerged with new-found strength to bring disputes into the political arena, alarming establishment elites and channeling social discontent into a sort of Latin Americanisation of Europe, as some have claimed (Cely and Mantilla, 2016; Padoan, 2016; Roberts, 2019).

Left-wing movements – old and new – articulated their discourse strategies in a manner similar to the binary division present in the message of Latin America's national-popular movements. In Spain, PODEMOS directed their discourse to the majority, i.e. 'the people,' urging resistance to the misrepresentations of a minority elite, referred to as a 'caste,' and enforcing a dyadic vertical discursive logic by pointing to the existence of enemies within. At the same time, the articulation of far-right populist discourses expanded globally, appealing to social discontent with even greater skill. In France, Marine Le Pen maintains the binary division of 'the people' within a particular political establishment. Le Pen's slogan 'Au nom du Peuple' [in the name of the people] highlights her appeal to such a collective subject. Yet, this articulation seems to be fixed not in the distortions of a local 'caste' per se, but in the danger represented by a contingent 'other,' embodied by different figures such as immigrants, Muslims, or terrorists. This forms a horizontal discursive logic articulated mainly by a constitutive outside.

Fukuyama's assertion of 'the end of History' seems to have dissolved amidst this expanding political uncertainty and brewing social discontent, against the backdrop of a tenacious and apparently inexhaustible social outbreak. The 'P' word often spreads and directs these complex processes, characterising our times as a 'populist zeitgeist' (Mudde, 2004, p. 542) or even a 'populist moment' (Mouffe, 2018, p. 6), marking 'the arrival at a fully political era' (Laclau, 2005, p. 222). It is not by chance that scholars and pundits have made many attempts to shed light on the exact nature of populism as a political phenomenon in order to explain such a convoluted social and political backdrop. This is where psychoanalytic theory has provided fertile grounds for crucial progressions in the study of populism as a political phenomenon. Here, the most substantial and compelling contribution is undoubtedly associated with the work of Ernesto Laclau (and, to a certain extent, that of Chantal Mouffe). In light of this, the so-called affective turn in the social sciences, particularly as scrutinised by the Essex School of discourse theory, has made significant advances, increasingly pointing towards the study of emotions and the role played by 'affect' in collective (dis)identification processes.

When one observes the social demonstrations occurring worldwide over the last two decades, the passion, anxiety, and profound libidinal social energy expressed through them are obvious. Nevertheless, despite the recurrent references to the significance assumed by affect, desire, and emotions in populism, few systematic steps have been taken to articulate their formal theoretical account an/d these have remained very much at the margins in the study of populism. I believe this to be a fundamental entry point. By claiming that 'desire' precedes any concrete form of 'social demand,' I argue that attention to the place to which these demands are addressed assumes a much more dominant role than that taken by the fleeting symbolic character conveyed by them. Yet, even this place, as observed throughout social demonstrations, remains far from being univocal, requiring a closer link between the 'psychic' and the 'social' in order to fill this gap productively.

This search will be conducted with reference to the psychoanalytic examination of hysteria, mainly as developed in the Lacanian theory of the four discourses. Here, the work of Slavoj Žižek – even when taking into account his recalcitrant scepticism towards populism (see Biglieri and Perelló, 2019) – lays essential grounds for rethinking the key analytical focus on the (dis)articulation of a social bond, presenting the functions of metaphor and metonymy as key to analysing the concrete forms of identifications at stake in a social displacement. Let me start by problematising some of the most compelling efforts which have aimed to make populism a category.

Problematising Populism

A review of the main literature that conceptualises populism shows these developments can be narrowed to two main fields: those focusing on substantive contents; and those which endeavour to formulate a more formal account. The approaches related to the former have struggled to come to terms with the substantive elements which restrict the particularity of populism, as exceptions regularly shed doubt on their theoretical validity, thereby threatening the soundness of their empirical contribution.

Kurt Weyland's (2001) conceptualisation of populism as a strategy certainly fits the case here. Weyland sees populism 'as a political strategy through which a personalistic leader seeks or exercises government power based on direct, unmediated, uninstitutionalised support from large numbers of mostly unorganized followers' (p. 14). For Weyland, populism assumes a bi-fold character, exhibiting two main tactical angles: (i) it promotes a discourse of incorporation through the early phases of social participation; or (ii) it follows anti-organisational tactics, aiming at displacing established groups and parties (p. 15). In any case, control over the masses – whether by organising the organisation-less or by dissembling mainstream forms of organisation – is kept under tight control by the leader.

My initial objection arises from the distance assumed by the strategic approach from the etymological grounds of populism – *populus*, i.e. the people – which are 'sufficiently clear, recent and compelling for us to take seriously' (Knight, 1998, p. 226). By abandoning the category of 'the people,' Weyland devises the peculiar unity of populism in the form of a personalistic strategy. Yet, this unity is thought in such comprehensive terms that one could easily recognise in it diverse expressions of leadership (such as the Latin American *caudillismo* or the Brazilian *coronelismo*) which, regardless of the conceptual definition, would raise serious doubts over the specificity of populism as a strategy. Indeed, the search for a rigid taxonomy of a political phenomenon could direct the sails towards favourable conditions for naming particular attributes and yet fail to spot the constitutive logic underlying them.

Moreover, as raised by Moffitt and Tormey (2014, p. 386), there are various contemporary examples where populism has flourished in contexts of strict party discipline, such as Le Pen's Front National. One could also think of cases where a populist leader took over a mainstream organisation run for the benefit of the elite, as was the case with Jorge Elicer Gaitan and the Colombian Liberal Party. Exceptions are regularly found, weakening Weyland's bifold tactical attribution, and thereby highlighting the sheer lack of credibility of the conceptualisation of populism as a strategy.

The thin-centred approach – the grounds of which were first laid by Margaret Canovan (2002) but were adequately formulated in Cas Mudde's (2004) work – focuses more sharply on providing a formal account and has taken a leading role in the literature over the past decade. By defining populism as 'a thin-centred ideology that considers society to be ultimately separated into two homogeneous and antagonistic groups, 'the pure people' and 'the corrupt elite'' (p. 543), populism is seen as a parasitic ideology which seeks to thicken out by attaching itself to a host.

The ideational approach's merit lies in distancing itself from previous efforts that persisted in the pitfall of a merely descriptive effort. The definition is therefore released from any bases of a specific type of organisation, in which – for instance – a strong leader, rather than defining populism as such, is taken as an element which facilitates it, and thus provides, through an opposition between 'the people' and 'the elites,' a straightforward operationalisation for conducting empirical research.

However, Moffitt and Tormey (2014, p. 385) are not alone in noting that it makes little sense to conceptualise populism as an ideology since – unlike feminism or environmentalism – there is no evidence that populism ever seeks to thicken its ideational density. Freeden (2017)

– father of the morphological approach adopted by Mudde – has himself admitted having 'considerable doubts about the applicability of thin-centrism to populism,' precisely because 'thin-centred ideologies have the potential to become full if they incorporate existing elements of other ideologies; whereas the truncated nature of populisms seldom evinces such aspirations or potential' (p. 3). Therefore, 'if one tries to avoid this pitfall by identifying populism with a dimension that cuts across ideological and social differences, one is burdened with the task of specifying what that dimension is' (Laclau, 2005, p. 15). The thin-centred approach thus fails to develop such a task in a sufficiently convincing way.

Alan Knight (1998), Margaret Canovan (1999), and Carlos de la Torre (2000) are among the leading scholars who have identified the genus of populism in the form of a style. Their approach is centred on rhetorical appeals and particular discursive frames. As expressed by de la Torre, populism constitutes a 'style of political mobilization based on strong rhetorical appeals to the people and crowd action on behalf of a leader' (p. 4). This appeal to 'the people' recovers centrality by challenging 'both the established structure of power and the dominant ideas and values of the society' (Canovan, 1999, p. 3). As a result, populism consists not merely in a reaction against power structures, but in an appeal to the question of authority by claiming legitimacy on the grounds of popular sovereignty (p. 4). This particular style would be accompanied by a characteristic mood, as in an emotional investment that can draw 'normally unpolitical people into the political arena,' arising from a direct and straightforward plea (p. 6). One way of refreshing this perspective is by paying attention to emotions in political engagement. This last point is fundamental in recognizing the role played by affect in subjective identity positions, and in processes of collective identification which are vital in populism. However, as we know, Canovan never makes this breakthrough as she refers solely to the above mentioned 'mood.'

It is worth noting that the dominant strands of literature either do not mention the role played by 'affect' in populism or do so only minimally without proper elaboration, merely relying on a broad social mobilisation and the displacement of the predominant structures of power. Yet, one of the most compelling efforts to conceptualise populism claims the importance of 'the affective investment on a partial object.' I am referring here to the work of Ernesto Laclau (2005, p. 116).

Ernesto Laclau, along with the political theorist Chantal Mouffe, had been trying since the 1970s to overcome the essentialist constraints in Marxist theory. However, it was not until their breakthrough publication *Hegemony and Socialist Strategy* that a post-foundational approach was formally laid, whose theoretical formulations were gripped by the 'post-Marxist' label. Through it, Laclau and Mouffe (1985/2001) consider society to be a discursive articulation sustained within an ontological horizon of negativity. As no symbolization can render (social) reality complete, representation therefore becomes a necessary function (p. 114). However, if any form of social representation supposes a partial effort to construct society, then antagonism would function as the expression of the excluded possibilities by the predominant structure (Biglieri and Perelló, 2019, p. 333). As aptly put by Glynos (2001), '[f]rom this perspective, the opposition is not between representations of society on the one hand and society as such on the other, but between representations of society and the failure of representation itself' (p. 197), where such a failure is expressed in terms of a 'dislocation' (Laclau, 1990, p. 60). These theoretical matrixes relied heavily on the Gramscian concept of hegemony and the Lacanian categories in psychoanalytic theory, where the latter played an even larger role in Laclau's (2005) solo publication *On Populist Reason*.

For Laclau, populism is a logic marked by the simplification of the antagonistic boundaries between an underdog ('the people') and its 'other.' It entails establishing a 'chain of equivalence' by the articulation of various 'social demands,' which had hitherto been displaced, through an 'empty signifier' (p. 67–83). Laclau (1996) had been considering the 'empty signifier' since the 1990s and saw in it a means of subverting the signifying function of the Saussurean sign (p. 36). Its formal account in his theory of populism functions as a way of representing the radical challenge to the predominant system, by articulating unsatisfied demands. Stavrakakis (2017) lays it out clearly:

> In conditions of increasing inequality, exclusion, and failed representation, the "people" can function as such an empty signifier, expressing the need to address the perceived lack in equal rights, inclusion, and representation, calling forth a political subject in need of restoring its lost power/sovereignty and claiming the representation of its true will against an anti-popular/anti-populist power bloc that has allegedly hijacked it. (p. 539)

Although the antagonistic relationship between 'the people' and its other resonates strongly with the ideational approach, rather than claiming populism as a form of ideology Laclau (2005) takes it as a form of constructing the political. Populism, therefore, requires 'making an object the embodiment of a mythical fullness' through a radical investment of affect that he explicitly links with the logic of Lacan's object *a* (p. 116). These general remarks point to more concrete grounds within a chorus that has been echoing throughout the critical literature over the years, and to the exploration of emotions and affect in social identification as a promising dimension for the conceptual refinement of populism.

As previously stated, Canovan (1999) already sensed the relevance of a 'characteristic mood' in the specificity of populism (p. 6). Stavrakakis (2004) took this seriously enough to claim that 'it might be necessary to distinguish populism not only in terms of its discursive structure but also in terms of its intensity, the nature of the investment leaders and followers exhibit in their identifications' (p. 264). Moffitt and Tormey (2014) endorse such intuitions, arguing that much work needs to be done in this direction (p. 396). Yet, such remarks have found no concrete shores, extending recurrently without any proper elaboration and thereby opening grounds for articulating new theoretical venues.

If anyone has systematically stressed the importance of 'affect and passions' throughout her theoretical corpus, it is Chantal Mouffe. In her latest work, *For a Left Populism*, Mouffe (2018) analyses the crisis of the neoliberal hegemonic formation through the post-2008 financial downturn. By identifying new outspoken demands that emerge outside the productive processes, she recognizes the necessity of recreating the political frontiers through what she calls a 'populist transversal mode' (p. 6). This is identified through the 'political awakening after years of relative apathy' where the mobilization of common affects constitutes the central axis of the present political dispute (p. 19).

While Laclau remarked on the relevance of Lacan's object a for political identification, Mouffe foresees in the 'protest movement' a broad canvas for the theoretical and strategic advance of populism as a fundamental logic in the discursive mobilisation of common affects. Allow me to offer a possible theoretical link between both remarks. Following the work of Jacques Lacan on discourse – which will be introduced in the next section – one can consider the existence of common significant features in the public protests. One can discern within them a set of unsatisfied grievances (a) which triggered mass mobilisations and directed heterogeneous demands towards the political establishment (S1). Through a radical questioning of the predominant order, the expansion of these processes has stressed the boundaries of the social imagination, leading to the articulation of new forms of social knowledge (S2). Much like Lacan's provocation of the '68 student movement, this is bound to result in a new hegemonic form (M). If my formulation encompasses theoretical validity, it would invariably be embedded in the discourse of the hysteric.

The Squares and the Hysteric

A number of scholars in the field of social movement studies have conducted case and comparative analyses aimed at understanding the wave of mobilisations that began to develop after 2008. As della Porta and Mattoni (2014) point out, at first glance, the protests share some similar conditions, namely in the approach of the protestors, who appear to be independent of the mainstream political actors, widely employing 'social-networking sites, combined with older web applications and Internet tools, in conjunction with face-to-face gatherings and the deployment of quite radical, contentious performances, amongst them the physical occupation of public spaces' (p. 1). On a second level, they are often seen to be the climax of decades of anti-capitalist struggles, now centred as the social anguish from the neoliberal hegemony, and assuming different forms of transnational diffusion (Sotirakopoulos and Rootes, 2014; Mouffe, 2018; Gerbaudo, 2017)

Gerbaudo (2017), Tuğal (2013), and Solty (2013) suggest that, although different triggers or groups were initially responsible for organizing the post-2008 mobilisations, the subsequent protests were spontaneous and exceeded any previous expectations. This implies a lack of prior formal means of social organisation that could have accounted for their rapid expansion. The protests were demographically diverse and made up of people from different ethnic, socio-economic, and age groups. This also seems to be the case in relation to their demands, which encompassed a wide range of grievances (from public transport and environmental issues to healthcare and police brutality).

Mouffe (2018, p. 12) and Solty (2013) see in this transitional stage of crisis a set of contradictions condensed in the thought of Antonio Gramsci. Gramsci (1971) explicitly refers to a 'crisis of authority', which 'is precisely the crisis of hegemony' (p. 210). This is described as the moment when 'the ruling class has lost its consensus,' thereby resulting in the detachment of the masses 'from the traditional ideologies' (p. 275). As we know, not only do Gramsci's insights on crisis inform Laclau's concept of dislocation (Mouffe, 2018), but the Lacanian theorisation of the inherent lack in the symbolic proves critical to its understanding (Stavrakakis, 2007, p. 73).

Encompassing the dual character found in the literature on populism, dislocation assumes a disruptive context and a discursive articulation (Stavrakakis, 2017, p. 547), explicitly linking a crisis of representation to the 'root of any populist or anti-institutional outburst' (Laclau, 2005, p. 137). In Gramsci's (1971) words, 'the crisis consists precisely in the fact that the old is dying and the new cannot be born; in this interregnum a great variety of morbid symptoms appear' (p. 210). Therefore, the detachment of the masses from the ruling class entails a lack which bursts an interrogation over the predominant order, where the appearance of 'morbid symptoms' – as the expression of unsatisfied grievances previously kept silent – marks a 'return of the repressed' (a *return of the political*, in Mouffe's (2005) terms) and may be directly associated with the psychoanalytic notion of hysteria.

Since Freud (1921/1955) did not use the term 'collective hysteria,' what can be taken from his work is rather the way in which he describes the dynamics of group processes through the concept of identification. In his 'Boarding School Girls' example, he describes a girl who receives a letter from a loved one, causing jealousy and, successively, a hysterical crisis. This crisis arouses a similar reaction in her friends through a mechanism Freud calls 'mental infection' or 'identification based on the possibility or desire to be placed in the same situation' (p. 60). From this hysterical attack en masse, it is possible to detect within Freudian theory an outline of a hysteria that is collective. For Freud, this is the type of identification present among the members of a group that can also be referred to as the bond the group establishes with their leader.

This clear-cut elaboration did not go unnoticed by Laclau (2005) and is seen in his work as a vital elucidation for the characterization of populism via Freud's key notion of identification. Nevertheless, he regards it as 'patently insufficient,' in which Laclau undermines its specific significance associated with the hysterical symptom and loses sight of the radical libidinal investment populism bears in the reconstitution of subjectivity by bringing about new identity positions (p. 83). This is not to say that Laclau ignored the role that desire plays in any form of identification (especially in a populist one), but the particular nature of such recalcitrant libidinous forces intertwining in the (dis)articulation of a social bond remains marginal and underdeveloped – and, as will be seen, brings with it substantial implications. I believe Freud did not rely on hysteria by chance and it is precisely through this particular factor that Lacan recognised in hysteria a productive analytical lens for his reflections on the May 1968 events. Therefore, one could say that the Lacanian interest in 'hysteria is, in many respects, a 'return to Freud'' (van Haute and Geyskens, 2012, p. 139).

The theoretical formulations in the psychoanalytic work of Jacques Lacan have been exalted by other scholars for their promising potential to conduct social and political analysis (Feher-Gurewich, 1996; Stavrakakis, 2002, 2007). Particular interest has emerged from the post-structuralist field, as 'Lacanian theory can provide poststructuralism with a new conception of subjectivity compatible with its own theoretical foundations,' filling some persisting theoretical lacks in the sciences (Stavrakakis, 2002, p. 13).

While objectivist perspectives in the (social) sciences tend to take the subject as a positively foreclosed entity, psychoanalysis commits itself to dealing with the drama of instability which constitutes subjectivity, providing solid ontological foundations for Laclau's theoretical developments. The fundamental point of departure here is the Freudian discovery of the unconscious as marking the constitutive excentricity of the human condition by a characteristic *Spaltung* (splitting). Interestingly enough, Freud reached this conclusion in his ground-breaking work with hysteric analysands (Giraldo, 2017, p. 95). On the face of it, Lacan takes such a split 'as something constitutive of subjectivity in general,' that is, as a radical subversion and opposition to the subject-as-cogito which, in short, keeps psychoanalysis alive and kicking (Lacan, cited in Stavrakakis, 2002, p. 15).

After the 1968 events in Paris, Lacan (2007) formulated his XVII Seminar, widely known as *The Other Side of Psychoanalysis*, bearing through its formulation an explicit provocation to the pervasive 1968 students' slogan: 'structures do not walk the streets.' If anything, Lacan tries through this Seminar to prove how structural shifts can explain social upsurges, thus stressing, in contrast to the demonstrators' provocative slogan, how structures can (and often do) walk the streets. Through it, he outlines four fundamental elements ($S1$, master-signifier; $S2$, knowledge; $\$$, split subject; a, object) that may occupy different discursive positions (agent, other, product, truth). This allows a distinction to be drawn between four types of discursive formations: the discourse of the master (to govern); the university discourse (to educate); the discourse of the hysteric (to desire); and the discourse of the analyst (to analyse). Through the 'mathemes' – as formal mathematical functions – Lacan attempts to offer a systematisation of psychoanalysis into core discourses, 'reveal[ing] how one discourse can be the other side (*l'envers*) of another' (Schroeder, 2008, p. 6). Notably, the discourse of hysteria is located a quarter-turn clockwise from the discourse of the master, where the latter is taken as a river-mouth of the former.

The discourse of the master refers to nothing else than to a normative structure which provides an order to the signifying chain of knowledge by telling the subject what to do (Schroeder, 2008; Fotaki and Harding, 2013). But Lacan, '[f]ar from winding up praising the act that inaugurates the Master,' shows it to be a sham, for in its discourse the space of production is taken by the object a, the object of desire, as an irreducible residue that inhibits the subject to be absolutely subsumed under the master's symbolic mandate (Žižek, 2014, p.

221). It is precisely under the hysterical discourse that the object *a* is hidden beneath *$*, and referred to a traumatised subject which remains divided by what of an object he represents to the Other. Ultimately, such a division triggers the fundamental hysterical question: 'What am I, if I'm what you've just been saying I am?' (Lacan, 1993, p. 279), defining 'the status of the subject as a speaking subject, which is to say, a divided [one]' (Žižek, 2014, p. 221).

As Joan Copjec (2015) has recalled, the psychoanalytic notion of hysteria is indeed 'the first analysed instance of the subject's essential division' precisely because of 'its questioning and refusal of social dictates,' taken as the paramount challenge to the subject's social identity (p. 51). As a result, hysterical desire is seen by Lacan (2001) not only as inherently unsatisfied, but also as 'the desire to have an unsatisfied desire' (p. 196). So, the captive-controlled subject, ordered by the master, lectured to in the discourse of the university, with 'even the analyst, supposedly on her side, interrogat[ing] her,' and full of doubts and uncertainties, finally reaches a voice when taking the place of the hysteric by refusing to embody the Other's dictates (Schroeder, 2008, p. 149).

Lacan (2007) famously pointed out the political consequences of assuming such a discursive position through his reading of the 1968 events in France. During the 'Intervention of Vincennes,' he responded to a provocation from the audience by pointing out that revolutionary aspirations were bound to the discourse of the master. In Lacan's own words:

> If you had a bit of patience, and if you really wanted our impromptus to continue, I would tell you that, always, the revolutionary aspiration has only a single possible outcome - of ending up as the master's discourse. This is what experience has proved. What you aspire to as revolutionaries is a master. You will get one. (p. 207)

As a result, the 'revolutionaries' are presented as agents of the hysterical discourse, in relation to a master placed in a position of knowledge, perpetuating the hysteric in that place of dissatisfaction and, therefore, aggressiveness in relation to the master. This is in line with Tomšič's reading (2019), through the formal discursive structure of the hysteric, of Marx's critical method of interpreting the capitalist mode of production. As Tomšič points out, Lacan did 'not shy away from identifying Marx and Lenin with the hysteric, suggesting that in the revolutionary discourse, the split subject assumes the position of agency, which 'interpellates' the master (capital) in order to extract knowledge of the contradictions that mark the sphere of production' (p. 304). Knowledge, far from signifying a logical and objective understanding, refers to mythical and unconscious fantasies that are hidden behind the master signifier (Fotaki and Harding, 2013).

Laclau did well to notice how a social displacement is the source of freedom, as dislocation of the symbolic structure is necessary for new knowledge to be (re)articulated, thus providing new identity positions that subjects can assume discursively. As we now know, his ontological grounds are deeply rooted in the Lacanian notion of the lack in the symbolic, adding to the concept of 'emptiness' with a valid theoretical standpoint for representing the absent fullness in existing socio-symbolic structures. Yet, if Freud's finding of the subject's division provided psychoanalytic theory with its point of departure, Laclau (2005) set the pace in a different trend: 'What is our minimal unit of analysis going to be? Everything turns around the answer to this question' (p. 72). Indeed, the analytical focus of Laclau's entire theoretical foundation would rest on such a minimal unit which, as we know, in his theory of populism 'corresponds to the category of 'social demand'' (p. 73). The key notion of 'the people' thus results from the articulation of heterogeneous demands by a nodal point: the empty signifier. Here, the signifying chain would result from the interaction of isolated and well-structured (almost positively foreclosed) 'demands' in becoming a 'broader social subjectivity we will call *popular demand*' (p. 74; emphasis in original). So, the 'demands,' as smaller social units, 'determine the kind of unity that populism brings about' (p. 73). It is at this point that one can have a greater appreciation of Laclau's refusal to accept Freud's formulation of the formation of a group as organised by an essentially 'libidinal tie' (p. 82), involving 'fleeting situations, such as the contagion of a fit of hysterics' (p. 83). By assuming the demand to be the minimal component in the articulation of populism, he relegates 'desire' to a subsidiary status.

The hysteric discourse, on the contrary, takes the lack in the Other seriously, as formulating the articulation of social knowledge by the constitutive lack which makes the subject a subject of desire, thus foregrounding a consistent minimal unit of analysis. It is, therefore, in a sort of dialectical process between the hysteric and the master that new knowledge is produced, as the hysteric 'asks himself a question while at the same time presupposing that the Other has the answer' (Žižek, 2014, p. 109). Yet, surprisingly the 'question asked of the Other is resolved through a reflexive turn in which the question begins to function as its own answer' (p. 109). Therefore, the role of the hysteric is not a minor one, as it is only through this radical questioning that the precarious character enclosed in the master's socio-symbolic structure can be fully rendered visible. As noted by Žižek (2004), the hysterical subject is regarded as the subject par excellence since, by radically resisting symbolisation, it assumes the logic of protest and resistance, and

[the logic of] of demands which, according to Lacan's formula, really want to be rejected because "*ce n'est pas ça*" (because, if fully met, the literal satisfaction of the demand robs it of its metaphoric universal dimension – the demand for X "really was not about X"). (p. 398)

In a similar vein, Lacan returns to some of Freud's patients as a means of illustration when reflecting on the hysteric form of identification. In one of these cases, the 'Butcher's Beautiful Wife,' a woman's 'desire to have an unsatisfied desire is signified by her desire for caviar,' presented as inaccessible (Lacan, 2001, p. 196). Nevertheless, 'as soon as it [desire] slips as desire into the caviar, the desire for caviar becomes its metonymy – rendered necessary by the want-to-be in which it is situated' (p. 197). Metonymy is taken as the effect where signification can only appear 'by the fact that there is no signification that does not refer to another signification' (p. 198), so caviar, as the object of the hysteric's desire, acts as a replacement for the Other, which organises her desire. 'For this desire of our witty hysteric (Freud's own description) – I mean her aroused desire, her desire for caviar – is the desire of a woman who has everything, and who rejects precisely that' (p. 198). The demand for X was not really about X.

If one takes the various claims that spread throughout the public square protests, a number of outstanding demands could indeed be identified. For example, Eklundh (2019) examines the online interaction within the Spanish Indignados movement and observes how 'some words and terms, regardless of their content, rise to become the signifiers of the movement,' (p. 178) such as 'people' and 'money' (p. 168). Yet, as she notes, 'the demands are plural, change over time, or are not recognized as demands in the first place,' so that political identities cannot be 'constructed around well-defined demands' (p. 148). As in the case of the hysteric, the desire of desiring repetitively can find no concrete satisfaction or univocal symbolisation and is only signified through various (shifting) specular objects that function as semblants of desire. To put it in Lacan's (2014) words, the demand 'comes unduly to the place of what is spirited away, a, the object' (p. 65).

In a broad examination, della Porta and Mattoni (2014) state all the social demonstrations involve rather radical and contentious performativity that certainly overwhelms any form of spoken signification. Such a character directly relates, as Lacan (2001) would put it, to 'the hysterical subject, for whom the technical term 'acting out' takes on its literal meaning' (p. 67). Žižek (2008) expresses it nicely:

> when we take a hysterical [subject] in the act of such a theatrical outburst, it is of course clear that she is doing this to offer herself to the Other as the object of desire, but concrete analysis has to discover who – which subject – embodies for her the Other. (p. 118)

Laclau and Mouffe (1985/2001) aptly pointed out the relevance of synonymy, metonymy, and metaphor, not as a means of adding 'a second sense to a primary [one],' but instead, as 'part of the primary terrain itself in which the social is constituted' (p. 110). The discursive articulation through which the Other is represented will embody different forms, depending on the ontic significance within concrete social spaces of inscription, and proving to be pivotal when one analyses the nodal cleavages at stake in a hysterical (social) outburst. In the 'Butcher's Beautiful Wife' case, for example, the demand for 'caviar' should not be taken for granted as it represents a key nodal point of signification. Yet, it is useful to the extent that, as in a metonymic function, it allows a more in-depth analysis of a much more involved process of identification to be conducted.

So, if the literally verbalised and utterly convoluted demands that may spring from a social outrage are of high analytical relevance, the key focus in the discourse of the hysteric compels us to ask: Which gaze is taken as the one from where I am being observed? From where do I appear likable to myself? If Eklundh's (2019) productive work on the *Indiganados* movement is taken into account, rather than focusing on nodal words such as 'people' or 'money,' the main focus should aim to find the place from where these expressions are supposed to be heard. In a similar vein, Žižek (2014) notes that

[t]he question we must ask about the hysteric is not "What is the object of his desire?" but, rather, "Where does his desire come from?" "What is the other subject through which he organizes his desire?" In the case of Freud's patient Dora, it is clear that, for her, Madame K [Frau K] is the other who embodies "knowing how to desire." (p. 145)

To state his point here, Žižek refers to Freud's most famous hysteric analysands. By recognising Dora's homosexual identification with Frau K, Žižek ends up creating an opposite analytical frame from that strongly taken up by Freud himself, whose 'constant attempt to convince Dora of her (hidden) heterosexual desire for Herr K is undoubtedly a result of reigning cultural prejudices' (van Haute and Geyskens, 2012, p. 57). However, if Žižek correctly identified Dora's desire for Frau K and her 'adorable white body' (Freud, 1905/1953, p. 60), he missed the point that 'Dora is here [actually] identifying with both Frau K and Herr K,' meaning that her object of desire is not only 'uncertain, but also that the place from where she desires is far from univocal' (van Haute and Geyskens, 2012, p. 57). Van Haute and Geysken were pointing in the right direction when they claimed that

[r]ather than [defending] heterosexual normality [and normativity], perhaps what Freud wants to protect at all cost is the idea of an identifiable desire at the basis of the symptoms from which Dora is suffering. Bisexuality confronts Freud – and all of us? – with structural uncertainty regarding not only the object of desire but also the place from where this desire takes shape. (p. 58)

Similarly, I believe Laclau, if he is basing his theoretical grounds on a post-foundational approach and certainly recognising the centrality of desire, wanted to protect at all costs the idea of an identifiable demand at the basis of a social dislocation – a conundrum which obliges us, by the ferocity of the social outrage (as the hysteric does), to reconsider. While van Haute and Geysken noted that hysteria presumes 'a structural uncertainty regarding gender identities,' (p. 58), Copjec (2015) felt this condition referred to social identities in general (p. 52). Therefore, one could surely stress such a structural uncertainty as a general condition within the hysteric proper.

The structural uncertainty over political (dis)identification processes within the public square protests appears to have been widely noted. As Eklundh (2019) so perceptively recognised, the shifting character of the antagonisms expressed in the recent demonstrations signals the difficulty (even impossibility) of recognising a one Other supposed to know. In her estimation, '[e]ven though Laclau would argue that the antagonist is indeed a congregation of many Others, there might not be one stable Other for today's protest movements' (p. 116).

So, if the place where the hysteric subject desires is indeed far from being univocal, a careful detailed analysis should instigate the 'libidinal constellation that expresses itself' historically (van Haute and Geyskens, 2012, p. 39). This requires, as Glynos and Howarth (2007) would suggest, profound analytical investment only attainable through the descriptive mastery of the specific social surface of inscription. Eklundh (2019) rightly asserts that 'denying the existence of nodes is to deny the possibility of political articulation' (p. 118). But if desire precedes demands, then the articulations would be made up of much more complex libidinal networks than those assumed within well-structured intertwining demands. Not only should affect not be disjoined from meaning-making, but what the hysteric teaches us about identification is that desire, rather than being instrumental, is emphatically constitutive, highlighting the need to link the 'social' and the 'psychic' more intensely. The latter forces researchers and academics, particularly in the field of populist studies, to take the affective dimension in the structuring of social meaning seriously.

Conclusion

The hysteric structure can provide populism with a productive formal logic in the interconnection between social displacement and political articulation by filling some important gaps seen in mainstream views in the field of populism studies. In particular, the post-structuralist field has advanced greatly by incorporating the psychoanalytic framework for political and social analysis, providing fertile grounds for understanding populism as a category. Yet, the central position which desire plays in such a framework has been persistently evaded by the pursuit of an objective unit from where a straightforward analysis could be established.

As Laclau and Mouffe (1985/2001) once stated: 'Any substantial change in the ontic content of a field of research leads also to a new ontological paradigm' (p. x), and so the current context of social eruption compels us to reconsider some of our leading theoretical assumptions. Hysteria not only provided psychoanalysis with the findings of the unconscious, but posed key questions for understanding collective (dis)identification and the production of social knowledge. I argue that the hysteric logic lays down a consistent framework from which social meaning-making can be understood from a perspective of desire.

From the structure of the hysteric, knowledge is produced not by the articulation of positively foreclosed demands within the realm of signification, but by a far-reaching embrace of negativity in the radical resistance of being subsumed within such an existing realm. This is not to say that signification ceases to exist, but that the 'demands,' rather than fully-fledged units, function as provisional emulators within a much more complex libidinal structure. So, the hysteric discourse consists of the essential engine of (a constitutive) desire that, by the relentless interpellation of the socio-symbolic structure, stresses in turn the structuring of new subjective identity positions. This eventually leads to the transformation – to put it in Freudian terms – of 'hysterical misery into common unhappiness' (Freud and Breuer, 1895/1995, p. 305).

2. Thesis Conclusions

By placing the research focus at the frontier of populism studies, this thesis is concerned with problematising, exploring and constructing meaning-making dynamics with reference to Brazilian politics. This is done by engaging with discourses explicitly drawing on populism rhetorical elements and by exploring the analytic positive points of the discourse theory of populism to study and explain political antagonism beyond strong forms of charismatic leadership and phenomena conceived as being populist as such. In other words, this thesis explores the politics of discourses about populism and raises questions, through the political logic of populism, on the dominant role personalism has taken in the political science literature, using Brazil as an ontic study reference. In so doing, I pay close attention to the role affect and desire play in the political (dis)articulation of social reality. In advancing these aims, the sequence of papers embodying this four-step research project follows my conceptual and contextual reasoning rather than the chronological order of their formal elaboration.

The first paper emphasises how discourses on populism were first introduced as central discursive elements in Brazil in the 1940s through a dynamic interplay of political and journalistic actors, further triggering the articulation of research projects on populism in Brazilian academia. This is done so through the creation of a multi-sited framework which renders intelligible processes of mutual feedback for the study and explanation of concrete discursive compositions (in this case, related to populism).

Moreover, this thesis' second paper takes issue with constructing contemporary journalistic debates about populism in Brazil and untangling the modes of fantasmatic enjoyment underlying these discursive approaches. Building on these discourses, I construct a more anchored picture of political antagonism featuring Lula and the PT political party as main (populist) foes, explaining some affective layers in the construction of Rousseff's impeachment, Lula's imprisonment and Bolsonaro's victory in the 2018 election through an upmarket journalistic standpoint.

Having constructed some core discursive valences and main figures from the anti-PT demonstrations (2013-2016) to the 2018 elections in Brazil (as explored by paper 2), paper 3 then moves away from mainstream debates drawing on the PT/anti-PT antagonistic frontiers and prominent figures in Brazilian politics. Instead, it comes to grips with the appearance of prefigurative electoral experiences setting alternative emancipatory horizons from a more grassroots standpoint. As such, paper 3 questions the sole scholarly focus on charismatic leaders and populist figures standing for the presidency, drawing the research attention to underlying local dimensions which provide a more complex and wider frame of (political) articulation and (social) meaning-making.

The preceding papers prompted my interest in how the link between desire and meaning-making can be thought of at the ontological level. As such, papers 1, 2 and 3 engaged with demands and articulatory practices enabling the construction of significant layers arising in some core political disputes in Brazil. Through them, a close link between affect and narrative is sensed, particularly through paper 2. Paper 4 goes into psychoanalytic theory to attempt to explain articulatory processes and the appearance of social demands from a perspective of desire, thus drawing on affect and meaning-making from a negative ontological standpoint. Before commenting on each paper's concluding remarks, allow me to draw the reader's attention to some limitations I have encountered in conducting this work.

2.1.Limitations

Every research project in the social sciences demands decisions and choices from the practitioner. These choices range from the research approach and strategy to the theoretical and empirical objects of study. Whether they are premeditated or contingent, rationally justified or emotionally led, the principles and content underlying these choices underpin the horizons and scope of what can and cannot be descriptively questioned, analytically explored and critically explained in a given field of investigation. Furthermore, no application of a rule, law or even logic can automatically link a concept to an object of study as every research project in the social sciences relies on the mastery of the theoretical and empirical research dimensions and the analytical perception attained by the practitioner in the process. This research project is no different. As formally stated in my research approach, no generalisation can be derived from this thesis by inductive or deductive means. As such, the plausible scope of generality that may go beyond the restraints of the concrete theoretical and empirical objects of analysis can only be weighed on a judgment of considerable resemblance to other such theoretical and empirical objects. Moreover, although I am very familiar with political and social developments in Brazil and have a good command of the Portuguese language, my limitations as a Colombian and Spanish native speaker should be stressed. Therefore, these are the general limitations within which this research project has been developed.

Having acknowledged the general limitations of this thesis, I can now point out some inherent boundaries and restraints underlying the formulation and findings of each paper. In engaging with political debates from 1946 to 1964, through paper 1 I have tried to gather and construct a credible archive research body of work. In doing so, I have used the media as an 'entry point' to study the dynamic interaction of discourses about populism across social spheres. In examining all occurrences within my dataset, I have gained access to some material from the political sphere (mainly public speeches, brochures, press releases and campaign leaflets). However, such material has gone through editorial curatorship intermediation of media actors, for paper 1 loses sight of relevant feedback dynamics and mutual constitution processes enacting within the sphere of politics. Due to time-economy questions in the development of this paper and the lack of digitalised archives of party material at the time, I could not make a more in-depth exploration of populism discursive interaction in the sphere of politics as such.

Moreover, Brazilian readers have been following the global trend and steadily migrating from traditional journalistic outlets and magazines to seeking online information through podcasts, YouTubers, Instagrammers and much else besides. By centring the research focus on the upmarket magazine *Veja* and its news coverage of populism, paper 2 retains its scope to a media-centric analysis. Specifically, this study takes issue with this approach tailored to a well-off targeted readership. Although *Veja* has an impact on so-called decision-makers in the private and public sectors and has been the most read news magazine in Brazil for over three decades, no generalisation or judgment can automatically be made about the impact of its coverage of and engagement in the public debate. Neither can it be inferred that populist discursive elements are a central feature of the contemporary Brazilian means of communication by focusing solely on *Veja*.

In terms of paper 3, the scant coverage by commentators and journalists of the political experience and electoral victory of the *Bancada Ativista* meant I had limited material available to approach this prefigurative collective experience. Therefore, I chose to conduct a series of interviews and managed to talk to one of the co-deputies of the *Bancada*: Anne Rammi. As a result, to a good extent, the analysis has been restricted to her speech. I had difficulties contacting other *Bancada* co-deputies and activists involved in the structuring of this collective initiative due to the COVID-19 crisis. Besides, the early campaigning process for the 2020 elections ruled out further interviews or even follow-ups with Rammi. Within these limits, I consulted Brazilian writings on the social movements and backdrop since 2013 in a bid to fill in this gap and bring coherence and plausibility to the explanations presented in paper 3.

Finally, my last article (and main theoretical contribution) has distinct limitations due to the nature of the reflections of which it is composed. As such, paper 4 is restricted to the theoretical perspectives and conceptual accounts that mark its development. Consequently, its analytical and strategic points may only be judged in light of further research confronting its theoretical and ontological scope with empirical objects at the ontical level.

2.2.Papers and Findings

Paper 1: *Populism in the Making: A Multi-sited Discursive Approach to Brazil's Fourth Republican Period (1946-1964)*

Created as a point of departure in navigating the study of populism as a concept and a signifier in Brazilian politics, paper 1 presents the first instances when the words 'populism' and 'populist' appeared as central features of Brazil's public debate. This paper takes issue with a gap in the literature identified by discourse scholars concerning the need to take discourses about populism more seriously, particularly the way they interact with and help constitute populist discourses.

In seeking to formulate a formal framework for this study, I have affirmed the utility of the concept/signifier pair and the double-hermeneutic perspective, and sought to advance these insights further. References to the key roles played by journalism, politics and academia often appear in discourse theory debates as core social spheres in the dynamic structuring of contemporary meaning-making. Drawing on these three spheres has shown a valuable strategy in tracing and (de)constructing complex discursive dynamics in the Brazilian case. However, this framework may be adjusted in light of context-specific considerations regarding more prominent spheres in other cases of analysis not necessarily restricted to the study of populism[12].

---

[12] The cinematographic sphere, for example, could assume a relevant role in a study drawing on American cultural anti-communism during McCarthyism.

In terms of the Brazilian case, I use this framework to shed light on the Fourth Republic (1946-1964), a period referred to by academic and non-academic players as the 'Populist Republic'. I am able to supplement existing accounts of this period by showcasing in greater detail and nuance the significance of key moments through a corpus-based study. The very fact that the first examples of where the words 'populism' and 'populist' were first used in Brazilian politics takes me back to 1946 is already a significant finding. The so-called *Populist Republic* was the first time in which popular layers of society (including female and rural social segments) played a significant role in setting the contours of electoral processes in Brazilian politics. Indeed, Varga's corporativist dictatorship had boosted a modernisation process which attracted peasant farmers from the rural areas as an available labour force for Brazil's main urban centres. This demographic realignment opened up new political dynamics in the democratic development taking place between Varga's *Estado Novo* [New State] and the dawn of the military regime, with the appearance (and construction) of new political subjects and identity positions.

In this sense, the Brazilian case resonates with other cases which have been analysed where the rhetorical label of 'populist' is employed as a means of political (and scholar) exclusion. This was the case with the late-19th-century United States People's Party (Stavrakakis, 2017b). The People's Party was a left-wing agrarian force resisting the powerful expansion of industrial modernisation in the United States and has assumed a central role in historiographic literature on populism, primarily through the work of Richard Hofstadter. By drawing on this experience, Hofstadter's (1955) work has been identified as the root of widespread academic anti-populism, triggering similar replications elsewhere, as was the work of Gino Germani (1962) in Argentina. Interestingly enough, by following academic responses to the political figure of Adhemar de Barros, I found published work drawing pejoratively on populism a year before Hofstadter's Pulitzer-winner *The Age of Reform* was published. I am referring to Jaguaribe's *Que é Ademarismo?*, published in 1954. To this day, Brazilian populism scholarship remains virtually absent from the international literature on populism studies. Therefore I believe this finding should be taken with all due seriousness and incorporated in and problematised through populism studies historiographic body of work.

In terms of the concrete case analysed, the figure of Adhemar de Barros takes on a central role in the discursive disputes (and victories) of populist and pro-populist elements in Brazil (at least until the first half of the Fourth Republic), with Vargas' PTB often rebuffing the populist/anti-populist frontier. This is yet another rather insightful discovery, as the figure of Vargas is often overblown in the study of populism in Brazil and de Barros' legacy is rather underplayed or simply unexplored. This can be seen in former IDA/PhD projects at the University of Essex, as is Alejandro Groppo's PhD work published under the book title *The Two Princes. Juan D. Perón and Getulio Vargas. A Comparative Study of Latin America Populism* (Groppo, 2013).

As far as the primary and secondary research questions of this paper are concerned, allow me to recall and elaborate on them one by one.

i.   (How) did the signifiers 'populism' and 'populist' first became central features of Brazil's political debate and how have these discursive articulations impacted Brazilian society?

Although the words 'populism' and 'populist' were first introduced in Brazil in 1946 by the fascist *Integralist* movement, led by Plínio Salgado, these two signifiers assumed a central political role through Dutra's Petropolis Scheme from March 20, 1949. As such, it is through the electoral succession disputes prior to the 1950 presidential election that populism elements are introduced as central discursive features of Brazilian politics. These two signifiers then assume a dominant role in setting the antagonistic electoral frontiers after Adhemar de Barros' appropriation of such labels. As in other such analyses (Nikisianis et al. 2019), the Brazilian case depicts how the construction of populist and pro-populist discourses came about in opposition to anti-populist forces. These discursive articulations were central to subsequent social and political processes in Brazil. Indeed, by the prevalence of anti-populist stances after Vargas' shocking suicide in 1954 and the humiliating defeat suffered by Adhemar de Barros at the end of the Fourth Republic, the democratic resistance to the military regime firmly rebuffed the so-called populist experience. As such, the main political parties opposing the military went out of their way to oppose so-called populist (charismatic and personalist) leaders (MDB) and coordinate a workers' movement standpoint (no longer being people- or populist-centric) in opposition to Vargas' (and de Barros') legacy (PT). Furthermore, anti-populist intellectuals (such as Weffort and Cardoso) were promoted within these party organisations, gaining traction and influence in the political sphere. This may be seen in more detail through my secondary research question regarding Paper 1.

ii.   Which sphere in the media-politics-academia matrix takes on a privileged discursive role, and how might this inter-sphere relational 'weight' affect the (feedback) dynamics influencing discourses about populism?

When examining the Brazilian case, I found the political sphere to have a more prominent role in mutual constitution processes on discourses about populism throughout most of the fourth republican period. As it comes, the inter-sphere disputes in politics and the relational weight of participants within this sphere not only enable and help account for the appearance of journalistic discourses about populism but also the antagonistic and non-antagonistic discursive modes taking place in the media sphere. For example, the lesser Dutra's political (and popular) appeal given de Barros' inter-sphere victories in politics is, the more mainstream journalism draws on 'populism' as a neutral description with even pro-populist discourses proliferating (in higher or lesser degree) in most media outlets. These principles gain greater exposure with the intra-sphere movement of players. For example, when the PTB politician Danton Coelho became *Última Hora*'s managing director in 1955, pro-populist discourses appeared more often in journalism.

However, once attention is drawn to the academic field, a shift of inter-sphere relational weight is observed, mainly after Jaguaribe's work on Adermaism was published. Why such a delayed appearance of academia in the tripartite sphere complex? Moreover, how did such a shift come about? Blinded peer-reviewed processes enclose closed-set intra-sphere dynamics in academia. As such, scholarly disputes are only visible once a body of work has gone through peer-review publishing processes in relation to other peer-reviewed bodies of work. This is to say, the intra-sphere dynamics in academia quietly draw from other social spheres and build antagonistic and non-antagonistic modes within peer-reviewed processes (with the editors and the blinded referees) and outside peer-reviewed processes (with peer-reviewed published work). As has been constantly stressed since this thesis' introduction, the very conditions for articulating social meaning in academia are no different from those in other spheres in ontological terms. However, academic production and publication processes present delayed mutual constitution and feedback dynamics at both inter- and intra-sphere levels. In the Brazilian case, this meant that academia was, in the first instance, influenced by the media-politics dynamics taking place in the first half of the Fourth Republic. However, academic actors would come to play a central role in the sphere complex once the main body of work drawing on populism went through editorial processes. And again, this influence was broadened by the movement of players – this time moving from academia to the political arena.

Given the prominent role of anti-populist scholars as partisanship intellectuals (such as Cardoso in the MDB and Weffort in the PT), anti-populist academic discourses, initially influenced by the dynamics in the political sphere, gained relational weight throughout the dictatorship, organising the democratic resistance of this period in anti-populist and class-based terms. As such, my findings invite further research in order to properly explore the politics of discourses about populism throughout the military period (1964-1985) and beyond.

My findings regarding populism discourses in Brazil's Fourth Republic may be summarised as follows:

1. Anti-populist discourses enable and animate the articulation of populist and pro-populist discourses through antagonistic discursive modes.

2. While there is no necessary correspondence or fixed role in the sphere complex, political discourses present an enabling character in terms of the dynamic interplay of populism discourses within and across spheres. Therefore, intra-sphere debates in politics lay the initial signifying turns on populism discourses. Other spheres later build and draw their intra-sphere debates from there (e.g. after the Petropolis Scheme, the main journalistic articles referring to Brazilian politics establish a core antagonistic frontier between *democratic-conservatives* and *populist* forces, as structured by Dutra). In this point, the question of media ownership is key in understanding the salient political discourses being replicated and restructured in the media.

3. While there is no necessary correspondence or fixed role in the sphere complex, discourses in the media play an invigorating and refining part of the discursive dynamics and disputes taking place in the political sphere. Therefore, journalistic feedback dynamics are significant in influencing later political debates, articulating adjacent meaningful elements into the relational discursive framework drawing upon populism as a nodal signifier. (For example, the differential logic established between

popular and *populist* as an antagonistic anti-populist journalistic opposition to the core pro-populist differential logic established between *populism* and *elitism.*)

4. While there is no necessary correspondence or fixed role in the sphere complex, academic discourses appear to have delayed responses to mutual constitution processes and present more stable structures of meaning in relation to political and journalistic discourses about populism. Therefore, scholarly discourses on populism are parasitical from political and journalistic discourses (e.g. Jaguaribe describes populism explicitly as de Barros has been described in public debate). In turn, however, they help sediment and crystalise meaning within and across spheres. For example, populism is dictionarised and thus pinned down conceptually after the main academic perspectives on populism are published.

5. The movement of individuals at both inter- and intra-sphere levels has a significant impact on mutual feedback and mutual constitution dynamics. Therefore, future research drawing on populism discourses should pay close attention to the inter- and intra-sphere movement of people and their effects on discursive valences.

6. Populism discursive dynamics in Brazil hint at the existence of path dependence processes as the study of discursive interactions regarding populism as a signifier should be studied historically and in a context-specific manner.

Paper 2: *From Lula to Bolsonaro: unravelling Veja Magazine's (anti)populist fantasies*

From the literature drawing on the politics of discourses about populism, most studies have committed to studying journalistic coverage. To a reasonable extent, the discourse theory scholarship focus on journalistic discourses on populism is justified, as has been formerly stressed, by the leading role media players have come to assume in contemporary communicational dynamics. However, by exploring the broad correlation of rhetorical and linguistic aspects, these studies circumvent a more lively and profound analytical engagement in terms of context and tenor animating and sustaining such formal signifying dynamics. This is especially so when it comes to the affective investment through which discursive elements come to grip subjects. And indeed, the words 'populism' and 'populist' are often used indiscriminately in a negative way by the news media. As such, paper 2 provides a media-centric analysis, aimed at bringing the category of fantasy back into the gist of the study of discourses about populism.

Therefore, having explored discursive turns and political disputes on discourses about populism in my first thesis paper, I then move onto exploring underlying affective narratives, taken as the driving force endowing normative and ideological preferences with reference to populism discourses. Fantasy has been deployed as an analytical category for the study of mainly tabloid-like news coverage. In turn, I have decided to explore distinctive modes of fantasmatic enjoyment underlying journalistic coverage of populism by drawing on the Brazilian magazine *Veja* which has an upmarket readership. For this study, I rely on prolific psychoanalytically informed scholarly work to further flesh and advance the analytic potential of fantasy orbiting concepts *vis-à-vis* contemporary political developments in Brazil. These orbiting concepts refer to *thief of enjoyment* (Zizek, 1989; Glynos, 2001) and *guarantor* (Chang and Glynos, 2011). Before moving on, I would like to recall in this discussion the research question underlying the development of paper 2.

    i.   (How) are the signifiers 'populism' and 'populist' articulated and constructed in Brazil's contemporary journalistic language, and (in what ways) do they invite forms of enjoyment and endow normative responses to perceived problems?

By constructing the linguistic operations, contextual references and main subjects involved in and sustaining *Veja*'s populism-referenced discourses, a connection between papers 1 and 2 can be seen. Setting the horizon for future exploration on the interaction of discourses about populism in Brazil's Fourth Republic, the influence of academics over political dynamics not only throughout the military regime but also in the democratisation process is referred to in paper 1. In concrete terms, Francisco Weffort seems to play a rather ambivalent role in the Workers' Party. While Weffort initially saw great potential in the PT by challenging Vargas' union corporativism, taking an active part in its class-based organisation, he would later become highly sceptical about this political force by identifying Lula as a populist, acting as a modern day Adhemar de Barros (*Folha de S. Paulo*, 2006). Interestingly, moreover, *Veja*'s mobilisation of the words 'populism' and 'populist' are saliently used as negative code words creating the bogey man figure of Lula.

Veja uses a populist descriptor in the construction of a dangerous other. At the core of this dreadful otherness-construction is Lula, seen as a thief of economic enjoyment through state interventionism (corrupt/evil) as opposed to market economy dynamics (free/idyllic). Other menacing figures such as Rousseff and the PT appear, condensed into a wider populist menace embodied by the frightening phenomenon of *Lulopetismo*. The antagonistic construction of a dangerous otherness, as has been elaborated, serves as a means of accounting for loss. With high approval rates and upholding Brazil's profile in the international arena, Lula became a central national political figure. To a reasonable extent, the legacy set by Lula was not restricted to a widespread success perception in both political and economic terms at national and international levels by invigorating the role of the State in social dynamics. His humble origins and absence of scholarly background made this perceived success a genuine watershed, as Brazil's face came to be represented for the first time by a humble former factory worker with no scholarly background from the impoverished north-eastern region. Why does Lula's legacy awaken *Veja*'s anti-populist anxiety?

Through *Veja*'s anti-populist discourses, I have constructed some libidinal structures highlighting not only the identificatory processes in terms of how the magazine's desire is structured but, more importantly, how such processes construct fantasies through which readers are invited to take part in distinctive modes of fantasmatic enjoyment. In a nutshell, a fantasy of elite expertise and market-economy rule are the main props which sustain *Veja*'s blind opposition to Lula. As such, Lula embodies the limits of this technocratic consensus reaching fantasy. Paradoxically, however, the frightening populist embodiment of Lula represents a limit to elite expertise and market rule being fully attained; at the same time, it serves as a means of sustaining and encouraging an emotional investment in such an ultra-liberal fantasy.

A psychoanalytic approach to subjectivity regards identity to be impossible. As such, the only way to reach an idea of the self is through identificatory processes which rely fundamentally on the construction of a constitutive otherness through which the subject explains the impossibility of reaching fullness (of attaining a full identity in positive and stable terms). As such, *Veja*'s characterisation of populist elements allows accounting for the limits of its own fantasmatic construction of social fullness. By doing so, it makes enjoyment partly accessible by both the anxious spur of losing sight of the self by the dangers of an other, while reaching a partial sense of joy by the failure of this other in affirming its own identity. As such, *Veja*'s anti-populist rhetoric allows a partial spur of joy by Rousseff's failure and Lula's desolation.

However, once the populist menace of *Lulopetismo* is kept at bay and the political limits of a plainly neoliberal and technocratic agenda are made clear (for example, by the absolute failure of the neoliberal candidate, Henrique Meirelles, at both popular polls and the 2018 elections), *Veja* engages in new populist constructions which can account for the limits of the self (thus also sustaining the idea of the self and animating an emotional investment in its own fantasy of fullness). This process can be seen by the shifting representation of Temer after Rousseff's impeachment (first beatific, then horrific) and by the antagonistic and non-antagonistic discursive modes the magazine adopts towards the figure of Bolsonaro after Lula's imprisonment. This libidinal game of affective proximities and distances is mediated by guarantor figures. To put it in plainly, *Veja*'s market-rule elite-expertise fantasy depends on constructing a populist nightmare that may account for the limit of such a fantasy. This is why there are constant references to the words 'populism' and 'populist' in its news coverage directed at its upmarket readership.

The findings of paper 2 may be summarised as follows:

1. Enjoyment is embedded in narrative and acts as the gripping force, sustaining or disrupting discursive structures.

2. Fantasy gives normative and ideological direction to narrative constructions. Studying fantasy allows unravelling discursive turns and responses to perceived crises and the shifting character of identificatory processes.

3. As such, *Veja*'s core fantasmatic antagonistic mode is directed towards Lula and the PT (telescoped of *Lulopetismo*) as left-populism represents a strong opposition to direct and unsupervised free market rule. As a result, no guarantor can make equivalential processes between *Veja* and left-populism ever possible, as the existence of such a left-populist thief encourages, in turn, *Veja*'s market rule and elite expertise fantasy. This explains the magazine's kneejerk endorsement of Rousseff's impeachment and Lula's imprisonment.

4. Right-wing populist thief representations awaken some concern in *Veja* through differential discursive processes by the representational strengthening of State function in the social functioning. However, the construction of economic and moral guarantors

may make equivalential processes between the magazine and right-wing populism possible as a left-populist menace is still discursively present as a bad guy from central casting. This point reinforces the focus on market and elite expertise in *Veja*'s fantasmatic narrative, setting political pluralism (identified by the magazine as core values of globalisation) into a more adjacent fantasmatic status.

Paper 3: *Collectivising political mandates: A discursive approach to the Brazilian Bancada Ativista's campaign in the 2018 elections*

This thesis's initial research steps (through papers 1 and 2) explore some crucial antagonistic practices in Brazil related to the discursive reference to 'populism' and 'populist' as signifiers. By examining formal discursive turns in articulating social meaning in the Fourth Republic and exploring affective narrative constructions in contemporary journalistic language, through papers 1 and 2, I affirm the distinctive qualities of discourse theory for studying the politics of discourses about populism in Brazil. These studies lead me to believe that every perceived form of social objectivity is politically installed (through the work of the negative) and that all forms of political action are constitutively affective (by the libidinal investment in a partial form of social representation).

In terms of these two steps in my overall approach, moreover, I have engaged with discursive constructions related to identificatory processes revolving around the importance of political figures and the dominant role of charismatic leadership in opposing and articulating political identities and social meaning (from Adhemar de Barros to Luiz Inácio da Silva). In doing so, I observe the representational principle of discourse theory regarding the necessary investment in a partial object as a means of representing a social totality (when the object is raised to the dignity of the Thing). I also believe, as Lacan did, that any form of social demand is ultimately a request for love (see Fink, 1999, p. 60). In this sense, a single figure or demand appears as a key partial object in the overall structuring of a signifying chain of various demands and meaningful objects (structured in both pro-populist or anti-populist terms).

However, the sole focus on a single demand or political figure should not exclude studying 'the emergence of a collective action, directed towards struggling against inequalities and challenging relations of subordination' (Laclau and Mouffe, 1985, p. 153). In this sense, the equivalential and differential logics enacted in structuring a chain of meaning are fundamental in sustaining or disrupting a single demand or political figure representing the overall signifying (social) structure. Therefore, these underlying (differential and equivalential) operations amongst various signifying elements (de)constructing a discursive social structure and affective ties should be studied seriously. What is more, '[t]here seems to be no reason why one demand should play this role - why not an amalgam or articulation of different demands?' (Howarth, 2008, p. 185).

While paper 2 has constructed critical discursive operations stimulating broad political disputes leading to the PT representational crisis and Bolsonaro's presidential victory in the 2018 elections, further layers of analysis of social practices and collective action processes are left unaddressed. In concrete terms, in the study of populism in contemporary Brazil, the figure of Jair Bolsonaro has taken over the research spotlight. He is seen by researchers and commentators as a populist leader who has taken over Brazilian politics by capitalising on widespread anti-PT social anger. In addressing this gap, paper 3 upholds the relevance of discourse theory to the study of collective action processes that prefigure alternative forms of political representation. For this purpose, I focus on the electoral debut of the *Bancada Ativista*. Allow me to bring the research question guiding the exploration in and development of paper 3 into this discussion.

i. Can the rationale endowed in *populism-as-a-logic* be employed analytically to explain the articulation of prefigurative forms of collective representation contesting personalism?

Drawing on the discourse theory understanding of populism as a political logic and articulating adjacent idioms from Critical Discourse Analysis, paper 3 makes a critical explanation of the appearance and composition of the anti-personalist *Bancada Ativista* in the 2018 electoral scene. Furthermore, responding to peer-review feedback and a reviewer's comments in the journal *Politics*, this research has engaged in discussion with broader strands of literature in political science and social movement studies that draw on questions related to *institutional crisis*, *personalism* and *collective action*. This has been done through a semi-structured interview with one of the *Bancada*'s representatives, Anne Rammi. As such, her self-interpretations are taken as an analytical layer in the overall analysis.

The study of the *Bancada Ativista*'s collective candidacy has allowed me to construct underlying dynamics of social contestation, political articulation and identity formation stemming from the upsurge of social protests in 2013 to the 2018 elections in Brazil. The articulation of this collective candidacy displays articulatory practices that sought to sidestep the dominant PT/anti-PT antagonistic frontiers by opposing the dominant form of personalist political representation. As such, the *Bancada* managed to articulate unsatisfied and fluctuating social demands that, while resisting right-wing collective organisation and opposing Bolsonaro's discursive platform, the Workers' Party failed to incorporate. At heart, the main positions the *Bancada* offers its followers saliently feature *female*, *black* and *non-heteronormative gender roles* and aim to articulate them on a wider scope of collective action.

In short, the new identification processes and forms of collective identification upheld by the *Bancada* derive from a dual displacement: the crisis within the hegemonic project of the

Brazilian left (mainly related to the PT under Lula's leadership), and the limits of traditional forms of personalist political representation. The space crafted by this dual displacement provided the conditions required for staging new subject positions outside the PT/anti-PT antagonistic frontiers, inviting agents to 'identify with new objects and discourses to fill the void made visible' (Howarth, 2013, p. 246).

It is worth mentioning, at this point, that the *Bancada Ativista*'s experience has gained traction in Brazil's present political situation since this paper was written and published. A number of individuals are grouping together to create a new kind of political leadership in Brazil. Inspired by the *Bancada*, over 400 collective candidacies sought to gain a seat in the 2020 elections. Twenty of these were successfully elected and now operate as formal political representative bodies in Brazil. Moreover, as a result of this new electoral process, Erika Hilton, a *Bancada* member, was the first transgender councillor elected in the city of São Paulo and the most voted councillor in Brazil. As such, this paper invites further research to study the proliferation of collective mandates in Brazil, the configuration of new forms of representation derived from them and the new discursive compositions reshaping institutional arrangements conforming to these prefigurative political experiences.

The main findings of paper 3 can be therefore summarised into three main correlated points.

1. The lack of political representation in Brazil, seen in the mass demonstrations since 2013, opened up vital space in the dispute and appearance of new subject positions. While the PT/anti-PT antagonistic frontier has indeed favoured personalist forms of emotional investment and modes of political identification (chiefly centred on the figures of Lula and Bolsonaro), the articulation of the *Bancada Ativista* points to a broader crisis in democratic representation constituted by the limits of personalist forms of political leadership.

2. The discursive exploration of the *Bancada Ativista*'s campaign in 2018 reveals a much broader picture of political dispute in terms of democratic representation in Brazil, raising questions over the central role Bolsonaro has assumed in Brazilian politics. Moreover, this electoral experience displays unsatisfied demands derived from alienating tendencies instilled at the heart of existing forms of democratic representation rather than by the populist and demagogic appeal of charismatic political leaders. This last point provides critical insights into the increasingly notorious 'personalised hypothesis' in political science and populism studies which assumes the crisis of (liberal) democracy to be a consequence of personalism. By studying the candidacy of the *Bancada Ativista*, the explanation constructed in paper 3 suggests that personalism is one of many symptoms deriving from the representational limits in existing forms of democratic representation in Brazil.

3. The scholarly focus on a single aspect of a political and social crisis neglects meaningful elements which provide further layers from which this crisis can be explained and assessed. As such, the literature studying 'personalism' and 'populism' should consider the limits these aspects have in wider social and political dynamics. Moreover, the underlying plurality of elements and relational processes enacting and conforming populist or personalist experiences should be accounted for from a bottom-up perspective, as this bottom-up approach could raise tough questions over the assumptions deriving a top to bottom research scope.

Paper 3: *Hysteria in the squares: Approaching populism from a perspective of desire*

Drawing on the interconnection between political identification and affective investment in social meaning-making processes, the three initial steps of this research project undergo a context-specific expedition of discursive antagonism, political articulation and identity formation. As such, I have made a critical exploration of complex social interactions and political dynamics, presenting the construction of concrete forms of antagonism in Brazil. New insights have emerged from the to-and-fro movement I have engaged in between the context of discovery and the context of justification as well as between empirical and theoretical work throughout all steps of this study. Distinct puzzling features have also appeared, demanding further (de)constructive engagements in articulating putative explanations to the underlying logics sustaining or disrupting social and political regimes and practices.

By focusing on the politics of discourses about populism (Papers 1 and 2) and constructing grassroots interactions that prefigure new forms of political representation (Paper 3), I have drawn on the discourse theory ontological standpoint. By discourse, I do not mean simple words, texts or mere symbolic representations but rather an articulatory practice that links together and modifies elements into relational systems of meaning. The articulation of these elements yields incomplete social systems, which are always marked by their limits (i.e. an outside). Therefore, from a discourse theory standpoint, the very condition of possibility for any social representation depends upon antagonistic relations between competing forces and political projects trying to deal with social reality.

Following these ontological presuppositions and placing the research focus at the frontier of populism studies, my work has aimed to show the political character and the relations of power giving way to concrete historical forms of social representation. This quest has allowed me to explore how contingent forms of meaning are structured through relational dynamics and how such articulatory practices are endowed by the desire to achieve the impossible mediation between representations of society and society as such.

Interestingly enough, a core theoretical puzzle has emerged by drawing on discourse theory populism related insights to study political and social dynamics through a horizon traced beyond the study of populist phenomena in its strictest terms. The exploration of widespread social contestation enacting in the so-called *Journeys of June* in paper 3 has caught my attention and put my research focus on prefigurative forms of political organisation. These Brazilian protests have been analysed against a much broader international scope of political resistance and social uprisings after the 2008 financial downturn. Paper 4 takes the widespread spark of social backdrop seriously and moves from prefigurative forms of political organisation to account theoretically for a desiring stage that prefigures the appearance of social demands.

As seen, DT conceives social meaning as an effect of transference as it arises at the margins of signification, not at its core. Yet, how can we think of meaning-making outside the realm of signification proper? As we know by now, the figure of 'demand' in the work of Ernesto Laclau is assumed as the minimal unit of investigation. However, which logics underly a stage that prefigures the formal appearance of the demand itself? At the heart of this question lies the role desire plays in meaning-making processes, as can be seen in the formal problem-driven question animating the theoretical exploration underlying paper 4:

i.   Can (dis)identification and meaning-making be conceived from a perspective of desire?

Through paper 4, I go back to psychoanalytic theory in order to explore some logics underlying the production of social knowledge from a perspective of desire. I do not intend to discredit or oppose Laclau's oeuvre by doing so. On the contrary, I further explore (dis)identificatory dynamics, which, as I take it, resonate with his ontological presuppositions and theoretical reflections. Indeed, as stated in the extended introduction of this thesis, I believe that Laclau's theory of political identities (reflecting on populism and hegemony) draws on a conception of *the political* (ontological) that circumvents the emotion/reason divide. However, by going back to psychoanalysis, some theoretical elements in Laclau's theory of political identities collapse while others appear.

Among the many theoretical turns undertaken through his return to Freud, Lacan put forward an idea of subjectivity as lack and drew on hysteria as a form of discourse that accounted for knowledge production from a perspective of desire. Through this conception, knowledge comes about not by articulating objectively endowed underrepresented social demands inscribed in the field of (social) signification but animated by a far-reaching embrace of negativity in the radical resistance of being subsumed within such an existing realm. As I see it, these formulations are directed at providing insights into the theory of identity formation.

In this view, demands assume the role of desire-emulators (*faux-semblants*) in striving to conform a radical opposition to the system as a whole as its nature, which is intrinsically lacking, is rendered visible. I regard this as an important point as it brings Gramsci´s thoughts on crisis and Lacan's ideas of lack (and the domain of the *Real*) to mind. As has been noted, these thoughts were whetted by Laclau through his idea of dislocation, from where demands allegedly detach from the dominant social structure, opening up avenues for a social (discursive) reconfiguration.

Where Laclau's scope relied upon the articulation of demands, a psychoanalytic perspective on identity formation focuses, through desire, on processes that prefigure demands which have not yet appeared on the social stage. In this view, demands lose centrality when reflecting upon identity formation and, in consequence, the main analytic energy is then drawn into underlying affective processes related to, at least, two main factors:

a) the place to which these demands are addressed (i.e. where they are supposed to be heard or 'gazed' from);

b) underlying processes of signification building through metonymic and metaphoric functions enacting in the shifting appearance of signifiers.

Thinking about hysteria confronts me with a pre-symbolic stage of collective identity formation brought about by a social dislocation. Of course, all political action relies upon signification processes. However, making desire a central element in the construction of political identities directs the analytic energy into affective narratives and libidinal structures coursing through common and everyday life aspects of collective processes at the micro and meso levels. This seems a breakthrough research endeavour, paving a way ahead, as few discourse theory studies are preoccupied with local-level collective action processes. Examining these aspects in a context-specific manner will allow an analytic engagement with social meaning-making processes mediated by historically constructed libidinal structures. Whereas from a demand-based populist reason strategy, the focus lies in articulating and structuring already given demands, a desire-based approach invites an analytical engagement with the prefigure shaping-processes of social demands from an embracing contingency perspective.

2.3. Reflective essay: populism studies and the research to come

Necessarily partial in nature, every form of contribution derived from a deep and systematic dialogue opens up horizons of meaning instead of perfected avenues of knowledge. By delving into the exploration of puzzling features underlying certain practices and regimes in Brazil, which are closely related to questions of populism, affect and meaning-making, I have touched on meaningful antagonistic aspects configuring the contours of Brazil's political dispute. In so doing, I have constructed plausible (yet limited) explanations of paradigmatic events. The thought-process and rationale behind my four-step approach can be seen in detail through sections 1.3 and 1.4, and the general conclusions derived from this analytical engagement with empirical elements have been formally elaborated through the preceding sections in this chapter.

As contended in the introduction of this thesis, every deconstructive exercise conveys the exploration of aporias within a gesture of totalisation, in which such aporias appear as constitutive and essential components in the formal functioning of such gestures without whose presence the entire system of meaning would simply collapse. A Lacanian-inspired framework adds some flesh to this framework by arguing that the possibility of identity lies in the impossibility of signification proper, since every form of meaning is intrinsically lacking. As such, every form of positive affirmation is at war with itself. In this sense, *de*construction allows one to untangle the exercise of power enacting in the articulation of processes which otherwise seem natural and spontaneous, exhibiting how these have been *politically* installed.

However, the mere act of untangling the tensions within a system of meaning habilitates novel forms of conceiving social reality, for such acts bring to the fore attempts of positive affirmation, which have, thus far, been neglected and repressed. Following Norval (2007), I understand that de*construction* allocates response-ability and decision to the subject in its encounter with constitutive difference (meaning undecidability, in Derridean terms). Let us remember that no act can extinguish the other, for difference (*différance*, for Derrida) and lack (in Lacanian terminology) make signification both an impossible and necessary function. To be sure, to conceive the subject as a subject of responsibility and decision means also to call upon the subject to account for its actions and desires in relation to an other. From this follows a democratic ethos relying upon the awareness of difference and awareness over elements of contingency in the moment of decision and the instalment of a practice or regime, for no act can institute the hegemonic completeness of democracy. To put it in a rather straightforward manner, and by paraphrasing Derrida, democracy is always yet-to-come (*l'avenir*), and the awareness over the other allows for its limited articulation and plausible maintenance and rearticulation. My view about future research on populism takes its bearing through such a deconstructive, discourse-theory-based, ethical stance.

Laclau's work has been hailed by many, and, despite his material departure from this world, he remains, as laid by Butler, 'one of the truly great thinkers in our lifetimes'. His meticulous writing and formal style or reasoning are committed to a reflective and critical stance, one which compels us to engage with the social world by confronting and questioning our own pre-conceptions of what society *is* and *should be*. His work, however, has been interpreted in many different ways. Categories such as *contingency, dislocation, hegemony* and *empty signifier* feature prominently in opinion pieces and stimulate much scholarly work, giving way to manifold analytical turns and slippages conforming with a wide span of discursive repertoires. In essence, such a broad ecology of intellectual production deriving from the Laclaunian discourse theory framework should be welcomed and encouraged, especially given the distinctive anti-objectivist stance which enlivens Laclau's oeuvre. However, the direct application of these apparently immutable principles to social and political dynamics have become frequent by discourse theorists and fellow travellers alike. This is especially so when it comes to the concept of *populism*.

Since the outset of this work, as a means of constructing this thesis' entry point, I addressed the problematic and reified (over)use made by social and political scientists of the concept of populism. As argued, populism, as a category, is widely present in political and social science literature. However, lack of consistency is apparent through most works intending to conceptualise populism, and research implying the importance of populism without making any defining effort has become frequent in and outside populism studies literature. These trends are exacerbated within Brazilian scholarship.

In assuming an agonistic distance with most schools of thought which take populism as a thing as such (and ascribe this thing a central role in contemporary politics), I take my bearings from a literature that reflects upon populism at the frontier of populism studies. This is to say, I gladly position myself at the Essex School and undertake this thesis to be a profoundly Laclaunian effort. Nevertheless, I also reflect critically upon my own intellectual stance.

Increasingly, populism has become a hallmark of supporters and allies of Laclau and Mouffe's legacy. Discourse-inspired analysts devotedly advocate for populist strategies to reshape, usually towards the left, the political agenda. Moreover, Essex-school practitioners constantly develop book-length articles elaborating on what populism is not and how crudely and repetitively intellectual contenders miss the point. Indeed, many Essex-school articles deal with developing a mere discredit or defence of a determinate view about populism, or aim at descriptively verifying the presence of a *chain of equivalence* condensed by a *nodal*, *master* or *empty signifier* to claim the presence of a *populist logic* at work. I believe populism is becoming both a means and an end to research production, and this trend takes its own shape within discourse theory scholarship.

In some of his later reflections about populism, Laclau grounds the political logic of populism at the ontological level. This is evident through his famous and, to many, infamous equivalence made between populism and politics. In one such case, Laclau states:

if populism consists of postulating a radical alternative within the communitarian space, a choice in the crossroads on which the future of a given society hinges, does not populism become synonymous with politics? The answer can only be affirmative (Laclau, 2005b, p. 47).

Such equivalence is also established with the concept of hegemony (see Laclau, 2005a; 2006). Contra standard views, which take such an argument to be too abstract and analytically lacking (Arditi, 2010; Katsambekis and Kioupkiolis, 2019, p. 8; Moffitt, 2016, p. 24), I contend that embracing Laclau's argument that all politics are hegemonic struggles based on the logic of populism is vital for the fruition of the profoundly critical and analytical commitments underlying his work. I believe the objective here is set in rather explicit terms: the ultimate analytic stake lies in untangling, explaining and taking issue with articulatory practices and meaning-making processes in the political dispute and instalment of social life. Inscribing populism at the ontological level points at the need to reflect critically about the political disputes over the construction of a communitarian space so as to grasp and to engage in relations of power. I previously stated that such an equivalence circumvents the emotion/reason divide and, as such, I now argue that it dissolves any immutable difference established between populist and non-populist subjects. Every discursive division between emotions and reason, populist and non-populist actors, should be studied as an attempt of political exclusion. The turn from studying populist discourse to closely explaining the politics of discourses about populism commits to such a deconstructive, discursive style of reasoning.

In so far as populism becomes a central discursive element in the antagonistic construction of political reality, the study of populism, as a signifier, becomes a central endeavour for untangling the discoursive operations through which the social space is being installed or contested. However, one must carefully reflect on how central the signifier populism actually is within social spaces of signification, for the will to explore the meaning of populism, above other discursive elements and operations, might distract the analyst from grasping more dominant logics and meaning-making processes reconfiguring political struggle and social representation processes.

Like many practitioners, commentators, politicians and journalists that today exhibit an overinvestment in the words populism and populist, structuring concrete fantasmatic narratives of social enjoinment, discourse theorists, in our own way, display an affective investment with representational constructions of social reality via populism discourses. However, few self-reflections critically draw on discourse theory, fantasmatic narratives of society, and the representational role populism plays in terms of enjoinment and loss in social, scholarly, and political discursive representations within discourse theory's academic and political circles. Might we be privileging populism discourses above other more salient discursive operations and articulatory practices?

Critically reflecting on the analytical and strategic limits of populism as a logic vis-à-vis contemporary social and political process and its usefulness in studying social phenomena overseen by the populist studies literature will instigate novel insights to appear and enrich discourse theory debates. This may also promote a more analytic and less descriptive intellectual stance, formulating more acute and perceptive explanatory insights into distinctive modes of political antagonism in a much more situated fashion. Ultimately, such self-critical engagements will habilitate novel emancipatory horizons, pointing at new possible articulations to be thought theoretically and empirically to engage in a more decisive way with contemporary political processes that are reshaping the contours of the research (and the society) to come.

3. References

A Manhã. (1949). Máscara para Esconder a Verdadeira Face, 5 August 1949. http://memoria.bn.br/docreader/116408/42786 [accessed 07/09/2021].

Alcantara, E. (2016). Legal versus ilegal, *Veja*, 09 March 2016, Pag. 36, https://veja.abril.com.br/acervo/#/edition/2468?page=36&section=1 [accessed 09 July 2021].

Almeida, E. M. (2019). O papel do Supremo Tribunal Federal no Impeachment da presidente Dilma Rousseff. *DESC-Direito, Economia e Sociedade Contemporânea, 2*(1), 52-75.

Almeida, R. (2018). Deuses do parlamento: os impedimentos de Dilma [Gods of parliament: Dilma's impediments]. In: Almeida, R, Toniol, R (eds) *Conservadorismos, fascismos e fundamentalismos* [Conservatism, Fascism and Fundamentalism]. Campinas: Editora Unicamp, 163–193.

Alonso, A. (2017). A Política das Ruas: Protestos em São Paulo de Dilma a Temer. *Novos Estudos CEBRAP Volume Dinâmicas da Crise* [Dynamics of the Crisis]. 23–40.

Altheide, D. L., & Schneider, C. J. (2012). *Qualitative media analysis* (Vol. 38). Sage Publications.

Alvarenga, B. (2016). No limite da imprudencia, *Veja*, 10 February 2016, pag. 78, https://veja.abril.com.br/acervo/#/edition/2464?page=78&section=1 [accessed 07/09/2021].

Alvarenga, B. (2017). Um sinal de luz, *Veja*, 15 March 2017, p. 61, https://veja.abril.com.br/acervo/#/edition/2521?page=60&section=1 [accessed 07/09/2021].

Alvarenga, B. (2018). Da para cumprir?, *Veja*, 17 October 2018, p. 47, https://veja.abril.com.br/acervo/#/edition/2604?page=46&section=1 [accessed 07/09/2021].

Anderson, P. (2019). Bolsonaro's Brazil. *London Review of Books* 41(3): 11–22.

Anderson, P. (1976). The Antinomies of Antonio Gramsci, *New Left Review*.

Anthony, G. (1984). *The constitution of society: Outline of the theory of structuration*. University of California Press.

Arditi, B. (2010). Review essay: populism is hegemony is politics? On Ernesto Laclau's on populist reason. *Constellations*, *17*(3), 488-497.

Avritzer, L., & Rennó, L. (2021). The Pandemic and the Crisis of Democracy in Brazil. *Journal of Politics in Latin America*. https://doi.org/10.1177/1866802X211022362

Balibar, É. (2007). Chapter Three. Constructions And Deconstructions Of The Universal. In *Recognition, Work, Politics* (pp. 47-69). Brill.

Balibar, É. (2010) Europe: Final crisis? Some theses. *Theory & Event* 13(2). https://muse.jhu.edu/article/384016, accessed 25 June 2020.

Barrett, M. (1991). *The politics of truth: From Marx to Foucault*. Polity Press.

Benetti, M. (2016). A ironia como estratégia discursiva da revista Veja. *LÍBERO*, (20), 37-46.

Benevides, M. V. (1981). *A UDN e o udenismo: ambiguidades do liberalismo brasileiro (1945-1965)*. Rio de Janeiro: Paz e Terra.

Benevides, M. V. (1986). Ai que saudade do MDB! *Lua Nova: Revista de Cultura e Política* 3 (1): 27–34. https://doi.org/10.1590/S0102-64451986000200006.

Berz, J. (2020). All the prime minister's glory? Leader effects and accountability of prime ministers in parliamentary elections. *Politics*, *40*(4): 444–459.

Bevir, M., & Rhodes, R. A. (2005). Interpretation and its others. *Australian Journal of Political Science*, *40*(2), 169-187.

Bhaskar, R., Collier, A., Lawson, T., & Norrie, A. (1998). Critical realism. In *Proceedings of the Standing Conference on Realism and Human Sciences, Bristol, UK* (Vol. 4).

Biglieri, P, and Perelló, G. (2019) Populism. In: Y. Stavrakakis, S. Frosh, L. Layton and D. Nobus (eds) *Routledge Handbook of Psychoanalytic Political Theory*. Abingdon: Routledge, pp. 330–40.

Blee, K. M., & Taylor, V. (2002). Semi-structured interviewing in social movement research. *Methods of social movement research*, *16*, 92-117.

Borges A. The Illusion of Electoral Stability: From Party System Erosion to Right-Wing Populism in Brazil. *Journal of Politics in Latin America*. 2021;13(2):166-191. doi:10.1177/1866802X211005164

Borges, L. (2018). Triplo cardapio, *Veja*, 7 November 2018, p. 45, https://veja.abril.com.br/acervo/#/edition/2607?page=44&section=1 [accessed 07/09/2021].

Bosi, L., & Reiter, H. (2014). Historical Methodologies. *Methodological practices in social movement research*, 117-43.

Bracher, M. (2018). *Lacan, discourse, and social change*. Cornell University Press.

Bronzatto, T. (2016). Fazendo historia, *Veja*, 20 April 2016, p. 67, https://veja.abril.com.br/acervo/#/edition/2474?page=67&section=1 accessed 09 July 2021.

Bronzatto, T. (2018). Vies autoritario, *Veja*, 11 April 2018, p. 93-95 https://veja.abril.com.br/acervo/#/edition/2577?page=72&section=1 [accessed 07/09/2021].

Brown, K., & Mondon, A. (2021). Populism, the media, and the mainstreaming of the far right: The Guardian's coverage of populism as a case study. *Politics*, *41*(3), 279-295.

Butler, J., Laclau, E., Žižek, S., & Žižek, S. (2000). *Contingency, hegemony, universality: Contemporary dialogues on the left*. Verso.

Cammaerts, B. (2018). The mainstreaming of extreme right-wing populism in the Low Countries: what is to be done?. *Communication Culture & Critique*, *11*(1), 7-20.

Cannon, B. (2018). Must we talk about populism? Interrogating populism's conceptual utility in a context of crisis. *New Political Science*, *40*(3), 477-496.

Canovan, M. (1999) Trust the people! Populism and the two faces of democracy. *Political Studies, 47*(1): 2–16.

Canovan, M. (2002) Taking politics to the people: Populism as the ideology of democracy. In: Y. Mény and Y. Surel (eds) *Democracies and the Populist Challenge*. London: Palgrave Macmillan, pp. 22–44.

Cardoso, F. H. (1962). Proletariado no Brasil: situação e comportamento social. *Revista Brasiliense* 41: 98-122.

Cardoso, F. H. (1976). Populismo: Uma Crise no Estado. *Cadernos de Debate* (1): 35-40.

Cardoso, F. H. (1977). Intervenção de Fernando Henrique Cardoso. In *Atas do Simpósio A Luta pela Democracia*, 18 June 1977. Mimeographed. Brasília: MDB.

Cardoso, F. H. (1985). A trajetória de um intelectual. In: *Revista Leia*. São Paulo, November 1985: 29-33.

Cardoso, F. H. (2010). O sociólogo e o político. Interview by Sérgio Fausto and Bernardo Sorj. In *Democracia, crise e reforma: estudos sobre a era Fernando Henrique Cardoso*. São Paulo: Paz e Terra, 29-60.

Carpentier, N., & De Cleen, B. (2007). Bringing discourse theory into media studies: The applicability of discourse theoretical analysis (DTA) for the study of media practises and discourses. *Journal of Language and Politics, 6*(2): 265–293.

Carpentier, N. (2020). Communicating Academic Knowledge Beyond the Written Academic Text: An Auto-Ethnographic Analysis of the Mirror Palace of Democracy Installation Experiment. *International Journal of Communication, 14*, 24.

Cely, A. and Mantilla, A. (2016) Left populism and taking back democracy: A conversation with Chantal Mouffe, 21 March. http://www.versobooks.com/blogs/2566-left-populism-and-taking-back-democracy-a-conversation-with-chantal-mouffe, [accessed 07/09/2021].

Chang, W. Y., & Glynos, J. (2011). Ideology and politics in the popular press: The case of the 2009 UK MPs' expenses scandal. In *Discourse theory and critical media politics* (pp. 106-127). Palgrave Macmillan, London.

Chauí, M. (2013). O inferno urbano e a política do favor, tutela e cooptação [Urban hell and the policy of favour, guardianship and co-optation]. *Teoria e Debate*, June. Available at: https://www.viomundo.com.br [accessed 07/09/2021].

Chicarino, T. (2020). A revista Veja e a produção de escândalos políticos (1985-2016). *Tese de Doutorado PUC-SP*.

Chicarino, T. S., Segurado, R., & Ronderos, S. (2021). Impeachment! Em nome do povo: uma análise discursiva da revista Veja nos governos Collor e Rousseff. *Mediapolis– Revista de Comunicação, Jornalismo e Espaço Público*, (12), 141-156.

Chicarino, T., & Ronderos, S. (2019). Entre a eliminação e o dissenso: soberanismo bolsonarista contra o ethos democrático. *Ponto-e-Vírgula: Revista de Ciências Sociais*, (26), 91-108.

Copjec, J. (2015) Read my Desire: Lacan Against the Historicists. London: Verso.

Costa, A. C. (2018). Há um risco claro, *Veja*, 31 October 2018, p. 46, https://veja.abril.com.br/acervo/#/edition/2606?page=46&section=1 [accessed 07/09/2021].

Cravo, T. A. (2019). The 2018 Brazilian elections and the global challenge to democracy. *Global Affairs*, 5(1): 1–4.

Critchley, S., & Marchart, O. eds. (2004). *Laclau: A Critical Reader*, London: Palgrave.

da Nobrega, M. (2015). Como o PT travou o crescimento do Brasil, *Veja*, 12 August 2015, p. 24, https://veja.abril.com.br/acervo/#/edition/2438?page=24&section=1&word=2438 [accessed 07/09/2021].

da Nobrega, M. (2016a). O PT mudou o Brasil?, *Veja*, 20 January 2016, p. 20, https://veja.abril.com.br/acervo/#/edition/2461?page=20&section=1 [accessed 07/09/2021].

da Nobrega, M. (2016b). Sem espaco para guinada, *Veja*, 09 March 2016, Pag. 24, https://veja.abril.com.br/acervo/#/edition/2468?page=24&section=1 [accessed 07/09/2021].

Dalton, R. J., & Wattenberg, M. P. (2000). *Parties without Partisans: Political Change in Advanced Industrial Democracies.* Oxford: Oxford University Press.

De Cleen, B., & Stavrakakis, Y. (2017). Distinctions and articulations: A discourse theoretical framework for the study of populism and nationalism. *Javnost – The Public, 24*(4): 301–319.

De Cleen, B., & Glynos, J. (2021). Beyond populism studies. *Journal of Language and Politics, 20*(1), 178-195.

De Cleen, B., Glynos, J., & Mondon, A. (2018). Critical research on populism: Nine rules of engagement. *Organization, 25*(5), 649-661.

De Cleen, B., Goyvaerts, J., Carpentier, N., Glynos, J., & Stavrakakis, Y. (2021). Moving discourse theory forward: A five-track proposal for future research. *Journal of Language and Politics, 20*(1), 22-46.

De Cleen, B., Moffitt, B., Panayotu, P., & Stavrakakis, Y. (2020). The potentials and difficulties of transnational populism: the case of the Democracy in Europe Movement 2025 (DiEM25). *Political Studies, 68*(1), 146-166.

de la Torre, C. (2000). *Populist Seduction in Latin America: The Ecuadorian Experience.* Athens, OH: Ohio University Center for International Studies.

Dean, J., & Maiguashca, B. (2020). Did somebody say populism? Towards a renewal and reorientation of populism studies. *Journal of Political Ideologies, 25*(1), 11-27.

della Porta, D., & Diani, M. (1999). *Social Movements: An Introduction.* Oxford: Blackwell.

della Porta, D., & Mattoni, A. (2014). *Spreading Protest, Social Movements in Times of Crisis*. Colchester: ECPR Press.

Diário da Noite. (1949a). Reconstituição da Histórica Palestra Milton Campos-Dutra no Salão de Despachos do Rio Negro. *Diário da Noite*, 21 March 1949. http://memoria.bn.br/docreader/221961_02/50101;http://memoria.bn.br/docreader/221961_02 /50106 [accessed 07/09/2021].

Diário da Noite. (1949b). Integralistas e Ademaristas Brigam Pelo "Populismo". *Diário Da Noite*, 7 July 1949, 2 edition. http://memoria.bn.br/docreader/221961_02/52294 [accessed 07/09/2021].

Diário da Noite. (1949c). Ademar Denuncia Uma Terceira Ofensiva Contra São Paulo, 13 May 1949, 2 edition. http://memoria.bn.br/docreader/221961_02/51146 [accessed 07/09/2021].

Diário de Notícias. (1949a). Teoria e Prática do Populismo Demagógico, 21 May 1949. http://memoria.bn.br/docreader/093718_02/45408 [accessed 07/09/2021].

Diário de Notícias. (1949d). 'Teoria e Prática do Populismo Demagógico', 22 May 1949. http://memoria.bn.br/docreader/093718_02/45421 [accessed 07/09/2021].

Eklundh, E. (2019). *Emotions, protest, democracy: Collective identities in contemporary Spain*. Routledge.

Eklundh, E. (2020). Excluding emotions: The performative function of populism. *Partecipazione e conflitto*, *13*(1), 107-131.

Elster, J. (1989). *The cement of society: A survey of social order*. Cambridge university press.

Fairclough, N. (2003). *Analyzing Discourse: Textual Analysis for Social Research*. London: Psychology Press.

Feher-Gurewich, J. (1996) Toward a new alliance between psychoanalysis and social theory. In: D. Pettigrew and F. Raffoul (eds) *Disseminating Lacan*. Albany: SUNY Press, pp. 151–70.

Femia, J. V. (1983). Gramsci's patrimony. *British Journal of Political Science*, *13*(3), 327-364.

Fernandes, S. (2017). O fim da ometra, *Veja*, 13 September 2017 p. 42 https://veja.abril.com.br/acervo/#/edition/2547?page=42&section=1 [accessed 07/09/2021].

Fink, B. (1997). *The Lacanian subject: Between language and jouissance*. Princeton University Press.

Fink, B. (2004). *Lacan to the Letter: Reading Écrits Closely.* Minneapolis: University of Minnesota Press.

Fleischer, D. (2007). A composição e o funcionamento das coligações no Brasil [The composition and functioning of coalitions in Brazil]. In: Avelar, L, Cintra, AO (eds) *Sistema político brasileiro: uma introdução* [Brazilian Political System: An Introduction], 3rd edn. Rio de Janeiro: Konrad Adenauer Stiftung, 303–348.

Flesher, F. C. (2014). *Social Movements and Globalization: How Protests, Occupations and Uprisings Are Changing the World*. London: Macmillan International Higher Education.

Folha de S. Paulo. (2006). Lula é o Adhemar de Barros do momento, afirma Weffort, 10. https://www1.folha.uol.com.br/fsp/brasil/fc1009200609.htm [accessed 07/09/2021].

Fotaki, M. and Harding, N. (2013) Lacan and sexual difference in organization and management theory: Towards a hysterical academy? Organization 20(2): 153–72.

Foucault, M. (1970). *The Order of Things: An Archeology of the Human Sciences*. New York: Random House.

Freeden, M. (2017). After the Brexit referendum: Revisiting populism as an ideology. *Journal of Political Ideologies, 22*(1): 1–11.

Freud, S. (1905/1953) *Fragment of an Analysis of a Case of Hysteria*. Standard Edition 7. London: Hogarth Press, pp. 1–122.

Freud, S. (1921/1955) *Group Psychology and the Analysis of the Ego*. Standard Edition 18. London: Hogarth Press, pp. 1–64.

Freud, S. (2014/1899). *On narcissism: an introduction*. Read Books Ltd.

Freud, S., & Breuer, J. (1895/1995) *Studies on Hysteria*. Standard Edition 2. London: Hogarth Press, pp. 1–335.

Fukuyama, F. (1992) *The End of History and the Last Man*. London: H. Hamilton.

Fuks, M., Ribeiro, E., Borba, J (2021) From antipetismo to generalized antipartisanship: the impact of rejection of political parties on the 2018 vote for Bolsonaro. *Brazilian Political Science Review* 15(1): 1–28.doi:10.1590/1981-3821202100010003

Garzia, D. (2019). *Personalization of Politics and Electoral Change*. New York: Springer.

Gazeta de Notícias. (1949). Populismo... Jogo do Bicho..., 5 November 1949, sec. Comentário do Dia. http://memoria.bn.br/docreader/103730_07/43581 [accessed 07/09/2021].

Geras, N. (1990). *Discourses of Extremity: Radical Ethics and Post-Marxist Extravagances*. London: Verso.

Gerbaudo, P. (2017) *The Mask and the Flag: Populism, Citizenism and Global Protest*. London: Hurst Publishers.

Gerbaudo, P. (2018). Social media and populism: an elective affinity?. *Media, Culture & Society, 40*(5), 745-753.

Giddens, A. (1984). *The Constitution of Society: Outline of the Theory of Structuration*. Berkeley: University of California Press.

Giraldo, M. (2017). Grant me the knowledge of what I want because all I know is that I want: A Lacanian view of hysteria. *Psychoanalytic Inquiry, 37*(2): 95–101.

Glynos, J., & Howarth, D. (2007). *Logics of Critical Explanation in Social and Political Theory*. Abingdon: Routledge.

Glynos, J. (2001). The grip of ideology: a Lacanian approach to the theory of ideology. *Journal of political ideologies*, *6*(2), 191-214.

Glynos, J. (2008). Ideological fantasy at work. *Journal of political Ideologies*, *13*(3), 275-296.

Glynos, J. (2021). Critical fantasy studies. *Journal of Language and Politics*, *20*(1), 95-111.

Glynos, J., & Howarth, D. (2018). The Retroductive Cycle: The research process in poststructuralist discourse analysis, in Marttila, T. (ed.) (2018) *Discourse, Culture and Organization: Inquiries into Relational Structures of Power*, London: Palgrave

Glynos, J., & Mondon, A. (2016). The Political Logic of Populist Hype: The Case of Right-Wing Populism's 'Meteoric Rise'and Its Relation to the Status Quo'. *POPULISMUS Working Paper Series*.

Glynos, J., & Stavrakakis, Y. (2008). Lacan and political subjectivity: Fantasy and enjoyment in psychoanalysis and political theory. *Subjectivity*, *24*(1), 256-274.

Glynos, J., & Stavrakakis, Y. (Eds.). (2018). *Lacan and science*. Routledge.

Glynos, J., & Voutyras, S. (2016). Ideology as blocked mourning: Greek national identity in times of economic crisis and austerity. *Journal of political ideologies*, *21*(3), 201-224.

Glynos, J., Howarth, D., Flitcroft, R., Love, C., Roussos, K., & Vazquez, J. (2021). Logics, discourse theory and methods: Advances, challenges and ways forward. *Journal of Language and Politics*, *20*(1), 62-78.

Glynos, J., Howarth, D., Norval, A., & Speed, E. (2009). Discourse analysis: Varieties and methods.

Goyvaerts, J., & De Cleen, B. (2020). Media, Anti-Populist Discourse and the Dynamics of the Populism Debate. In *Perspectives on Populism and the Media* (pp. 83-108). Nomos Verlagsgesellschaft mbH & Co. KG.

Gramsci, A. (1971). *Selections from the Prison Notebooks.* Edited and translated by Q. Hoare and G. Nowell-Smith. London: Lawrence and Wishart.

Gramsci, Antonio. (1996). *Prison Notebooks*. Vol. 2, Notebooks 3, 4 and 5. Edited by Joseph A. Buttigieg. New York: Columbia University Press.

Groppo, A. (2010). *The Two Princes: Juan D. Perón and Getulio Vargas: A Comparative Study of Latin American Populism.* Eduvim.

Gryzinski, V. (2021). A direita pos-Trump, *Veja*, 24 February 2021, p. 53. https://veja.abril.com.br/acervo/#/edition/186694?page=52&section=1 [accessed 07/09/2021].

Gryzinski, V. (2016a). ''nos'' contra ''eles'', *Veja*, 20 July 2016, p.73, https://veja.abril.com.br/acervo/#/edition/2487?page=73&section=1 [accessed 07/09/2021].

Gryzinsky, V. (2016b). Fim da era do consenso, *Veja*, 12 October 2016, p. 46, https://veja.abril.com.br/acervo/#/edition/2499?page=46&section=1 [accessed 07/09/2021].

Guandalini, G. (2016). Macri tem pressa, *Veja*, 16 March 2016, p. 60 https://veja.abril.com.br/acervo/#/edition/2469?page=60&section=1 [accessed 07/09/2021].

Guandalini, G. (2017a). A miopia de Davos, *Veja*, 25 January 2017, p, 71, https://veja.abril.com.br/acervo/#/edition/2514?page=70&section=1 [accessed 07/09/2021].

Guandalini, G. (2017b). A crise e os novos pobres, *Veja*, 22 February 2017 p.69, https://veja.abril.com.br/acervo/#/edition/2518?page=68&section=1 [accessed 07/09/2021].

Guandalini, G. (2017c). Eles não estão nem ai, *Veja*, 19 July 2017, p.67, https://veja.abril.com.br/acervo/#/edition/2539?page=66&section=1 [accessed 07/09/2021].

Gurewich, J. F., Tort, M., & Fairfield, S. (1996). The subject and the self: Lacan and American psychoanalysis.

Hall, S. (1991). Postscript: Gramsci and us. *Gramsci's political thought: An introduction*, 114-130.

Hofstadter, R. (1955). *The age of reform: From Bryan to FDR* (Vol. 95). Vintage.

Howarth, D. (2000). *Discourse. Concepts in the Social Sciences*. Buckingham: Open University.

Howarth, D. (2013). *Poststructuralism and After*. London: Palgrave Macmillan.

Howarth, D., & Stavrakakis, Y. (2000). Introducing discourse theory and political analysis. In: Howarth, D, Norval, AJ, Stavrakakis, Y (eds) Discourse Theory and Political Analysis: Identities, Hegemonies and Social Change. Manchester: University Press, p.11.

Howarth, D. (2004). Hegemony, political subjectivity, and radical democracy. In *Laclau: A Critical Reader,* Routledge (pp. 266-288).

Hunter, W., & Power, T. J. (2019). Bolsonaro and Brazil's illiberal backlash. *Journal of Democracy*, *30*(1), 68-82.

Jäger, A. (2017). The semantic drift: Images of populism in post-war American historiography and their relevance for (European) political science. *Constellations*, *24*(3), 310-323.

Jaguaribe, H. (1954/2013). Que é ademarismo?. In *Estudos Filosóficos e Políticos*, 287–304. Brasília: Fundação Alexandre de Gusmão.

Jørgensen, M. W., & Phillips, L. J. (2002). *Discourse analysis as theory and method*. Sage.

Junior, P. (2017). Temer, o reformista, *Veja*, 15 March 2017, p.65, https://veja.abril.com.br/acervo/#/edition/2521?page=64&section=1 accessed 09 July 2021.

Kaltwasser, C. (2019). La (sobre) adaptación programática de la derecha chilena y la irrupción de la derecha populista radical. *Colombia Internacional*, (99), 29-61.

Katsambekis, G., & Kioupkiolis, A. (Eds.). (2019). *The populist radical left in Europe* (Vol. 1). Routledge.

Kautsky, K. (1909). *The Road to Power*, trans. AM Simmonds. Chicago: Black.

Knight, A. (1998) Populism and neo-populism in Latin America, especially Mexico. *Journal of Latin American Studies, 30*(2): 223–48.

Kramer, D. (2017). Gato por lebre, *Veja*, 26 April 2017, p. 63, https://veja.abril.com.br/acervo/#/edition/2527?page=63&section=1 accessed 09 July 2021.

Krasny, E. (2020). HYSTERIA ACTIVISM. *Performing Hysteria*, 125.

Lacan, J. (1949). *The mirror stage as formative of the I function as revealed in psychoanalytic experience.* In *Écrits* Edited by: Fink, B. 75–81. New York: W. W. Norton & Company.

Lacan, J. (1991). *The Ego in Freud's Theory and in the Technique of Psychoanalysis, 1954-1955* (Vol. 2). WW Norton & Company.

Lacan, J. (1993). The Seminar of Jacques Lacan: Book III: The Psychoses. Edited by J.-A. Miller, Translated with notes by R. Grigg. London: W.W. Norton & Company.

Lacan, J. (2001) *Ecrits: A Selection.* Translated by A. Sheridan. Abingdon: Routledge.

Lacan, J. (2007) *The Other Side of Psychoanalysis: The Seminar of Jacques Lacan, Book XVII.* Translated by R. Grigg. London: W.W. Norton & Company.

Lacan, J. (2014). *Anxiety: The Seminar of Jacques Lacan, Book X.* Edited by J.-A. Miller. Translated by A. Price. Cambridge, UK: Polity Press.

Lacan, J., & Miller, J. A. (2013). *The psychoses: the seminar of Jacques Lacan.* Routledge.

Laclau, E. (1977). Politics and Ideology in Marxist Theory: Capitalism. *Fascism, Populism.*

Laclau, E. (1990). *New Reflections on the Revolution of Our Time*, London: Verso.

Laclau, E. (1991). Intellectual Strategies: Memorandum to PhD Students in the IDA Programme. *University of Essex*, https://tinyurl.com/laclau-phd-recommendations.

Laclau, E. (1993). Power and Representation. I Politics, Theory, and Contemporary Culture, red. M. Poster.

Laclau, E. (1996). *Emancipation(s)*. Verso.

Laclau, E. (1997). The death and resurrection of the theory of ideology. *Mln, 112*(3), 297-321.

Laclau, E. (2004). Glimpsing the Future. In S. Critchley, & Marchart, O. (Eds.), *Laclau: A Critical Reader* (pp. 279-328). London and New York Routledge.

Laclau, E. (2005a). *On Populist Reason*. London: Verso.

Laclau, E. (2005b). Populism: What's in a Name?. *Populism and the Mirror of Democracy, 48*.

Laclau, E. (2006). Why constructing a people is the main task of radical politics. *Critical inquiry, 32*(4), 646-680.

Laclau, E. (2014). *The rhetorical foundations of society*. Verso Trade.

Laclau, E., & Mouffe, C. (1985/2001). *Hegemony and Socialist Strategy*. London: Verso.

Lafer, C. (1970). *The Planning Process and the Political System in Brazil: A Study of Kubitschek's Target Plan (1956-1961)*. PhD Thesis. Cornell University.

Lafer, C. (1975). *O Sistema Político Brasileiro*. São Paulo: Perspectiva.

Lenin V. I. (1967). *What is to be done?* Trans. J. Fineberg and G. Hanna. London: Lawrence and Wishart.

Limongi, F., & Guarnieri, F. (2014). *A base e os partidos. As eleições presidenciais no Brasil pós-redemocratização* [The Base and the Parties. Presidential Elections in Brazil after Redemocratization]. São Paulo: Novos Estudos CEBRAP.

Luxemburg, R. (1985). *The mass strike, the political party and the trade unions.* Marxian Education Society.

Mair, P. (2013). *Ruling the Void: The Hollowing of Western Democracy.* New York: Verso Trade.

Mair, P, Müller, WC., & Plasser, F (eds). (2004). *Political Parties and Electoral Change: Party Responses to Electoral Markets.* London: SAGE Publishing.

Marchart, O. (2018). *Thinking Antagonism: Political Ontology after Laclau.* Edinburgh: Edinburgh University Press.

Marcus, G. (1995). Ethnography in/of the World System: The Emergence of Multi-Sited Ethnography. *Annual Review of Anthropology* 24: 95-117.

Marx, K. (1859). Preface to a Contribution to the Critique of Political Economy. *The Marx-Engels Reader*, 2, 3-6.

Marx, K., & Engels, F. (1845/1965). *The German Ideology.* London.

Marx, K. (1847/1976). The Poverty of Philosophy. In *Marx and Engels Collected Works*, 6:105–212. London: Lawrence & Wishart.

Marx, K. (1852/1979). The Eighteenth Brumaire of Louis Bonaparte. In *Marx and Engels Collected Works*, 11:99–197. London: Lawrence & Wishart. https://tinyurl.com/marxengels-11.

McAllister, I. (2007). The personalization of politics. In: Dalton, RJ, Klingemann, H-D (eds) *The Oxford Handbook of Political Behavior.* Oxford: Oxford University Press, pp.571–588.

McCombs, M., & Valenzuela, S. (2020). *Setting the agenda: Mass media and public opinion.* John Wiley & Sons.

Meirelles, H. (2017a). a posição populista, *Veja*, 30 August 2017, p.48, https://veja.abril.com.br/acervo/#/edition/2545?page=48&section=1 [accessed 07/09/2021].

Meirelles, H. (2017b). Sou presidenciavel, *Veja*, 08 November 2017, p.42, https://veja.abril.com.br/acervo/#/edition/2555?page=42&section=1 [accessed 07/09/2021].

Mills, A., & Mills, J. (2018). Archival research. In *The sage handbook of qualitative business and management research methods* (pp. 32-45). SAGE Publications Ltd, https://www.doi.org/10.4135/9781526430236

Moffit, B. (2016). *The Global Rise of Populism*. Stanford: Stanford University Press.

Moffitt, B., & Tormey, S. (2014). Rethinking populism: Politics, mediatization and political style. *Political Studies* 62(2): 381–97.

Molica, F. (2018). A dimensão histórica da derrotada, *Veja*, 11 April 2018, p 71, https://veja.abril.com.br/acervo/#/edition/2577?page=70&section=1 [accessed 07/09/2021].

Motta, R. (1993). O MDB e os intelectuais. *Varia História* 12: 104-113.

Motta, R. (1996). A formação do MDB e a influência do quadro partidário anterior. *Revista de Sociologia e Política* 6: 201-212.

Mouffe, C. (1979). *Gramsci and Marxist Theory*. Routledge & Kegan Paul.

Mouffe, C. (2005) *The Return of the Political*. London: Verso.

Mouffe, C. (2018) *For a Left Populism*. London: Verso.

Mouzelis, N. (1990). *Post-Marxist Alternatives: The Construction of Social Orders*. Basingstoke: Macmillan. https://doi.org/10.1007/978-1-349-12978-2

Mudde, C (2007). *Populist Radical Right Parties in Europe*. Cambridge University Press.

Mudde, C. (2004) The populist zeitgeist. *Government and Opposition* 39(4): 541–63.

Mudde, C. (2019). *The far right today*. John Wiley & Sons.

Mudde, C., & Kaltwasser, C. R. (2011). *Voices of the peoples: Populism in Europe and Latin America compared*. South Bend, Indiana: Helen Kellogg Institute for International Studies.

Mughan, A. (2000). *Media and the Presidentialization of Parliamentary Elections*. New York: Springer.

Müller, J. W. (2016). *What is populism?*. University of Pennsylvania Press.

Nicolau, J. M. (2011). *Sistemais eleitorais* [Electoral Systems]. Rio de Janeiro: Fundação Getúlio Vargas.

Nikisianis, N., Siomos, T., Stavrakakis, Y., Markou, G., & Dimitroulia, T. (2019). Populism versus anti-populism in the Greek press: Post-structuralist discourse theory meets corpus linguistics. In *Discourse, Culture and Organization* (pp. 267-295). Palgrave Macmillan, Cham.

Norval, A. (2004). Hegemony after deconstruction: the consequences of undecidability, *Journal of Political Ideologies*, 9:2, 139-157, DOI: 10.1080/1356931041000169187

O Cruzeiro. (1949). O Cidadão Eurico Dutra, 26 March 1949. http://memoria.bn.br/docreader/003581/63585 [accessed 07/09/2021].

O Estado de S. Paulo. (1946). Partido de Representação Popular, 26 October 1946. https://tinyurl.com/estadao-19461026 [accessed 07/09/2021].

O Estado de S. Paulo. (1950). Elites e Populismo, November 14 1950. http://tinyurl.com/estadao-19501114 [accessed 07/09/2021].

O Estado de S. Paulo. (1958). A Linha Popular da UDN, 10 January 1958, sec. Espaço Publicitário da UDN. http://tinyurl.com/estadao-01101958 [accessed 07/09/2021].

O Jornal. (1946). A Batalha Carioca, 20 December 1946. http://memoria.bn.br/docreader/110523_04/36549 [accessed 07/09/2021].

O Jornal. (1947). Interessado o Governo na Reabilitação Comercial do Zebú, 1 October 1947, 2 edition. http://memoria.bn.br/docreader/110523_04/36863 [accessed 07/09/2021].

O Jornal. (1949a). Quase Certa a Candidatura Vargas, 6 June 1949. http://memoria.bn.br/docreader/110523_04/49277 [accessed 07/09/2021].

O Jornal. (1949b). Coordenação Partidária ou Perigo para o Regime, 16 February 1949. http://memoria.bn.br/docreader/110523_04/47662 [accessed 07/09/2021].

O Jornal. (1949c). A Solidariedade Democrática, 26 February 1949. http://memoria.bn.br/docreader/110523_04/47821 [accessed 07/09/2021].

O Jornal. (1949d). Candidato do PSD Mineiro ou Candidato Extra-Partidário, 29 September 1949. http://memoria.bn.br/docreader/110523_04/51296.

O Jornal. (1958). Regime: os primeiros sinais de maturidade, 5 July 1958. http://memoria.bn.br/docreader/110523_05/64471 [accessed 07/09/2021].

O Jornal. (1960). Liderança pessedista em 61 vai passar às mãos de JK: o sentido do retôrno, 24 August 1960. http://memoria.bn.br/docreader/110523_06/6354 [accessed 07/09/2021].

O Jornal. (1963). Esta é a notícia, 20 July 1963. http://memoria.bn.br/docreader/110523_06/28968 [accessed 07/09/2021].

Padoan, E. (2016). A Latin Americanization of southern Europe? A typology of antineoliberal turns in dualized societies. *Paper presented at the Conference of the European Consortium for Political Research*, Trento, Italy, June 16–18.

Padua, L. (2017). Da para ser optimista, *Veja*, 13 September 2017, p. 72-73, https://veja.abril.com.br/acervo/#/edition/2547?page=72&section=1 accessed 09 July 2021.

Paduani, R. (2018). Luz no fim do tunel, *Veja*, 14 November 2018, p. 17-19, https://veja.abril.com.br/acervo/#/edition/2608?page=17&section=1&word=James [accessed 07/09/2021].

Panizza, F., & Miorelli, R. (2013). Taking discourse seriously: Discursive institutionalism and poststructuralist discourse theory. *Political Studies, 61*(2): 301–318.

Pequeno Dicionário Brasileiro da Língua Portuguesa. (1951/1957). 'Populista', 971. Edited by Hildebrando de Lima and Gustavo Barroso, 9th ed. Rio de Janeiro: Civilização Brasileira.

Pequeno Dicionário Brasileiro da Língua Portuguesa. (1961a). 'Populismo', 955. Edited by Aurélio Buarque de Hollanda. Rio de Janeiro: Civilização Brasileira.

Pequeno Dicionário Brasileiro da Língua Portuguesa. (1961b). 'Populista'. In *Pequeno Dicionário Brasileiro da Língua Portuguesa*, 955. Edited by Aurélio Buarque de Hollanda. Rio de Janeiro: Civilização Brasileira.

Pereira, D., & Bronzatto. (2016). O Pecado Original, *Veja*, 7 September 2016, p. 49, https://veja.abril.com.br/acervo/#/edition/2494?page=48&section=1 accessed 16 July 2021.

Pereira, D. (2015a). Um dialogo de surdos, *Veja*, 12 August 2015, p. 46, https://veja.abril.com.br/acervo/#/edition/2438?page=46&section=1&word=2438 [accessed 07/09/2021].

Pereira, D. (2015b). O fim da farsa, *Veja*, 12 August 2015, 51, https://veja.abril.com.br/acervo/#/edition/2438?page=50&section=1&word=2438 accessed 09 July 2021.

Pereira, D, Rangel, R., & Bonin, R. (2016). O exxx-presidente, *Veja*, 03 February 2016, pag. 41, https://veja.abril.com.br/acervo/#/edition/2463?page=41&section=1 [accessed 07/09/2021].

Petry, A. (2015). A cabeça de Moro, *Veja*, 30 December 2015, p. 50, https://veja.abril.com.br/acervo/#/edition/2458?page=50&section=1 accessed 09 July 2021.

Plekhanov, G. (1883/1974). Socialism and the political struggle. *GV Plekhanov, Selected Philosophical Works, Volume One*, 49-106.

Prentoulis, M., & Thomassen, L (2013) Political theory in the square: Protest, representation and subjectification. *Contemporary Political Theory, 12*(3): 166–184.

Rae, M. (2021). Hyperpartisan news: Rethinking the media for populist politics. *New Media & Society*, *23*(5), 1117-1132.

Rangel, R., & Bronzatto, T. (2016). So eles não sabiam..., *Veja*, 20 April 2016, Pag. 67, https://veja.abril.com.br/acervo/#/edition/2474?page=66&section=1 accessed 09 July 2021.

Roberts, K. (2019). Bipolar disorders: Varieties of capitalism and populist out-flanking on the left and right. *Polity* 51(4): 641–53.

Ronderos, S. (2020). La transformation de la violence en Colombie. *Multitudes*, (4), 254-259.

Ronderos, S. (2021). Hysteria in the squares: Approaching populism from a perspective of desire. *Psychoanalysis, Culture & Society*, *26*(1), 46-64.

Ronderos, S., & de Barros, T. Z. (2020). Populismo e antipopulismo na política brasileira: Massas, Lógicas Políticas e Significantes em Disputa. *Aurora. Revista de Arte, Mídia e Política*, *12*(36), 31-48.

Ronderos, S., Chicarino, T., & Segurado, R. (2021). Collectivizing political mandates: A discursive approach to the Brazilian Bancada Ativista's campaign in the 2018 elections. *Politics*, 0263395721990276.

Ronderos, S. & Marín-López, D. (2021). Rebels at War, Criminals in Peace: A Critical Approach to Violence in Colombia, *Rethinking Marxism*, DOI: 10.1080/08935696.2021.1999764

Rydgren, J. (2017). Radical right-wing parties in Europe: What's populism got to do with it?. *Journal of Language and Politics*, *16*(4), 485-496.

Sakate, M. (2016a). A economia a deriva, *Veja*, 23 March 2016, p.74, https://veja.abril.com.br/acervo/#/edition/2470?page=74&section=1 [accessed 07/09/2021].

Sakate, M. (2016b). O governo repete seus erros, *Veja*, 13 April 2016, pag. 71-72, https://veja.abril.com.br/acervo/#/edition/2473?page=70&section=1 [accessed 07/09/2021].

Sakate, M. (2016c). Uma safra de retomadas nas usinas, *Veja*, 22 June 2016, pag. 92, https://veja.abril.com.br/acervo/#/edition/2483?page=92&section=1 [accessed 07/09/2021].

Sakate, M. (2017). Não pedale, Meirelles, *Veja*, 12 July 2017, p.56, https://veja.abril.com.br/acervo/#/edition/2538?page=56&section=1 [accessed 07/09/2021].

Sampaio, Regina. 1982. *Adhemar de Barros e o PSP*. São Paulo: Global.

Saussure, F. (2011). *Course in general linguistics*. Columbia University Press.

Schroeder, J. L. (2008). *The Four Lacanian Discourses: or Turning Law Inside Out*. Abingdon, Oxon: Birkbeck Law Press.

Shapiro, S. P. (2005). Agency theory. *Annu. Rev. Sociol.*, *31*, 263-284.

Simon, ed. 1996. *Deconstruction and Pragmatism*. London: Routledge.

Simon, R. (2015). *Gramsci's political thought: An introduction*. Lawrence & Wishart.

Singer, A. (2013). Brasil, junho de 2013: Classes e ideologias cruzadas [Brazil, June 2013: Crossed classes and ideologies]. *Novos Estudos CEBRAP* 97(31: 3) 23–40.

Singer, A. (2010). A segunda alma do partido dos trabalhadores. *Novos estudos CEBRAP*, no. 88 (December): 89–111. https://doi.org/10.1590/S0101-33002010000300006.

Singer, A. (2012). *Os sentidos do lulismo: reforma gradual e pacto conservador*. São Paulo: Companhia das Letras.

Solty, I. (2013) The crisis interregnum: From the new right-wing populism to the Occupy movement. *Studies in Political Economy, 91*(1): 85–112.

Sotirakopoulos, N., & Rootes, C. (2014). Occupy London in international and local context. In: D. della Porta and A. Mattoni (eds) *Spreading Protests: Social Movements in Times of Crisis*. Colchester: ECPR Press, pp. 171–92.

Souza, J. (2016). *A radiografia do golpe: entenda como e por que você foi enganado* [The Radiograph of the Coup: Understand How and Why You Were Deceived]. Rio de Janeiro: Leya.

Stavrakakis, Y. (2002). *Lacan and the Political*. London: Routledge.

Stavrakakis, Y. (2004) Antinomies of formalism: Laclau's theory of populism and the lessons from religious populism in Greece. *Journal of Political Ideologies* 9(3): 253–67.

Stavrakakis, Y. (2004). Antinomies of formalism: Laclau's theory of populism and the lessons from religious populism in Greece. *Journal of Political Ideologies*, *9*(3), 253-267.

Stavrakakis, Y. (2007). *Lacanian Left*. Edinburgh University Press.

Stavrakakis, Y. (2014). The return of "the people": Populism and anti-populism in the shadow of the European crisis. *Constellations*, *21*(4), 505-517.

Stavrakakis, Y. (2017). Populism and hegemony. In: C.R. Kaltwasser, P.A. Taggart, P.O. Espejo and P. Ostiguy (eds) *The Oxford Handbook of Populism*. Oxford: Oxford University Press, pp. 535–53.

Stavrakakis, Y. (2017, January). How did 'populism' become a pejorative concept? And why is this important today? A genealogy of double hermeneutics. In *Populism in Theory: Towards an Anthropological Frame workshop, Universidad de Barcelona*.

Stavrakakis, Y. (2017a). *Populism and hegemony*. In *The Oxford handbook of populism. Oxford University* Press Kaltwasser, C. R., Taggart, P. A., Espejo, P. O., & Ostiguy, P. (Eds.).

Stavrakakis, Y. (2017b). How did 'populism' become a pejorative concept? And why is this important today? A genealogy of double hermeneutics. In *Populism in Theory: Towards an Anthropological Frame workshop, Universidad de Barcelona*.

Stavrakakis, Y. (2017a). Populism and Hegemony. In *The Oxford Handbook of Populism*, edited by Cristóbal Rovira Kaltwasser, Paul Taggart, Paulina Ochoa Espejo, and Pierre Ostiguy, 535–53. Oxford: Oxford University Press. https://doi.org/10.1093/oxfordhb/9780198803560.013.26.

Streeck, W (2014) The politics of public debt: Neoliberalism, capitalist development and the restructuring of the state. *German Economic Review, 15*(1): 143–165.

Taylor, C. (1985). II. Connolly, Foucault, and Truth. *Political Theory, 13*(3), 377-385.

Teixeira, D. (2017). A ONU esta com medo, *Veja*, 08 March 2017, p. 58 https://veja.abril.com.br/acervo/#/edition/2520?page=58&section=1 [accessed 07/09/2021].

Teixeira, D. (2018). Ele não e o primeiro, *Veja*, 11 April 2018, p. 59 https://veja.abril.com.br/acervo/#/edition/2577?page=60&section=1 [accessed 07/09/2021].

The Economist. (2009). Brazil takes off, *The Economist*, 14 November 2009, https://www.economist.com/leaders/2009/11/12/brazil-takes-off [accessed 07/09/2021].

Thomassen, J. (ed.) (2005). *The European Voter: A Comparative Study of Modern Democracies.* Oxford: Oxford University Press.

Thomassen, L. A. (2016). Hegemony, populism and democracy: Laclau and Mouffe today. *Revista Española de Ciencia Política.*

Tomšič, S. (2019) The unconscious and the economy. In: Y. Stavrakakis, S. Frosh, L. Layton and D. Nobus (eds) *Routledge Handbook of Psychoanalytic Political Theory.* Abingdon: Routledge, pp. 296–306.

Tønder, Lars, and Lasse Thomassen, eds. 2005. *Radical Democracy: Politics Between Abundance and Lack.* Manchester: MUP.

Trotsky, L. D. (1986). *The permanent revolution & Results and prospects.* Trans. B. Pearce. New York: Pathfinder.

Tuğal, C. (2013) Resistance everywhere: The Gezi revolt in global perspective. *New Perspectives on Turkey, 49*: 147–62.

Última Hora. (1957). O Populismo da UDN, 25 November 1957. http://memoria.bn.br/docreader/386030/43619 [accessed 07/09/2021].

Última Hora. (1958). São Paulo: Influência econômica sobre a política e os políticos, 17 November 1958. http://memoria.bn.br/docreader/386030/51245 [accessed 07/09/2021].

Última Hora. (1963a). Flávio Tavares: Informa de Brasília, 28 October 1963. http://memoria.bn.br/docreader/386030/91005 [accessed 07/09/2021].

Última Hora. (1963b). Paulo Francis: Informa e Comenta, October 29 1963. http://memoria.bn.br/docreader/386030/91028 [accessed 07/09/2021].

Urbinati, N. (1998). Detecting democratic modernity: Antonio Gramsci on individualism and equality. In *Philosophical forum* (Vol. 29, No. 3-4).

van Haute, P., & Geyskens, T. (2012) A Non-Oedipal Psychoanalysis?: A Clinical Anthropology of Hysteria in the Works of Freud and Lacan. Leuven: Leuven University Press.

Veja. (1980). Longe da praia, *Veja*, 23 January 1980, p. 27, https://veja.abril.com.br/acervo/#/edition/594?page=26 [accessed 07/09/2021].

Veja. (1992). Pedagogia das urnas, *Veja*, 30 September 1992, p. 39, https://veja.abril.com.br/acervo/#/edition/1254?page=38 [accessed 07/09/2021].

Veja. (2014). Eles sabiam de tudo, *Veja*, 29 October 2014, https://veja.abril.com.br/acervo/#/edition/2397?page=1&section=1 [accessed 07/09/2021].

Veja. (2015a). O Brasil perde a calma, *Veja*, 12 August 2015. p. 42-43 https://veja.abril.com.br/acervo/#/edition/2438?page=42&section=1&word=2438 [accessed 07/09/2021].

Veja. (2015b). Moro, pop star, *Veja*, 07 October 2015, p. 40, https://veja.abril.com.br/acervo/#/edition/2446?page=40&section=1 [accessed 07/09/2021].

Veja. (2015c). As trevas contra a luz, *Veja*, 30 December 2015, p. 85, https://veja.abril.com.br/acervo/#/edition/2458?page=84&section=1 [accessed 07/09/2021].

Veja. (2016a). Bencao ou maldição?, *Veja*, 20 January 2016, pag. 10, https://veja.abril.com.br/acervo/#/edition/2461?page=10&section=1 [accessed 07/09/2021].

Veja. (2016b). O dinheiro dos outros, *Veja*, 03 February 2016, pag. 10, https://veja.abril.com.br/acervo/#/edition/2463?page=10&section=1 [accessed 07/09/2021].

Veja. (2016c). O 'chefe' e a 'madame', *Veja*, 24 February 2016, https://veja.abril.com.br/acervo/#/edition/2466 [accessed 07/09/2021].

Veja. (2016d). A exploacao da crise, *Veja*, 23 March 2016, p. 49, https://veja.abril.com.br/acervo/#/edition/2470?page=48&section=1 [accessed 07/09/2021].

Veja. (2016e). issue cover 2474, *Veja*, 20 April 2016, https://veja.abril.com.br/acervo/#/edition/2474 accessed 09 July 2021 [accessed 07/09/2021].

Veja. (2016f). Os tipos da direita, *Veja*, 12 October 2016, p. 42, https://veja.abril.com.br/acervo/#/edition/2499?page=42&section=1 [accessed 07/09/2021].

Veja. (2016g). A revolta nas urnas, *Veja*, 28 December 2016, p.67, https://veja.abril.com.br/acervo/#/edition/2510?page=66&section=1 [accessed 07/09/2021].

Veja. (2018). a ameaça e real, *Veja*, 19 August 2018, p. 27, https://veja.abril.com.br/acervo/#/edition/2593?page=36&section=1 [accessed 07/09/2021].

Ventresca, M. J., & Mohr, J. W. (2017). Archival research methods. *The Blackwell companion to organizations*, 805-828.

Ventresca, M. J., and Mohr, J. W. (2017). Archival research methods. *The Blackwell companion to organizations*, 805-828.

Weffort, F. (1965a/2003). Estado e massas no Brasil. In *O populismo na política brasileira*, 5th ed., 49–65. Rio de Janeiro: Paz e Terra.

Weffort, F. (1965b/2003). Política de Massas. In *O populismo na política brasileira*, 5th ed., 13–47. Rio de Janeiro: Paz e Terra.

Weffort, F. (1967/2003). O populismo na política brasileira. In *O populismo na política brasileira*, 5th ed., 69–89. Rio de Janeiro: Paz e Terra.

Wells, C., Shah, D., Lukito, J., Pelled, A., Pevehouse, J. C., & Yang, J. (2020). Trump, Twitter, and news media responsiveness: A media systems approach. *New Media & Society*, *22*(4), 659-682.

Weyland, K. (2001) Clarifying a contested concept: Populism in the study of Latin American politics. *Comparative Politics, 34*(1): 1–22.

Weyland, K. (2001). Clarifying a contested concept: Populism in the study of Latin American politics. *Comparative politics*, 1-22.

Weyland, K. (2001). Clarifying a contested concept: Populism in the study of Latin American politics. *Comparative politics*, 1-22.

Winch, P. (1990). *Value and Understanding: Essays for Peter Winch*. Psychology Press.

Wittgenstein, L. (1963). *Philosophical Investigations*. Transl. by GEM Anscombe. Blackwell)

Wolf, E. (2016). Quem criou Bolsonaro, *Veja*, 11 May 2016, pag. 72, https://veja.abril.com.br/acervo/#/edition/2477?page=72&section=1 [accessed 07/09/2021].

Zicman de Barros, T. (2020). Desire and Collective Identities: Decomposing Ernesto Laclau's notion of demand. *Constellations*.

Žižek, S. (1989). *The sublime object of ideology*. Verso.

Žižek, S. (1990). Beyond discourse analysis. *New reflections on the revolution of our time*, 249-260.

Žižek, S. (1993) *Tarrying with the Negative: Kant, Hegel and the Critique of Ideology*. Durham, NC: Duke University Press.

Žižek, S. (1997). *The plague of fantasies*. Verso.

Žižek, S. (2004) The structure of domination today: A Lacanian view. Studies in East European Thought 56(4): 383–403.

Žižek, S. (2006a). Against the populist temptation. *Critical inquiry, 32*(3), 551-574.

Žižek, S. (2006b). Schlagend, aber nicht Treffend!. *Critical Inquiry, 33*(1), 185-211.

Žižek, S. (2014) The Most Sublime Hysteric: Hegel with Lacan. Translated by T. Scott-Railton. Cambridge: Polity Press.

Mazzolini, S. (2020). Populism Is not Hegemony: Towards a Re-Gramscianization of Ernesto Laclau. *Theory & Event, 23*(3), 765-786.